Inheritance

An Autobiography of Whiteness

~~BAYNARD WOODS~~

LEGACY
LIT

New York   Boston

Cover design by Henry Sene Yee
Cover art image of street by Getty Images; texture image by Shutterstock
Cover copyright © 2022 by Hachette Book Group

Legacy Lit, an imprint of Grand Central Publishing
Hachette Book Group
1290 Avenue of the Americas
New York, NY 10104
LegacyLitBooks.com
Twitter.com/LegacyLitBooks
Instagram.com/LegacyLitBooks

First Edition: June 2022

Grand Central Publishing is a division of Hachette Book Group, Inc. The Legacy Lit name and logo is a trademark of Hachette Book Group, Inc.

The publisher is not responsible for websites (or their content) that are not owned by the publisher.

The Hachette Speakers Bureau provides a wide range of authors for speaking events. To find out more, go to www.hachettespeakersbureau.com or call (866) 376-6591.

Library of Congress Control Number: 2022931331

ISBN: 9780306924194 (hardcover), 9780306924187 (ebook)

Printed in the United States of America

LSC-C

Printing 1, 2022

To T.W., C.W., D.K., I.W., and S.W.—for the future

Author's Note

More than 200 million Americans carry whiteness around with us all the time. It defines our mothers and our fathers and so many of the people we love. And yet we don't understand our whiteness at all. Just as our skin is the place where our body intersects with the world, our whiteness is where our experience of the world is shaped by power.

Because it defines us, we cannot see our own whiteness and how it lies at the root of so many of the seemingly novel problems we've witnessed in recent years. And this is why it is so dangerous. Even when we are shocked by the racist demagoguery of Trump or the Nazi flags in Charlottesville, we tell ourselves that it is not about us. And since whiteness is the lens through which we see the world, we believe that lie.

This book is an attempt to see my own whiteness.

It might strike people of color strangely, that the force of whiteness remains so obscure to us white people. This lack of self-knowledge is why we have offloaded the labor of thinking about whiteness to Black writers. We lean on them, and it allows us to see whiteness as something external, and so we continue to feel safe in the invisibility of our personal whiteness.

In the first draft of this book, I tried to do a version of this external story, to outline my whiteness as social history, without really putting my own skin in the game. It felt safe that way, because the idea of "structural racism" protects me from thinking about myself or my family as racist. It is useful, but it can also give us an excuse not to examine our own lives.

As a reporter I covered the first Tea Party rally, the Baltimore Uprising, the massacre of nine Black churchgoers in Charleston, the Trump regime, the alt-right, and the racist rally at Charlottesville, and I imagined that by investigating these moments and interrogating the totalitarian history of my home state, South Carolina, I could draw an outline of whiteness without involving myself too much. It was an unconscious move—it was how whiteness works.

My editor noticed the distance immediately. "Write about whiteness from the inside," she said.

So, in a fit of furious self-recognition, I wrote this as rawly as I could. I tried to feel my whiteness, assessing its impact on the present, tracing it back to the past, and attempting to figure out how to defuse this bomb for future generations.

I sought out the gaps between my self-perception and reality because in those lacunae, I might catch my whiteness at work. This account is as honest as I can make it, but the process has taught me how much I cannot see. The task is urgent. History has shown that the problems posed by whiteness will not fade. White fury will get worse as it exacerbates the other problems we're facing. Whiteness fuels fascism, surveillance capitalism, mass incarceration, ballooning police budgets and shrinking social services, toxic masculinity, the ecological crisis, Trumpism, and countless other catastrophes befalling us.

The stakes could not be higher. We cannot outsource the effort of dealing with whiteness to those most targeted and harmed by it. We white people must accept that responsibility.

I have changed the names of many people in this book because accepting responsibility for my whiteness, recognizing it as an obligation, is not about blaming others or proving myself superior or even inferior to anyone else. But I could not change my own name, Baynard Woods, however much I may want to.

My family held people in bondage for centuries. In 1860, for instance, the Baynards and the Woodses combined held more than seven hundred people in bondage. My name is a Confederate monument, a testament to a totalitarian slavocracy. That is the truth of my family's past—the source of my identity as white. To change my name would only continue the cover-up that has constituted whiteness for the last 150 years. And so I leave my name here, on the cover of this book, but I cross it out, both marking off that history and acknowledging it. The mark through my name is a reminder of my civil, psychological, and ethical obligation.

In what follows, I seek to use memory to strip my whiteness of its defenses and see it for what it has always been.

Baynard Woods

Inheritance

Chapter 1

I WOKE UP LATE, Dad yelling at my door.

"Move it or lose it," he hollered.

It was early for me to be out of bed on a summer morning, but my friend Chuck and I were going to ride downtown to skateboard when Dad went to work today, and I'd hit snooze one too many times. Dad was never late for work. I threw on some shorts, a T-shirt, socks, and my smelly Vans skateboard shoes and hurried down the stairs.

In the kitchen I gulped down a glass of milk, and as it coated my throat with coolness, I stared absently out the window at the woods that extended for miles behind our wooden two-story house in Irmo, South Carolina, a leafy suburb ten miles from the state capital, Columbia. Then I noticed that the thermometer mounted outside the kitchen window read 87 degrees already. It wasn't even eight o'clock yet. It was going to be hot.

"Make sure you drink enough," said Mom, handing me a five-dollar bill and a small plastic bottle of Coca-Cola. "And don't get hurt. You've got to take the SAT this weekend."

I ignored her and picked up my skateboard from where it was leaning against the wall, the glittering grip tape refreshingly rough against my fingers.

"Just think," she continued. "Next summer you could go to Duke."

"Mom," I groaned. "I told you, I don't want to go to Duke next summer."

"You've got to think about your future, Son," Dad said, walking into the kitchen wearing a blue button-down shirt and a red tie, holding his sport coat on a hanger in his hand. His graying hair was washed and parted to the side, his mustache neatly trimmed beneath his nose.

I was about to turn thirteen and had no interest in thinking about the future.

"If you go for this talent scout program," Mom said, "then you'll get a scholarship to go there for college and then law school and—"

"You can get a good job," I said, mimicking her. That was my parents' promise, their spiel, their litany, and I'd heard it over and over again all my life: work hard, go to a good college, get a good job, and you will live happily ever after.

It was a seemingly democratic pledge, the idea that anyone can succeed with a little sweat. But everything that surrounded that promise already made it ring hollow. For them, it was about going to the *good* schools, which meant living in the *good* neighborhoods, which meant wearing the *right* clothes and having the *right* friends and playing the *right* sports. And being the *right* race.

"We can talk more about this later," Dad said. "We've got to go. I have a meeting and can't be late."

Dad identified so deeply with the insurance company where he worked that, until that year, I'd thought Seibels Bruce was something akin to God. Sometimes, when I'd thank him for a toy he'd brought me back from a business trip, he'd say, "Thank Seibels."

I grabbed my Coke and tucked my skateboard under my arm, happy for the chance to spend one of the final days of summer skateboarding downtown, where the terrain was far more interesting than in our leafy subdivision.

When we got into his company car, which was square and boxy and looked like a police car, Dad turned the radio to his favorite station for his morning commute. The morning DJ was the father of one of my old friends, David, from elementary school.

"Have you seen David lately?" Dad asked.

"Not this summer," I said.

If a kid didn't skateboard, I was not interested in hanging out with him. I had been a chubby, clumsy loser throughout my life, and now that I was a skateboarder, I felt cool and confident for the first time.

Skateboarding was an unlikely passion for me. At least one doctor in a series of specialists had described me as "retarded" when I couldn't use scissors or skip in kindergarten. My parents had sent me to a special school that summer.

"You're so smart, you're going to college," my mom had said, describing this remedial program. She wasn't technically lying, since the program was located on the university campus, but one look around and even I knew that the other kids in the program were not there because they were geniuses. We were the kids who couldn't learn to tie our shoes.

I'd hated it, and I couldn't believe they expected me to want to go to another summer program at a university. "But it's Duke," Mom would plead, as if that was supposed to impress me. *Hell no*, I thought as we pulled out of the garage. *I'm going to be skating.*

Just hearing David's dad on the radio brought back memories I wanted to put behind me.

In addition to going to the special school, the doctors said I should play as many sports as possible to develop coordination since I was so awkward and clumsy. Instead, I'd developed a thick skin as the worst player on any team. The kids made fun of me, and I had to decide that I would not care, or I would have perished under the mockery. But Dad's disappointment was different. He tried his hardest, but he couldn't quite manage to hide that look of pity in his eyes.

Dad loved sports and he could see that I did not, even though I attempted to fake it because I loved being with him, sitting with him at college football and basketball games or at NASCAR races, which I liked better than the other sporting events. When I first got on a skateboard, all of that changed. I felt a sense of competence for the first time in my life. I felt freedom and passion while moving through the air, and it changed my body, transforming it from a soft mass of undefined boy-flesh into the rangy, wiry body of an adolescent athlete. And my parents just kind of looked on in awe—and fear. As an insurance claims adjuster, Dad had seen numerous cases involving gruesome skateboard injuries.

Dad pulled out of the long driveway lined with tall, prickly bushes, and we drove two blocks through our subdivision, Murraywood, most of whose houses sat, like ours, up on a hill on either side of the valley where a creek ran along beside the road, before pulling up in front of my friend Chuck's single-story house at the end of a cul-de-sac. Dad gave a quick toot on his horn, and a moment later Chuck fluttered out his door like a gangly bird and approached the car, his skateboard under his arm, his ripped Chuck Taylor tennis shoes flopping on his feet.

"He needs some new shoes," Dad said.

"So do I," I said, trying to show him the hole in the side of my duct-taped sneaker as Chuck opened the door.

"What's up, dude?" I said as he got in.

"Nothing much."

"Hi, Chuck," Dad said.

"Hi, Mr. Woods," Chuck replied through the long bangs hanging out of his baseball cap with an upturned bill and the circled *A*, symbolizing anarchy, scrawled over the stitches on its green underside. Dad looked in the rearview to make sure Chuck hooked his seat belt.

For a few hopeful minutes, as we passed from our subdivision into the commercial area with its gas stations, video rental places, and pizza joints, we listened to the radio in silence. Then Dad had a question.

"Your father works for John Deere, right?" he asked Chuck, catching his eye in the rearview.

"Yessir," Chuck said. His family had just moved to town from West Virginia when the company transferred his dad a year earlier.

"That's great. That's a good, solid company. That's what you've got to do. Find somebody solid, somebody that you can trust. For me, nothing is so certain as Seibels Bruce," he said. "They have been around since the eighteen hundreds and will be around hundreds of years more. We're about to buy one of the biggest international insurance companies in the South.

A homegrown business from right here in Columbia. Yessir, God, taxes, and Seibels."

"Come on, Dad," I said, groaning. "This isn't a commercial."

"And Xerox," Dad added. "Our neighbor, George Scoff, he's been with them for years. And John Deere. Great company."

I turned around in my seat and looked at Chuck and rolled my eyes. But as embarrassing as Dad was, I still liked him better than most of my friends' fathers, including Chuck's, who seemed to me often cold, distant, and imperious.

An illuminated bank sign said it was already 90 degrees. Chuck and I were going to be out in it, skateboarding around downtown Columbia all day while Dad was at work. And even though I was soaking up the AC before plunging into the intensity of the heat, I couldn't wait to get out of the car.

We pulled off the interstate onto Huger Street and we were downtown, the buildings made of dirty red brick and speckled gray granite the color of a stormy sky. We cruised past a mural depicting George Rogers, a USC football player who'd won the Heisman Trophy and led Dad's beloved Gamecocks to their most successful season in modern memory several years earlier.

"I hope that getting out of New Orleans will help straighten him up," Dad said.

Then he looked in the rearview.

"You probably don't know who that is, do you?" he asked Chuck, pointing out the window at the giant, smiling brown face of number 38 painted on the passing wall.

I'd gone with Dad to games during that 1980 season when Rogers ran hundreds and hundreds of yards, and I'd gotten swept up in the general excitement of the cheering crowds, even though I didn't care about the sport. But that had been almost six years earlier, and this was just embarrassing now, listening to Dad tell Chuck all about Rogers's glorious run as a Gamecock.

"After the Heisman, he was the first-round draft pick and went to the

New Orleans Saints, where he led the league in rushing—until he was implicated in a cocaine sting," Dad said. "He just got traded to Washington. But through it all, he still has his house here, over in Cold Spring."

Neither Chuck nor I said anything. I was cringing. Dad's earlier adulation and current condemnation of this man struck me as strange, out of whack somehow, and it was embarrassing.

We were silent again, and the radio DJ said that we might get a big thunderstorm that afternoon.

When we'd made the deal to come downtown with him, Dad had said he had meetings and we couldn't come to his office, so we had to be sure we wanted to be out all day.

"And Phyllis is on vacation, so she can't help you either," he'd said of his long-time secretary.

But now he was relenting.

"Call me if it gets too bad," he said.

"We'll hide in a parking garage," I said. "No problem."

The statehouse dome loomed up ahead. The traffic was backed up as everyone streamed into the center of the city, cars sputtering along beside each other as pedestrians dodged back and forth at crosswalks at a density so different from that of my subdivision, where packs of kids were the only ones who walked down the street.

I turned in my seat.

"I'm gonna pull a boneless off those steps today," I said to Chuck, pointing out the window and deflecting the conversation away from Dad with our private skateboard argot.

"Me too," Chuck said.

We drifted into daydreams about the tricks we might try on our skateboards until we rolled up in front of Seibels Bruce.

"See that?" Dad said as we pulled into a parking space marked "Vice President." "I started at the very bottom. If you work hard, you can do anything."

Dad turned off the car, and Chuck and I scampered out. Dad opened the back door behind him and pulled the sport coat down from where it was hanging and put it on as if it were a piece of shining armor. He quickly ran his fingers through his mustache, ensuring there were no odd breakfast crumbs hanging on to one of the coarse salt-and-pepper hairs. I hated that mustache. He looked like a cop. And because of skateboarding, I had started to hate cops.

"I'll see you boys back here at five," he said. "Don't be late."

"Can I have five bucks for lunch?" I asked.

"Didn't your mom give you five?"

"No," I lied.

He took out his wallet. A car pulled into the lot.

"Thanks," I said, and stuffed the bill into the pocket of my shorts. Then I jumped on my skateboard and rode off.

Gliding down the sidewalk, I looked up for just a second at the strange, angular shape of the building that housed Dad's office. I'd been to his office plenty—but I had no idea what he did up there all day.

When he had been an adjuster, I'd understood. He'd take me around with him sometimes, and we'd look at wrecked cars, or he'd sit in body shops talking to guys about parts in rooms that smelled like grease while I lolled on an old car seat serving as a couch and watched a fan lazily blowing flypaper, or I'd gaze out the window at the mountains of crashed cars and retired yellow school buses. Once, when I was in third grade, he'd taken me to Montreal, where we'd picked up a stolen-and-recovered 1976 Corvette Stingray with T-tops and driven it back down to SC.

But now I had no idea what his job was, no clue what a vice president did all day in the office, but it seemed like school to me, where he just did busywork and memos, and with the summer ending, that was the last thing I wanted to think about. Outside on my skateboard, cutting between the people passing by on the way to work, popping the tail of my board and flying off the side of the curb and into the street, the rumble of the polyurethane wheels beneath my feet, reinventing the architecture, repurposing the curbs for fun as the wind blew my long blond bangs back away from my face—this was the life for me.

There were so many places to skate downtown—the trick was not getting kicked out. The university was the best spot, especially in the summer, when it was mostly deserted. But we also liked to climb to the tops of parking garages and bomb down them as fast as we could, cooled by the shady breeze against our faces, dodging the security guards when we got to the bottom.

Occasionally we would try the statehouse because we thought the multiple flights of granite stairs, the stone benches, and the plinths of statues were perfect props for our four-wheeled antics. But we always knew we would be chased away after a trick or two.

Mom would bring me to the state capitol when I was little to watch the squirrels and play in the grass, and every year or so my class would go on a field trip. A couple of years earlier, when I was in the fourth or fifth grade, we had gone on a class trip to the state capitol and all waited in a big line to shake hands with Senator Strom Thurmond, who sat aged and brittle, his eyes barely open and drool hanging from the right side of his crusty lip beneath the state scepter. He held out his frail and ancient hand to us, and we each shook it. "He is a great man," our teacher told us.

As the afternoon wore on and Chuck and I exhausted the university spots, we found ourselves there once again at the historic capitol building. I skated by the hulking stone edifice and looked up to see the bronze stars that marked where Yankee cannonballs had bombarded the dome roof, and I noted the statue of George Washington standing in front of the colossal stairs holding a broken cane, which Mom had told me had been smashed by Yankees who hated freedom so much that they'd stoned the statue of the father of our country. "Sherman's men weren't content to burn the city," she said of the Union attack on the birthplace of secession. "But then they had to go and attack the statue of George Washington."

I popped an ollie, sending my board up into the air with my feet still on it, and came down on an acorn. My wheels stopped. I flew forward down onto the hot concrete. My palms burned; twigs and pine straw stuck to my sweaty chest and face. I heard Chuck say something and looked up to see his heel, level with my face, pushing away as his wheels whirred across the rough concrete.

I turned and saw cops running for me in gray uniforms. I climbed up from the pavement and threw down my board so that it was rolling and jumped on it. As far as we knew, these cops had jurisdiction only on the statehouse grounds, and so, I surmised, once I made it down these steps and onto the sidewalk, I should be safe. And what were they really going to do if they caught us, anyway?

One of the cops got close for a second, his gun belt bouncing against his leg as he tried to run and yell at the same time, but soon enough he stopped, bent over and coughing. I jumped down the steps as the rebel flag flapped above my head.

"Fuck you, man, I'm having fun," Chuck cried from ahead of me, almost across the street.

"Fascist pigs!" I yelled as I rode away.

After the chase, we needed some AC. We made our way to the Burger King that served as our home base when we skated downtown. It was close to everything, food was cheap, and the parking lot had an embankment we liked to ride. I ordered a Whopper. We sat at one of the booths and gulped down ice water from the waxy cups.

I took a bite of my burger.

"These things taste good," I said. "But they smell like BO."

"Dude, that's sick. Why would you eat it, then?" Chuck asked, chewing on a chicken strip.

"Because once you take a bite you don't smell it anymore," I said, shoving the ketchup-slathered buns into my mouth. "And it tastes good."

A police car passed outside the window, reminding us of our escapade at the statehouse.

"Stupid cops," I said, swallowing. "They're just like the Yankees who attacked the city. They're just trying to take our fucking freedom."

"What?" Chuck said.

"I mean, all we're doing is expressing ourselves. Being free. Having fun. And then they come running and tell us what we can't do," I said. "They don't even have the right to fly a rebel flag. We're the rebels and they chase us away."

"I don't think that's why the Union Army came down here," said Chuck.

When I was growing up, it was clear to me that everyone in Columbia walked around with this tragic sense that we lived in a conquered city, a city that had been burned. All the white people, at least. The ones who weren't Yankee transplants. And we all were simultaneously sad, angry, and aggrieved. And it all felt justified. Even for a man like Dad, who believed in the system, or the American dream, more than anything, there was a sense that something was irrevocably lost, something in the universe deeply askew. In my house, both Christ and the South would rise again.

"Sure it was," I said. I'd always been proud that my great-grandfather had fought in the Civil War and had been wounded at Gettysburg. That was my dad's grandfather, only three generations back, and there was a sense of veneration around the Confederate dead.

"Dude, the Civil War was about freeing the slaves," Chuck said.

"I mean, not really," I said. "It's called the rebel flag and not the slave flag. That was just one of the things, but really it was about rebellion. Think of the Duke boys in the *General Lee*. It had the flag on it, and they were running from cops and jumping over stuff just like us."

Chuck laughed.

"We're just some good ol' boys," I sang from the show's theme song, making sure I mocked the twang of the singer, Waylon Jennings, who had once been my favorite.

"West Virginia broke off from Virginia because the poor mountain men up there didn't want to fight for the slave owners down here," Chuck said. "Or at least that's what *we* learned in school."

I was pretty sure that a lot of people in my family had been slave owners. My grandmother had always told me that the slaves had been happy. I didn't have any reason to question her. When I was small, she'd lived in an ancient house with her hundred-year-old mother, and I assumed she knew the past better than I.

"I mean, it's not like I love that flag or 'Dixie' or anything," I said in a quick deflection. "I was just saying. It's a funny coincidence."

"What's funny is how our different schools teach different things," he said.

Here in Columbia, they taught us the Civil War had been about Southern independence, and at Chuck's old school in West Virginia, they'd taught him it had been about slavery. It was just evidence to us of how ridiculous our teachers and education system were.

"Yeah," I said.

"It's like nobody really knows anything," he said.

"No shit," I said. "That's so true. Nobody knows nothing. Not for real."

We sat there a minute in sweaty reflection. I looked at my watch.

"I know one thing," I said, crumpling up the ketchup-smeared paper that had been wrapped around my Whopper. "We have another two hours to skate before we meet my dad."

"Yeah," he said. "Let's get."

We walked out of the restaurant and back into the blinding concrete heat of the city. But it felt as if our wheels had sunk into the overheated asphalt, and our movements were slow and dragging for the rest of the afternoon.

When I saw Dad walking out of his office at the end of the day, stripped of the buffer between work and home that his commute must have normally provided, he looked even worse than we did.

He had always been pudgy—his brothers sometimes called him Porky—but now that he was thirty-eight, Dad's belly was beginning to balloon so that at the end of the day his dark-blue coat looked like an overstuffed trash bag that had ripped up the middle as he carried it out the door.

The other afternoon commuters seemed as weary and beaten down as Dad did, horns honking around us in a mad call and response before the mass of cars lurched slowly forward, their exhaust making the thick evening heat even more unbearable. The air felt like blue balls. Pedestrians now dragged their wilting bodies down molten sidewalks. We stopped at a red light. The news played softly on the radio. The light turned green. A horn honked. A Black man in a loose-fitting, short-sleeved button-down ambled slowly in front of us.

"Damn bear," Dad sighed with slow frustration. "Can't you read the damn signs?"

I glanced nervously between Dad beside me and the rearview mirror, where Chuck appeared smaller underneath all his sweat, the way a dog does when it gets wet.

I was embarrassed by what Dad had said because it sounded so country and dumb. *Bear* was one of many idiosyncratic turns of phrase he had picked up from his father, who, like Dad and his five brothers, had grown up in the small town of Manning, about an hour and a half southeast of Columbia. I loved barbecue from Manning, but other than that, I didn't want anything to do with it. But that hick town was crystallized, along with everything else that embarrassed me about Dad, in the word *bear* as it filled the air-conditioned car while we waited to drive through the intersection.

The word didn't bother me just because it was country. I knew it was somehow wrong. I didn't know how or why really, but it was a word he only used derisively and only of Black people.

Our suburban subdivision was almost entirely white, but downtown, Black and white people shared the same space, passing on sidewalks on the way to work or to college. I remembered once, when we were in the car on our way to Capri's Italian Restaurant, when Dad had referred to a "group of bears" who were standing at a bus stop downtown.

"John," Mom had protested, slapping him on the shoulder with a soft, not-quite-playful hand.

"You remember when we were kids," Dad replied. "It said 'Colored' above the doors. And 'Negro.' And some people said worse."

"Only rednecks talked like that," she said.

"I know. That's why my daddy said 'bear,'" Dad said, laughing. "It was polite in those days. Most of his customers at the furniture store were Black, and he didn't say it to them. He never said it until we got back into the car after making the rounds to collect the weekly payment on the furniture they'd buy on credit."

"Well, don't you teach it to our boys," she said. "It's low class and redneck."

Such exchanges always left me uncomfortable, feeling ill prepared, as if there was some big secret they were not letting me in on. A secret that involved my family. A secret that involved me. Dad reveled in the exploits of Black football players like George Rogers, but he also described Black people as bears, animals.

Those thoughts rushed through my brain as I glanced nervously back and forth between Dad, Chuck's reflection, and the Black man walking across the crosswalk, a slight pep in his slow step, despite the withering heat.

I started to say something to Dad, planning to approximate Mom's mannered rebuke, but I wasn't sure if Chuck had heard what Dad said at all. And if he hadn't, and I made a point of it, then I would just be drawing his attention to it, and I would have to explain it. And not only would I have to explain it, I'd have to explain it in front of Dad. I couldn't even imagine where to begin. I didn't know what white and Black were supposed to mean to us or how they fit with the gray and the blue in the Civil War that Chuck and I had talked about earlier.

Looking back, at that moment, unsure about how to act, I felt my whiteness materializing as a problem in the same way my sweat dried on my skin, giving me chills. I became aware of my own skin, aware that it wasn't just skin. It had meaning attached to it, meaning that went beyond me.

In the course of my daily life, whiteness was invisible to me. It was there, but it didn't carry any meaning. It was noise, not signal. We were just people, the Woods family. Of course, *this* Woods family happened to be white, but that was incidental. Other people, Black people, were marked by their race. But not us. We just *were*. As a result, whiteness was taboo, not to be spoken of.

But in moments like this, I felt as if I were bumping into it, like feeling something against your leg in a dark ocean and hoping it's a porpoise and not a great white shark.

I said nothing and turned away and stared out the window.

When the man finally reached the sidewalk, Dad drove forward, calmly. A Chevy Nova sped up to try to get around us, coughing exhaust into the air.

"Turkey," Dad muttered at the driver. That was not a race thing. *Turkey* was what he called people who drove too fast. "Slow down, turkey!" he'd yell from behind the lawn mower when someone sped down our street.

The tension created by *bear* had passed with *turkey*, and as Dad finally pulled the car off the highway and back into our mostly white suburb, I returned to the primal state of whiteness I had mostly occupied since my birth, a blissful unawareness.

For most of my life, whiteness was the freedom not to notice my race.

Chapter 2

I CONTINUED TO GET GLIMPSES of the ways my whiteness worked when we moved out of our insular, suburban neighborhood. It started when Dad's company, Seibels Bruce, acquired a firm in Winston-Salem and decided to transfer him there.

"It's an important promotion," Mom said.

"It will be good for the family," Dad said.

"OK," my brother Christopher said.

"Cool," I said.

I had been trying to reinvent myself, and a change of cities could give me a fresh start.

But then something happened.

When Christopher and I walked into the room, sweaty from skating, Mom and Dad were both sitting on the couch a little too close and a little too stiffly, as if they'd been waiting for us. Something was up.

"We need to talk to you boys," Mom said, sitting there, her face ashen, her eyes red.

We sat down. I could hear a woodpecker pounding on a tree outside the glass door.

"Your daddy quit his job," she said, casting a bitter look toward him.

"What?" Christopher and I said in unison. This made no sense. How could he quit Seibels Bruce? It was like Mom announcing that she had become a Buddhist.

"Well, you remember my friend Bob died a couple weeks ago," Dad said.

Christopher and I looked at each other. We did not remember that. We paid little attention to the parts of our parents' world that didn't affect us.

"He was my boss too," Dad said. "And after he died, they made some decisions that were just going in a different direction than me."

Mom looked at him sharply.

"A direction I didn't agree with," he added.

"What does that mean?" my brother asked.

"We won't be going to Winston-Salem," Dad said.

"Are we staying here?" I asked.

"We already sold the house," Mom said, grimly.

I looked around the room. There were two small rocking chairs, one red and one black, sitting up against the wall. They had been too small for us for years, but Mom had never been able to bear putting them away. We'd moved into that house when I was three, and as I looked at those chairs I realized that most of the things I remembered about my life had happened while I lived here, next to the Scoff family, in this two-story, four-bedroom house with a playroom downstairs, set back on a hill in the woods. I had been ready to leave, but seeing Mom's face quivering, I suddenly felt all that would be lost.

I didn't understand how Dad could do this, how he could quit his job. But I was surprised to find that I was also proud of him. It was the first time I'd ever actually seen a grown-up, one who wasn't on TV or in a movie, take charge of their life and use the freedom Americans are supposed to be so damn proud of. And I thought it offered hope for my own future.

When my older cousin Michael lived with us after his parents, my uncle Bully and his wife, Pat, got divorced, he had gone to see the punk band the Clash at the Carolina Coliseum and come home with a shirt that read, "It's more vital to have freedom than a job." I was in the fourth grade and the slogan puzzled me. It was the exact opposite of everything Dad believed in and pushed on me. And now Dad, who worshipped Seibels, seemed to embrace that idea as he quit his job because he didn't agree with what the company was doing. If Dad was going punk rock, the world was full of possibilities.

Mom didn't share this surging sense of potential—at all. The day we moved out of the house, most of our stuff already in storage, she could not stop wailing. She talked about hell a lot in the family devotions and Bible study sessions she led us through in the evenings, but I had never understood the phrase *gnashing of teeth* until that day. It is a horrible thing to see your mother gnashing her teeth. We had nowhere to live and were going to move in with my aunt and my cousin for the summer, and she could not bring herself to leave the house this final time.

"We're homeless," Mom sobbed as Dad walked out the door from the kitchen into the garage in front of her. "Homeless!"

The evening light looked eerie leaking in the window of the empty kitchen, as if the house were haunted. Then I realized that we were the ones who were haunting it, and I was ready to just get out and get on with it. But we were standing behind Mom, and we couldn't leave until she did.

She grabbed ahold of the doorframe, refusing to take her final step out of that door.

"Now, come on, Moth," Dad said, his Lowcountry accent shortening her name, Martha, to that of an insect.

Christopher looked at me, and then we both averted our eyes, awkwardly standing there in our long board shorts, not knowing what to do. We had never seen our parents shaken like this. I mean, Mom was tough. At this very door, she had stood down three juvenile delinquents who had escaped from jail and come to our house looking for a gun. I'd let them into the house when they asked to use the phone, and she had cornered them with a baseball bat until the cops got there. And now she was weeping and gnashing her teeth and refusing to take that first final step.

She tilted her head back so that her perm was like a mane and her mouth was aimed at heaven and screamed again. The curdled sound echoed through the empty house, coming back to me from the other side of our home. My brother gazed up at me, wondering what we should do. But she just kept screaming, her long thin fingers grabbing the doorframe, and we couldn't do anything.

"Mom," I offered, my voice low and hesitant.

"I won't leave, damn it," she sobbed. "I won't go. I won't, this is not right. We raised the boys here. All our memories are here. I won't leave, you can't make me."

That's when Dad slapped her. It was the kind of slap men give women in the movies to calm them down. It was the only time I'd ever seen him hit her, and, as in the movies, it worked. She quit crying and let go of the doorjamb.

She turned and looked at me and Christopher huddled together, attempting to hide our eyes from this shameful spectacle. Her bottom lip stuck out and quivered. She blinked rapidly, swatting away tears. She bit her lip, trying to gain control. She dug her nails into her palms as if she was about to fight, and then she turned and silently walked into the garage.

We followed behind her and climbed into the back of the van, which held the last of our belongings. The van, with its plush burgundy-and-gray interior with a bench seat in the back and captain's chairs in the center, had been designed for tailgating at college football games and wasn't outfitted as a moving van, our most used belongings cluttering the space, propped up at odd angles, so that I had to sit with one foot atop a box. But now that Dad didn't have a company car—for the first time in many years—he'd had to permanently borrow the van from his father-in-law, my grandfather Summey. For the first time since he was fourteen, Dad didn't have a car.

He backed out of the garage and tipped over the box that was under my foot as he drove down our long driveway for the last time. I straightened the box. Then I looked out the window and caught a glimpse of the creek across the street reflecting the sky in silver slivers as it trickled through the rustling bamboo and fragrant honeysuckle. We drove past the Scoffs' house and then by Chuck's and finally out of our neighborhood, which was no longer our neighborhood. But we weren't going far. We would be sleeping at the house that Gaile, Mom's sister, lived in with her son Eric, who was three years younger than I, about a mile and a half away, in a slightly less prosperous suburb.

Eric was an only child and his father was an asshole and Gaile had divorced him years earlier and she didn't drive, so we always went everywhere together: vacation, doctors' appointments, whatever. They were pretty much our immediate family anyway, long before we lived with them.

The house was full of adults—Gaile and her boyfriend, Jim, and both of my parents—but I hardly remember seeing them that summer. We lived off ham sandwiches and cereal and delivered pizza, and our parents paid little attention to us. We would fall asleep watching music videos on the couch or the living room floor most nights. It was a lot better than some dumb Duke program, which had been all but forgotten in the chaos, even though I had done well enough on the SAT to get in.

We kids spent a lot of time riding our skateboards down to the Pantry, a convenience store about a mile away, to buy sodas and candy. It was closer if we cut through the parking lot of an apartment complex across the main road and climbed a clay hill up through some small scrub pines poking out of the red dirt.

One humid evening we were heading back home a little late, the sugar of SweeTarts and gobstoppers already coursing through our veins and staining our mouths. We clomped down the hill, lazily kicking clods of red clay with our Vans. Music and the smell of grilling meat came from the parking lot.

As we cleared the trees and hit the asphalt, we noticed that there were small groups of people standing around or sitting on front steps, sipping on beers or sodas and talking. Then I noticed that everyone was Black except us. We'd driven through Black neighborhoods before, but this was the first time that I was in the minority in the flesh, and it felt uncomfortable. I felt as if people were looking at us. I felt vulnerable. And I was painfully aware of my white skin in a way I had not been before.

I started walking a little faster while trying to look more relaxed. Even though no one had ever really talked to me about racism, I knew it would look bad to be afraid of Black people, as if I was scared of them because they were Black, and so I did a chill, but fast, stroll.

"Hey, lemme see that board," one kid a little older than me said, walking quickly up beside me. He had a crisp white T-shirt and just a little bit of mustache growing above his lip.

"Nah," I said quietly. I looked around and saw that people were looking at us. A couple of other boys were walking our way. I threw my board down onto the sticky slow pavement and jumped on it. My brother and cousin did the same.

"Come on, give it here," the first guy said.

I used my back foot to push my board as hard as I could.

"Come on and give it to me," he said, swiping lazily at my cousin as we pushed faster.

"You better run," he yelled, half-heartedly coming after us, shoes slapping the pavement behind me.

As we roared ahead of him on our skateboards, the apartment buildings and brown faces a blur in our rattling polyurethane speed, a green translucent glimmer soared past my head. A plastic bottle thudded and bounced and skittered across the asphalt beside me. Then there was a rock.

"Fuck you white boys," an older woman, sitting on her steps near the exit of the parking lot, yelled at us, as the Michael Jackson song "Billie Jean" came from the radio on her stoop.

When we hit the edge of the parking lot and I paused to make sure the traffic was clear before trying to jet across the street, the guy who had been chasing us was just walking, laughing at us with a couple of friends who had joined him. He waved his hand dismissively. The woman with the radio was scowling, looking at me like a teacher about to get up and come whup my ass. We dashed across the busy street to the safety of Eric's largely white neighborhood.

"What the hell?" Eric said, out of breath, his board up under his arm, sweat staining his light-blue shirt.

I was the oldest, and they looked to me for answers about the world.

But I didn't know what to tell them. I didn't understand why the people had chased us. I mean, the kids, sure. That was what kids did. Jocks and preps tried to fight us all the time. But the older lady stunned me. She had used *white boy* as an insult and she'd had fury in her voice.

"I don't know," I said.

"Remember how worried our moms got when Black kids started coming to Columbia Mall?" Chris asked.

I remembered. When our white moms saw crowds of Black kids hanging around the arcade where they left us while they shopped, it had been a full-on panic until, after Mom and other white shoppers complained, the police started to patrol the mall more regularly and Mom felt that order had been restored.

"Yeah," I said.

"Maybe it's like that," he said.

"Yeah," I said. "You're probably right. Maybe they thought we were looking to rob or vandalize them."

"But we weren't," Eric said.

We kept walking along, holding our boards, kicking pebbles, and sipping sodas. Again, I had the feeling that there was something about race that our families and teachers were hiding from us. We knew there was an obvious difference between white and Black people, but we didn't understand the meaning that was attached to that difference. But this encounter showed me there was something about whiteness and Blackness that had nothing to do with skin color at all. At that time I felt it was more like chess and the colors told us where we could go.

"I guess there are white places and Black places," I said, and as I spoke the words, I knew that of course that was true. I had always known that. But I had never known that I knew it until right then.

Only by being in this different environment had I gotten a glimpse at the code that had been governing my life. Whiteness goes beyond our skin, beyond our bodies. It occupies space, including some people and excluding others.

I hadn't noticed this before because I was raised in an environment created by exclusion, one where I didn't have to see Black people seeing me. Black kids went to my school, but because they were in the minority, I never had to consider how I might appear to them. But finding myself in a majority-Black space, I could see myself as white more clearly than I ever had. I could see that my whiteness meant something to the Black people in the parking lot that it did not mean to me. Whiteness had created boundaries so close around me that I perceived them as my own skin.

I'd like to say I was the kind of kid who went home and asked my parents about it, asked them about race and segregation, but I was not. Still, we had learned a lesson about the way race worked that day—we had learned that we should not cut through those apartments, and we avoided them for the rest of the summer.

Chapter 3

"YOUR MOM'S COMING HOME TONIGHT, so don't stay at the mall too late," Dad said just before Christopher and I dashed out of the apartment on an autumn afternoon whose bright-blue sky and crisp, refreshing air felt full of possibilities.

"OK," I said, my mood dampening a bit as I closed the door, walked down the steps, and jumped on my board to ride to the mall at the bottom of the parking lot. Things had been a lot more lax—and easy—since Mom had started working in Greenville, about two hours away.

Dad hadn't been able to find a job, so Mom had to work. Her father had said he needed help in the carpet store he owned. So she'd left us and moved back home and started working about a month earlier, after the end of our summer at Gaile's, when I started the eighth grade and Dad and Christopher and I moved into the two-bedroom apartment that Dad's oldest brother, Uncle Bully, had bought when he went through his divorce.

This shuffling around to stay with different family members—from Mom's sister to Dad's brother while Mom moved to her parents'—felt surprisingly natural for us, because other family members had always stayed with us when there was a divorce or some other exigent situation.

But it was stunning to see how much my parents both transformed after Dad quit his job. Before I was born, Mom had worked as a chemical plant inspector, but she gave up the job when she got pregnant and, for the entirety of my life, she had not worked outside the home—except in capacities related to me and my younger brother. She volunteered at school and had worked on a committee to draft the governor's education plan, but she saw those things as part of her role as a homemaker. I had seen her virtually every single day of my life, and now we saw each other only on the weekends—and not every weekend.

On the other hand, for most of my life, if Dad was home, he had been either coming from or going to work. Now he woke up and cooked us breakfast. Then he drove us to school and picked us up in the afternoon and dropped us off at an old drainage ditch, where we'd skateboard, and then picked us up again when it was dark. Occasionally he'd go meet a friend for beers at a place he called Leo's Chicken Lips. Other than that, I had no idea what he did all day, when we were at school, but it seemed as if he rarely left the apartment.

Mom was already there when Christopher and I walked in that evening. We could smell the pizza and had started toward the small kitchen counter where it sat steaming when we noticed Mom and Dad, once again sitting too close to one another on the couch.

"We're going to move in with Nanny and Summey," Mom said, using the names we called her parents. "But don't worry, we're going to use Uncle Jimmy's address to make sure that you go to the best school."

"I don't want to go to the best school," I said, sitting on the couch. "I don't want to move. We just moved. I want to stay right here. I'm in love. I have friends. You're ruining my life."

"Your Daddy can't get a job here," Mom said, looking at Dad with a judgment as fierce as what she promised would come at the End of Days.

"It doesn't make sense for us to all live apart like this," Dad said.

I pushed past Mom and Dad on the couch and walked past the pizza and into the bedroom I shared with my brother and slammed the door. I did not want them to see my tears.

I switched on the college radio station. A punk rock song was playing. I didn't know what band it was, but I liked how aggressive it felt, and

I turned up the volume loud enough that it would annoy my parents. I knew I needed to call my girlfriend, Katie, but I didn't know what to say. She was older and cooler than me, and I was already afraid of losing her all the time.

I'd met Katie when I was skating alone at the mall by our apartment on Friday night at the end of the first week of school. I was trying to learn to ollie up onto a ledge when she walked up to me. I'd been trying to pull the trick for two hours, riding up to the wall again and again, popping my board up and turning it forty-five degrees in the hopes of landing with my axles on the ledge of a planter that was about a foot high. I almost pulled it, but then my axles slipped off the concrete and I fell. When I looked up, there she was, standing over me, her hair cut short in the back and on the sides, but long in front like mine. She had rings all the way up the cartilage of her ear, bangles and a Swatch watch on her wrist, ripped-up jeans that showed her pale thigh, and combat boots on her feet.

"You're the new boy, Bay," she said.

I nodded, stunned to be recognized by a girl. She even knew my name.

"We're going to see *Rocky Horror* at midnight," she said, gesturing toward the movie theater marquee. "You need to come with us."

"I'd have to ask my dad. But I just live in those apartments there," I said, pointing toward the fence I cut through to get from the apartment complex to the mall next door, which had a movie theater, a record store, and an arcade. It was also, as I was discovering, where kids hung out on Friday nights.

"Let's go," she said. She and her three friends walked with me up to the apartment. When I opened the door, Dad and Christopher were sitting on the couch watching TV.

"Hi, I'm Katie," she said. "Bay's our friend. Can he come to the midnight movie with us?"

"Please," the other three girls said in unison, as if in a chorus.

Dad looked at them, stunned.

"Be home by two," he said as we walked out the door. "Like Jenks said, nothing good ever happens after two."

"Who's Jinx?" Katie said.

"He's my granddad," I said. "Except I never knew him. But my dad is always quoting dumb sayings of his."

After the movie, she gave me her Swatch watch. And then, following a dramatic couple weeks of late-night phone calls and call-in requests to the college radio station to dedicate songs to each other, she was my girlfriend. But she also hung around with older punk rock guys, and I was sure that if I moved away, we would break up.

I felt ripped in two and utterly uprooted. I was also confused. What was happening to Dad? I thought he had quit his job. But it seemed there was no plan. This was all fucked up and chaotic. And if he was quitting jobs, didn't that mean the whole deal, the "work hard and get a good job you can keep forever" deal, was no longer valid? Why were we lying about our goddamn address? The world was insane. Or at least my parents were. And I still couldn't separate the wider world from my family.

Over Thanksgiving break, on a cold and rainy night just after I turned fourteen, we loaded up the Gamecocks van again, and Dad drove to Katie's, where I said a tearful goodbye in her driveway. She put a peace symbol ring on my pinkie and kissed me on the mouth in the glare of the headlights.

Two hours later, Nanny and Summey welcomed us into the fluorescent light of their kitchen. Nanny came up, pale and thin with her beauty-shop hair and a mauve outfit, and kissed both of my cheeks. Summey was standing there in boxer shorts and a white T-shirt, a New York Yankees cap covering his bald crown, a white foam spit cup in his hand.

We called him by his last name because when I was no more than knee high he had told me that if I ever called him anything like Grandpa or Pop Pop, he would kill me.

"Close the goddamn door," he said as Dad struggled with our cumbersome luggage. "It's cold."

Then he winked at me.

I carried my stuff down into Summey's finished basement, where I would live in what was essentially my own apartment, while my parents and my brother took the two extra upstairs bedrooms. At the bottom of the stairs, I entered the living room, furnished with bright-red carpet that my brother and I used to pretend was lava. I wished I could jump over this whole part of my life like lava as I walked through the room, past a piano on one wall and an electric organ on the other, toward the two bedrooms at the back of the basement.

I stuck my head in the room on the left, its carpet the color of lime sherbet. It had been the room my crib was in when we'd lived in that basement right after I was born. It smelled like mildew, and the curtains were white and lacy. I did not want to sleep in there. Moving here was bad enough, but I didn't need to be reminded of my infancy every goddamn night.

I walked into the other room and dropped my book bag onto the blue carpet covering the floor. The room was furnished with antiques—an old telephone on the wall, a Victrola on the dresser, and a giant wardrobe with a mirror on the door, all in an ancient shimmery dark wood that seemed to have soaked up centuries. On the dresser I spotted one of the foam heads Summey used to store his toupees when he wasn't wearing them.

I stood soaking in the spooky antique vibe of the room and looked around. The bed, up against the wall, was both bigger and higher up than any bed I'd ever slept in before—queen size at least and a foot higher than my bed at the apartment. That was one good thing. Since we'd moved out of our old house, where I'd had my own room, I'd spent far too much time in the bathroom jerking off while others banged on the door hoping to get in. Now I'd finally get some goddamn privacy.

There was a second door on the far wall of the room, one that had always been a source of wonderment for us as kids. I opened it. I smelled the mothballs and the dust and the mildew and the old clock oil. I turned on the fluorescent light, which hummed hectically overhead and then illuminated a cabinet of wonders with a staticky, woolen light.

Summey was a serial obsessive, a serious collector of ephemera, who spent weekends at flea markets, jockey lots, and auctions collecting Coke bottles, commemorative whiskey bottles, baseball cards, gold coins, and antique clocks in turn, and this big storage room, which ran the length of the basement, was piled high with endless examples of each. There must have been a hundred old clocks hanging there above me, all in various states of disrepair, their pieces scattered around the room in old cigar boxes, none of them telling time.

I walked back into my new bedroom and looked at the antique record player and remembered being fascinated by it as a kid. It had been fourteen years since I had lived in this basement as a baby, and yet everybody still treated me like a child. I had no say in the direction my life would take, and my parents moved me around based on their whims, as when they'd decided to move here but then lied about our address so we could go to a different school because someone had told my mother it was better.

"A little thing like that can determine everything about your future," Mom had said.

I punched the foam head. It bounced off the dresser and hit the corner of the room and tumbled down in front of the TV. It felt good. I picked the head up and tossed it in the air and punched at it again, but I missed and it fell on the floor. I needed to hook up my record player, but I was too tired and sad. I turned the TV on. It was only a little longer until David Letterman came on, and I had come to rely on his sarcastic sense of humor in forming my own. I fell asleep on the floor sometime after the opening monologue.

It was cold and rainy the next morning, and I did not want to go to school. I came up the stairs into the kitchen and saw Mom there with a new perm, wearing her work clothes, and ready to go.

"Come on," she said.

"We can't go to school," I said.

"Yeah, it's raining so hard. Let's just wait until tomorrow," Christopher said.

"This is a once-in-a-lifetime opportunity," I pleaded. "Since we aren't officially in the school yet, the absences won't even count against us. We could just come back after Christmas break."

Mom was usually incapable of resisting an argument, but for once, no matter how I angled, she refused to offer a retort. Her answer was firm.

"You are going to school, so get in the damned car right now," she said.

Christopher climbed in the front and I sat in the back, sullen, staring out the window, missing my old life at the apartment. Mom drove down the winding mountain road from Summey's house, past the carpet store, which was at the end of a shopping center beside a barbecue place, and then through a bunch of new suburbs that were outside the city limits on the east side.

Whether at Christmas break or during summer vacation, we'd spent weeks at a time at Nanny and Summey's house all my life, and when they went to work, usually we'd go with them and either play on rolls of carpet in the basement or hide under big metal racks holding displays of carpet samples and listen in as Summey held court with a colorful cast of characters who gathered at the store to talk sports, gamble, gossip, and tell jokes. I knew that part of Greenville well, the world of my grandparents. But as we drove east, toward Northwood Middle School, through suburbs filled with newer houses, I had no idea where I was or if I had ever been in this part of the city before. But I knew, even before Mom pulled up in front of the squat brick building with a covered walkway and two big blue doors, that I would hate it here.

On that first day, when it was finally time for lunch, the teacher told us to line up.

"What's going on?" I whispered to another kid.

"Lunch," he said.

"I know, but—"

"Who is talking?" said the teacher, who had fiery red hair, drawn-on eyebrows, and a long green dress. "Remember, there will be no talking at lunch until the end of this term."

No talking at lunch? Fuck this. At my old schools, when the bell rang, we just wandered to the cafeteria or the outdoor courtyard and conversed with anyone else who had the same lunch period. But here we had to walk in line like elementary schoolers and sit silently with our class.

I almost started to cry as we marched down the long, narrow, prison-blue hall in single file, the hushed sound of rain outside matching the sad streaks of water making diamonds on the windowpanes, but I knew that would only make everything worse. I hated the smell of the school. I couldn't name it, but it smelled like lonely institutionalized sadness. It smelled like plastic death. I was lonesome and forlorn, stuck in my own skin, watching the world as if from the inside of a nightmare.

We went down the line where lunch ladies slopped food on our trays, and when I sat down and scanned the room, I noticed that the kids at this third school looked just like the ones who had gone to my first middle school, with their Jordache jeans and polo shirts and cologne and feathered hair and gold chains and sports jerseys—and they were almost all white.

I was starting to associate white with uptight, the way Dad had been before he quit his job. Cop car, cop mustache. Everything but the badge. That was white. And that was what all these kids were shooting for. To live lives like their parents. I wanted something different. I was naive enough to think I could opt out somehow.

The next day, I wore a T-shirt for the punk band the Circle Jerks, which had a picture of a man pissing on a pile of records and the words "A Golden Shower of Hits." A teacher noticed it at lunch. She sent me to the office, and they made me button up the flannel that had covered the shirt when I left home and warned me never to wear it again.

A few days later, I got kicked out of class for talking back. While I waited for the teacher in the hall, I stuck a safety pin through my ear. When she walked out, blood was running down the side of my face and dripping onto the faux wood finish of the desk attached to the chair I was sitting in at the end of a long hall lined with gray lockers.

But I was learning. I could see the way the world worked a little more clearly. There were rules, but there were all kinds of ways for certain people to cheat—and cheating was part of the system. And, according to Mom and Dad, how you cheated could change your life, make you a success.

It was somehow all about *where* you were in relation to other people. In moving from a woodsy, affluent suburb to a less affluent suburb to an apartment off the highway to the old part of a city—and being a skateboarder who was constantly looking for new terrain—I was seeing even more clearly how where we are can determine who we are. And it pissed me off. Just by lying about my address, Mom could not make me be the person she wanted me to be. So I might have been sitting there secretly reading an F. Scott Fitzgerald story in the English class textbook that I was bleeding on, but I was never going to let them see that. I was going to show them the safety-pin piercing and the Circle Jerks and the blood.

I felt as if I was being suckered into a conspiracy, and I wanted out. But I had no idea how deep it even reached or how to buck against it. It was a desperate feeling, but if I gave up, I knew I would sink into a lie.

After the doctors told Mom I was "retarded" they had done dozens of IQ and aptitude tests and come back with a different, equally damning diagnosis. They told her I was supposed to be some kind of "genius." Of course I wasn't. I did very well on tests that had been created to cater to the cultural knowledge that a middle-class white kid would be expected to have but did little to measure my ability to succeed in a classroom, which was abysmal, especially in math.

A whole math class could go by, and I would awaken to realize I had been lost in a daydream the entire time and had not heard the assignment. Then I'd walk out without asking. Mom tried everything. She made me write down my homework and get it signed by teachers. She forced me to sit at the dining room table for three hours every day after school and do my homework. I would just sit there, a problem half finished so I could pretend to work when she approached, and daydream the rest of the time away. As a result, I'd been partially grounded since the fourth grade, and Mom and I spent the better part of our time together arguing.

However badly I did on my report cards, Mom kept pushing to pretend that I was good at school. When I was in sixth grade, she bullied the guidance counselor into letting me into the academically gifted program—which I flunked out of after one semester. When I was in the seventh grade, she did my science report for me and arranged for me to take the SAT for the Duke University Talent Identification Program, which I was still glad I hadn't attended, and now she'd determined which school I would go to by telling a lie rather than following the rules set up to make such things fair.

Whiteness was part of America's conspiratorial agreement on what mat-tered and what counted as success, including the color of our skin. In all these decisions that were supposed to determine my future, the skin color of the people I would be around mattered to my parents, although racial criteria were never directly mentioned. Still, whiteness influenced where we lived, how we dressed, and everything else about our lives, insisting that we do each of these things in accord with its silent dictates just as surely as if they had been encoded above the doors of the public bathrooms where we pissed and the restaurants where we ate.

Chapter 4

I POPPED MY SKATEBOARD INTO my hand and looked back over my shoulder as I approached the carpet store. It was just before six, when Mom was supposed to get off work, and I was going to ride home with her. Christopher had a cold, and I had been hanging out at the skate shop up the street since school finished.

The carpet store had become the symbol of all the forces that had made us move and left my teenage social life in wreckage. The store sat in a strip mall right across from Bob Jones University, a superconservative Christian college that controlled the town. Everywhere we went, Bob Jonesers would come up with their Bibles and their goofy shirts buttoned all the way up or their long dresses and they would accost us about Jesus and about how we were going to go to hell for skateboarding. The college was in the news because it prohibited interracial dating and said that AIDS was God's punishment for gay people, and there were rumors that it censored all the TV stations and movie theaters in town.

In Columbia we'd mainly gotten our Jesus at home, in the form of Mom's epic family devotions, and I hated having to contend with it in the streets because even just seeing the Bob Jones kids reminded me of how square, how depressed and sad and gray and empty this town was, as if the Rapture had already come and sucked up everything but these dorks. Mom would tell me how booming Greenville had once been. But when we moved there, the downtown was deserted, populated only by roaming hordes of religious zombies.

They approached me when I got off my board at a rough section of asphalt and started to walk as I approached Little Pigs Barbecue, which belched charcoal smoke beside the carpet store, reminding me how hungry I was with its ever-present odor of meat.

"Have you heard the good news?" asked a guy with very short hair and tiny eyes, two of his friends standing behind him like backup singers in an amateur morality play.

"Hell yeah I have," I said.

I threw down my board and pushed hard up to the carpet store's glass door.

The bell hanging from the handle clanged as I swung the door open, alerting Summey, who was sitting, as he did most evenings, in a rocking chair up front, by the plate glass windows, a spit cup in his hand and a Yankees cap on his head, talking to the sheriff and Judge Johnny Dobbs, one of his best friends.

"Hey, boy," Summey said when I walked in, his phlegmatic voice a smooth growl. "You remember Judge Dobbs, don't you?"

I nodded. The judge, a giant of a man, standing more than a foot above me and twice as wide, leaned over and slapped his big hand across my sweaty shoulder.

"I remember when you was just a little bitty thing and I brought a goat in here one time, a pet goat," the judge said. "And you were here and you just could not believe it. I still remember how your eyes looked when you saw it. They was as big as saucers."

"I remember that," I said.

"And this is Sheriff Jackson," Summey said. "And Jax, as much as I hate to admit it with him looking like that, this is my grandson."

Everyone laughed. Summey was quick with a quip, but he could also be casually cruel. He was a driven man. The story was that he would go up to Baltimore after the war to buy appliances you couldn't get in Greenville and then sell them on the side of the road. Then he'd opened an appliance store in this same spot, and after that, when television came around, he had gone exclusively into selling TVs. The store still had a Zenith sign, with a lightning bolt, on its roof. In those days the New York Yankees were the only baseball team whose games were broadcast on TV in Greenville, initiating Summey's devotion to the team. But eventually, since Greenville was a textile town and he knew a lot of the carpet guys, he had gone into the flooring business. He knew everybody in the town, but it always felt as if his ambition was bigger, as if there was something empty at his center that caused him to lash out or try to turn members of his family against each other through a shifting display of favoritism. He and the judge were getting along now, but it seemed as if Summey was feuding with him every other week or so.

"Nice to meet you, son," the sheriff said. "Now make sure to be careful skateboarding, and don't do it in the street or on private property."

Oh, so like, nowhere, I thought, but I said nothing.

"Remember," the sheriff said. "Private property is sacred. It's what this country is built on. We hate to get called over a skateboarding incident because some young men don't understand that principle."

"OK," I said. "Good to see y'all."

As I walked past the racks of carpet samples to the back of the store, where Mom had her desk, I muttered under my breath, "Fucking pig."

"Hey, honey," Mom said from her desk, her face made up and a kind of suit coat on.

"Can we go to Columbia this weekend?" I asked.

"I don't think we can go this weekend," she said.

"Come on," I said. "There is nothing to do here. It is miserable."

"We'll see," she said.

We went through this every weekend. I had tried to keep things up with Katie, but we'd only been together a couple of weeks before I moved, and after I was gone she'd started dating a skinhead and told me never to call her again. But I still wanted to go and hang out with my friends as much as possible. Moving away from people made them seem infinitely cooler than they had been when I lived there. My parents and my brother would stay with Aunt Gaile, and I would stay with one of my buddies, most often Chuck.

A couple of days later, when Mom finally relented and agreed we could go that weekend, Chuck's parents said I couldn't stay with them because his sister would be visiting. That was actually sort of fine, because Chuck had called me a couple of weeks earlier to tell me that he had been saved. Born again. The church we used to go to had built a bunch of skateboard ramps that its youth group was using, apparently with some success, to recruit. With Mom and all the Bob Jonesers around, I didn't need any more Jesus in my life.

I crashed with my friend Danny, who lived with his parents and his sister in a little white house up on a hill behind the middle school. Down below the house they had a fenced-in pasture with a pond and about half a dozen goats. One of them was named Tony Goat, because it had the same flip of hair over the eye as Tony Hawk, the skater we'd all stolen our hairdos from. But I was ready to cut mine off. I was feeling angry and mean, and this floppy bop of hair wasn't working. I decided to shave half of my head entirely bald—the most ludicrous hairstyle I could imagine. And Danny's mom was a hairstylist.

I was sitting in a tall chair with a hard plastic bottom in their kitchen. The winter light was a die-cast gray. I could feel each snip of the scissors as my once-prized bangs, which had hung down almost to my upper lip, fell in blond clumps to the tile floor.

"Now are you sure you want me to shave one whole side of it?" Danny's mom asked when she was done cutting the bangs.

"Yes, ma'am," I said.

Danny was sitting on a stool by the table, watching us with a certain glee. He was a year older than I, and he had a goofy athleticism to his skating and a wild sense of humor. But something about him also intimidated me. He had encouraged me to go ahead with this cut, and I half thought he just wanted to see what would happen.

"And your parents are OK with it?" his mom asked.

"Oh, definitely," I said.

36

They weren't OK with it.

As soon as the silver van pulled up the long gravel drive, I knew I was in trouble.

Dad got out of the driver's side.

"Get in the van," he said.

"I, um—" I stammered.

"Get in the goddamn van," he stated coolly.

I felt the winter air cold on the left side of my head. When I got in the van, there was absolute silence except for the sound of Mom sobbing softly in the front seat. Christopher wouldn't look at me. Danny stood in his driveway laughing, and I knew he couldn't wait to tell all our friends. All my *old* friends. Their world was moving on. I was just a sad, funny story to them now, half-bald riding back to Greenville to get my ass kicked by my dad.

But we didn't get on the highway. Instead, Dad drove toward Gaile's house, whistling something that didn't seem to be a tune. Just random notes that, I imagined, were supposed to represent the music before a showdown in a Western. We pulled into Gaile's driveway just as the streetlights came on. I opened the sliding door in the back.

"You stay here," Dad said.

I froze, scared but also defiant.

"You two go on," Dad said to Mom and Christopher. My brother edged past me and ducked out the door, still without looking, the way one walks past a condemned man.

As Christopher walked toward the house, he gave a quick glance back as Dad stepped into the back door and slid it closed, the metal portal slamming shut with an awful echoing sound like a cell door closing in prison movies.

"You know this has to be punished," he said, struggling to take off his belt from under his massive belly, crouched over the captain's seat in the middle of the van. "I'm going to have to beat you."

"Why does it have to be punished?" I shot back. "I didn't hurt anyone or do anything wrong."

"Didn't do anything wrong?" he barked, giving up on the belt to point at my head. "What do you call that?"

"It's nobody's business but mine," I said.

"It's everyone's business," he said, letting out one bitter burst of laughter. "Everyone has to look at it. And you know what they do when they look at it? They judge you, and when they judge you, they judge me and they judge your mother and your grandparents, and you are making us all look bad."

"I make you look bad?" I said. "You are the one who quit your job and messed up everybody's lives. You're the one who hurt people—who did wrong. I'm just expressing myself. It's you who caused all this."

He lunged forward to grab me, and then he stopped as if he had been restrained by wires hanging from the ceiling of the van. He just looked at me a second, his eyes glossy and bulging behind his glasses. Then he brought his hands to rest on his knees.

We were silent. I could hear kids playing football in the yard next door.

"You think I quit my job," he said.

His Adam's apple lurched up in his throat and settled down again as he swallowed.

"That's what you said."

"I quit my job so they wouldn't fire me," he said, his words full of an emotion I couldn't place. It was like all the bad emotions at once just bundled up and covered over with shame.

"What?" I said, more confused than outraged—but I felt the heat of anger slowly rising in my face.

"When Bob, my boss, died, they told me they were moving in a different direction and said I could either quit or be fired," he said. "So I quit."

I stared down at the twirled gray fibers in the carpet on the van's floor. I couldn't look at him. I had been so impressed by his courage to quit. And I had been angry and confused since we moved. And the whole thing had been a lie.

Sitting there, I felt a kind of pity that hovered between compassion and anger over the social pressure I realized my parents were under. Whatever was telling them that they had to be a certain way and that no other way was acceptable was a lot stronger than I'd thought. Every little infraction of this invisible code sent them into a terror, the kind of terror Dad said belonged to Communist countries.

I wondered where they got these rules and who had made the system we were supposed to abide by. Mom was always talking about the Bible, but it wasn't biblical rules at work here.

"Why didn't you tell us?" I asked, my voice cracking.

"'Oddamn it," he said with a sad frustration, dropping the *G* in his curse, as he sometimes did, to save himself from blasphemy. "We didn't know what else to say, and we thought I'd be able to find another job faster than I have been able to."

We sat there a moment, neither of us looking at the other, both hunched forward on our knees.

"That's why it's so important that you do well, so you can get a degree from a good college and get a good job," he said. "That's why we push, because we want your life to be better than mine. If I had gone to law school like my brothers, I wouldn't be in this situation. If I had finished college."

"But—"

"You ready to go back to Greenville?" he said. "Let's go get your Mom and your brother."

He slid the door open, and we climbed out into the cool evening air. I could smell someone's fire in the distance.

"Touchdown," screamed one of the kids throwing the ball on the lawn next door.

"Raaah," another kid said, mimicking the sound of a cheering crowd as he spiked the ball.

I looked up at Dad, walking toward Gaile's house, disappearing in the half light. My heart was broken for him, but I could no longer believe in the world that he offered. I walked behind him into the house, but I would never truly follow him again.

I'd come to see whiteness—the system of power governing Mom and

Dad's idea of success—as a way to cheat, a false criterion of value. But whiteness is also a lie we tell to save face when we have failed. Whiteness is the willingness to replace reality with a myth in order to protect our perceived worth.

A few minutes later, we all walked awkwardly out to the van. Neither Mom nor Christopher knew what had gone down between me and Dad. They thought he had beaten me. He started the engine and pulled out, and we began the long silent drive to Greenville as I stared out the window, my reflection on the window pale against the darkening night.

Chapter 5

DAD WOKE ME UP, HIS eyes boring into my blanketed body. It was early in the morning on New Year's Eve, on the cusp of 1988. He had finally found a new job, doing something with auditing that I didn't care to understand, and we'd moved into a house near the high school I'd started attending in ninth grade.

"I need you to take me to the hospital," he said.

I rubbed my eyes and tried to focus. I had been out at the park with some friends the night before, drinking Milwaukee's Best and Mad Dog wine, and I had a hangover.

"Your mother can't get out of bed because of her back, and I need to go now," he said, his eyes urgent. A couple of times a year, Mom's back would go out, bad, leaving her utterly immobile for days because the smallest motion could be excruciating.

I stumbled from the bed and threw on a pair of pants and a purple *Thrasher* magazine hoodie. I grabbed the keys to the car he had bought me when I got my license at fifteen and ran down the stairs. In the kitchen, Dad was already waiting, his jacket on.

"Let's go," he said.

I had a wretched taste in my mouth, and I grabbed a bottle of Coke from the fridge.

I could tell that something was wrong as we drove across town because he wasn't criticizing my driving. But he still hadn't told me what was bothering him.

"What's wrong, Dad?" I asked.

"Nothing," he said. "My chest is just hurting a little. I'm feeling better, but it's safer to check it out."

I stopped at a red light in front of Pete's Diner at the corner of East North Street and Stone Avenue. I turned to look at him. His face was red. He'd always been big, but he had gotten balloonishly fat since he started the new job and was working all the time again, spending many nights in Charlotte. It had happened so gradually that I hadn't noticed, but when I looked close I realized I hardly recognized him. His cheeks bulged in a way that obscured his eyes. The light turned green and I drove on, scared.

At the hospital, he told them his chest hurt. A nurse said they would take him up to a room for tests.

"Stay and fill out the insurance," he said, handing me a card. I sat down with an administrator, a Black woman wearing a floral dress, and answered a dozen or so insurance questions. I'd never done anything like that before, but I managed to get through it.

"He should be in room 428," the woman said. "You can go on up."

I rode silently in the elevator, and when the doors opened I stepped out into the antiseptic odor of the hallway. Someone rushed past me wheeling a big bag of fluid on a metal roller. I looked both ways down the hall, trying to figure out which way to go. I saw a nurse's station, but no one was there. Then I noticed the number 428 on a closed door to my left. I walked toward it and opened the door.

"Hey, Dad," I started to say, but then I saw what was happening. Half a dozen people in scrubs and surgical masks stood around him, pumping, pounding at his chest. He gasped. It seemed as if he was trying to say something to me.

One of the masked scrubs came to me, a doctor.

"You should step outside," he said, and used his body to turn me away from the scene of my father, his face now wan and pale and shocked into something like lifelessness as he gasped.

"We have a private waiting room just over there," the doctor said as he pushed me out into the hallway. "I'll have someone take you to it. Your father is in the middle of a massive heart attack. I will tell you when there is news."

I stood there in shock. In a minute, a white nurse with short, thick black hair walked up to me.

"You're Mr. Woods's son?"

I nodded.

"Come with me," she said.

She led me to a waiting room with the color scheme of a Howard Johnson's—orange and light blue—and it reminded me of traveling with Dad when I was just a kid and he would take me with him to Miami, where he worked a lot, to eat at Cuban restaurants with his Cuban friends and then for a couple of days in the Keys, where two of his lawyer buddies had houses and boats.

"We'll let you know as soon as we have news," she said. "There's a telephone here and a Coke machine in the hall."

She left the room. I looked at the phone. I could not bring myself to use it yet.

It was raining outside and water streaked the window and I looked out at the grayness and then back in at the blue and orange and then again at the phone.

I wondered what Dad's life had amounted to. He had another job now, and he worked as hard as ever. But he didn't love it the way he had loved Seibels. He didn't love it as much as the job that had fired him. And now he was lying in a hospital bed in the middle of a heart attack. Everything he had been striving for had amounted to nothing.

In a few minutes, the doctor who had taken me from the room came in.

"I'm sorry to tell you this," he said, taking the mask down from in front of his lips, letting it cover only his chin. "Your father is dying, and you need to go in and say goodbye."

I didn't register the words, but I walked behind him in a daze as he led me through the fluorescent glare of the hallway toward Dad's room. When the doctor opened the door for me, Dad was lying there gray and white. He looked alien, his mustache caked in dried white spittle, his chest caved.

"Don't tell your mother," he said, his voice so weak and papery that it barely reached me. "She'll try to come here. Just promise me you won't tell your mother."

"OK," I said.

"Tell her they are keeping me for tests," he said, and stopped, gasping, to catch his breath. "Only if I die . . . then of course you have to tell her."

His head fell back with its full weight on the pillow, and he closed his eyes. For a split second I thought he was dead. Then his gray eyes looked at me.

"Don't worry, Dad, there's nothing to live for after forty-two anyway."

I was so overwhelmed by the command to hide this catastrophe from Mom, by his physical condition, by the doctors, and by the fact that he was dying, that I have no idea what I actually said, but those words sum up my worldview at the time pretty well, even if I wasn't honest enough to utter them to Dad as he lay on his deathbed.

"Promise me you won't tell her," he said.

"I promise," I said, tears running down my cheeks.

Back in my little waiting room, I knew I had to call Mom. But I didn't know if I could pull off this lie. It was like how they'd lied to me about Dad quitting his job—but bigger. I knew it was all the pressure to find a new job and live the lie of the American dream that had almost killed him, causing this heart attack, and now he was roping me into this web of untruth with his dying wish. And he was right. I had to tell the lie. If not, Mom would hurt herself worse. She couldn't move anyway due to her back, so there was no reason to tell her tonight.

"Mom," I said when she answered.

"What's wrong?" she said. "I know something is wrong."

"Everything's OK," I said. "They're going to keep him overnight for tests."

"You're lying to me," she said.

"I'm not, Ma. I'm not," I said. "I'm just going to stay here a little while, and I'll be home soon."

She wept softly on the other end of the line.

"I'll call Nanny and Summey," I said.

"I'm gonna go and see her," Summey said. "Nanny will pick up your brother, and they'll come there to you."

"OK," I said. "But he made me swear not to tell Mom he had a heart attack. He made me swear that we tell her they're just keeping him for tests."

"Of course," Summey said. "For tests."

The doctor came back in.

"You should get your mother here," he said. "We are trying to stabilize him, but he could still go at any minute."

"She's laid up with a bad back and can't move," I said.

"Anyone else who can come?" he asked.

"My grandmother is on the way with my brother," I said.

When Nanny and Christopher walked into the room, she hugged me. Her brittle hair smelled like rain. Christopher and I just looked at each other in sad solidarity. Then we mostly sat in silence, the ambient hum of the hospital closing in on us.

The doctor came in. We looked at him, frozen. I knew he was going to tell me that Dad was dead.

"He has stabilized," the doctor said, pulling the mask from his mouth, and I felt as if I breathed for the first time all day. I noticed how exhausted he looked, heavy lines drawn down his cheeks by the mask, bags under his eyes, his pink skin damp.

"He needs open heart surgery. We're trying to get him scheduled for surgery at Emory as soon as possible," he said. "But everything is jammed up because of all the New Year's injuries and people taking time off. But we think he will make it through the night. You should go home."

We remained in the waiting room until later that evening, when another doctor came and said we should go home and that they would be in touch with us the next morning. Dad's oldest brother, Bully, was on the way to our house by then. My brother and I stopped at the Wendy's drive-through and ordered burgers, and we just sat in the parking lot and ate them, listening to Public Enemy's *Yo! Bum Rush the Show*, trying to figure out what was going to happen.

"Are you really not going to tell Mom?" Christopher asked.

"I can't," I said. "Dad told me not to. Like as a fucking final request."

We sat there, eating, listening to Chuck D and Flavor Flav. Rap was quickly taking the place of punk as the music of choice on the skate videos we made with Summey's camcorder, and it resonated with us because we also felt like the white world was a goddamn lie. We didn't think about it as the white world—because we were white, the white world was just the world. But the music, like some punk I listened to, offered a critique of the systems of power. The systems of power that, I now felt, were killing my dad and were coming for me.

"But I don't want to fucking lie to her," I said.

"Me either," Christopher said.

"You have to," I said. "I mean, I'll do it. I'll tell her. But you'll have to back me."

"OK," he said.

"Let's go and get it over with," I said, putting the car in reverse. "I was supposed to go out tonight."

"Are you going to?" Christopher asked. I could tell he didn't want to be alone with Mom.

"Bully is coming tonight. But I probably won't end up going anywhere. It's been such a long day."

"Do you think he'll die?" Christopher asked.

"I don't know," I said. "I thought he was dead when I saw him in there, and he looks a lot better than that now."

As soon as I walked in the house, I knew I would have to go out: the atmosphere felt suffocating. I walked up the stairs and into Mom's room. She was propped up against the headboard, rolled-up pillows under her knees. She looked so frail and fragile there. But her eyes were fierce, insistent.

"How is he?" she demanded.

"They're just keeping him for tests," I said. "He's OK."

"You're lying," she said.

I walked up to her, beside the bed.

"Come on, Mama, calm down," I said.

"You are lying to me," she said, and hit my solar plexus with her fists. It felt like a baby bird flying into me. "You are lying why are you lying what is wrong with him what is wrong what is wrong."

I wrapped my arms around her and held her still, her soft cotton gown and her smooth hair pressing against my face, and she started weeping. I could feel her tears on my face, and I did everything I could to keep from letting my own tears fall. She tried to hug me tighter, and then she shot forward, as if she'd been shocked, jolted by the paralyzing pain in her back.

"Just lay and rest, Mom," I said.

I sat with her, on the edge of the bed, holding her hand, until she fell asleep. I could hear my grandfather Summey and uncle Bully talking somewhere in the house, and I slipped out of the room and found the two men standing in the kitchen, watching a college football game on the small TV on the counter.

"You done good," Summey said to me when I walked in. He was wearing his toupee instead of a baseball cap.

I didn't say anything.

Uncle Bully walked up and gave me a meaningful look. He is the oldest and the tallest of the six Woods brothers, and he bent down to hug me. His hair smelled like Dad's. I did not want to break down.

"I'm going out for a while," I said, turning away.

I stole two bottles of Mad Dog 20/20 from the convenience store and drank them, quickly, with my girlfriend and her best friend as we drove around in the rain. I ended up crawling home from a party down the street.

47

I staggered into the kitchen, soaked and slurring.

"Whoa," Uncle Bully said. "You've had a little too much. Maybe you ought to go on up to bed."

"It's all bullshit," I said. "It's fucking bullshit."

"Yep," he said slowly, drawing the syllable out. "Yessir, sometimes it is."

As drunk as I was, climbing the stairs that night, I understood something that I wished I did not ever have to know. After I'd found out that my parents had lied to me about Dad quitting his job, I'd known that the whole culture they wanted to bequeath to me was a lie. That night, as the clock rang in 1988, I knew that my inheritance was not just a lie. It was the act of lying. The lie is active; it makes you complicit, forces you to carry its untruth forward, to pass it on like counterfeit cash or a chain letter, person to person, generation to generation. I'd lied to my mother and I'd made my brother lie.

My lie about Dad's health and his lie about his job were wrapped up in my mind, but they were parts of the other, bigger lie that dominated our lives—the attempt to keep up appearances as the All-American Southern White Christian Middle-Class family. It felt as if families like mine just passed down this lie over the generations.

I was a part of this farce, and it bothered me. We often think of whiteness as the complexion of our skin, but whiteness is a fantasy that tries to minimize our failings and maximize our power. I knew from spending time with my friends' families that this fabrication played out differently inside every white home, but that night at my house, the worst night we'd ever weathered, I felt as if I saw through the face of whiteness and glimpsed the hollowness inside.

Standing in the hallway in front of my door, I thought of walking down the hall to check on Mom in her room. But I knew I was too drunk, and I thought I might throw up.

All the pictures of skateboarders on the walls seemed to be spinning when I walked into my room and turned on the lights. I grabbed my dresser. The silence of the space swirled, whipping me up in it like a tornado. Mom was in a state of unreality that I'd knowingly kept her in. I had been initiated into the lie, and I had passed it on. It seemed cruel not to let her know the truth of what was happening. I didn't see how it was better to make her think Dad was OK when she would obviously know he wasn't soon enough. Maybe she would want to make the effort, endure the pain, to get up if I told her. But I knew I couldn't do it now.

I fell down in my bed and passed out.

Chapter 6

"**CAN YOU SLIDE THAT BOX** over there?" Dad said to me in the garage one bright spring day, two or three months after a quintuple bypass at Emory University Hospital in Atlanta saved his life. He was thinner than he had been since he was twelve years old, and his head seemed big on his frail body, his mustache too large over his lip.

"Sure," I said, and picked the box up and moved it.

"I said slide it," he bellowed when I laid the box down.

"I moved it," I said. "Whatever."

"It's not whatever," he said, lunging at me with both hands. "You do what I tell you to do."

He grabbed me by the front of my flannel shirt and shook me.

I ripped free of him and grabbed a hammer from where it hung on the wall.

"Get off of me," I yelled.

We stood there glowering at one another.

I threw down the hammer. It clanged against the concrete floor. I stormed out of the garage and got into my car and drove toward my friends' house.

I parked my rusting VW Bug in an empty spot in front of a small, low-rent apartment complex a couple of miles from my house. I looked in the mirror to make sure my tears were gone. My hair had grown long, and

I was wearing Dad's old jeans, slung low on my hips, and one of his old flannel shirts over a Bob Marley T-shirt.

I walked up to the brown door and knocked on it.

A small woman with curly black hair and a little elfin face opened the door.

"Are Glenn and Hector here?" I asked.

"They said if anyone came by to tell them that they're talking with Paco," she said sweetly, with the same look of good-humored puzzlement she always had on her face when it came to her two boys. I knew they lived in the small apartment on her disability, and she often seemed younger than her sons.

"OK, thanks," I said, and ran off before she even finished her sentence. Paco was the name they had given their pipe. As I got to the end of the parking lot, I could smell the weed coming from the patch of woods on the side of the building—the Grubs' makeshift clubhouse.

"Hola, motherfuckers," I said. "Yo hablo español con Paco todos los días."

The three guys standing in a circle turned to look at me and laughed.

Glenn handed me the bowl. He was short and powerfully built, with big shoulders and thick black hair. He was wearing a Black Flag T-shirt and combat boots. He reached into his pocket to pull out a Zippo and light a cigarette.

I managed to coax a small hit out of the nearly cashed bowl and passed it to Hector, Glenn's older brother, who was soft everywhere that Glenn was hard and round where Glenn was angular. Hector was always jocular and overly polite, until he got shit-faced, when he became sloppy and rude, the boyish politician's curl in his brown hair unable to cover up his fundamental contempt for the world.

He pulled a bag from his pocket and pinched out a little bit of shake and put it in the bowl.

"Did you get a hit?" he asked.

"Not really," I said.

"Bullshit," said Nash from the other side of the circle. I'd met him at the skate shop years earlier, when we were just visiting my grandparents, before we even moved to town, and now our parents went to church together and he'd introduced me to the whole crew.

"Me either," Glenn said, and laughed.

Hector handed me the bowl, and Glenn punched me in the arm.

These guys understood my contempt for my parents' world. We called ourselves the Grubs, short for "grubby campers," an accurate description of our state after a drug-fueled camping trip in the mountains outside of Greenville. But it wasn't just that; we were all misfits in some form or another, grubby not just on the surface but somewhere deep down in our souls. We didn't fit into Greenville because we didn't want to. If, as the Bob Jonesers told us, we were going to hell, we were going because we wanted no part of their heaven. We were heathens—the world was safest when we were up in the mountains camping and not on the roads. At least then we were a danger only to ourselves…most of the time. Unless we took hallucinogenic mushrooms and ran out of beer, as we had once at a place we called Hector's Pixie Pussy Lake.

It was a new campsite for us, one that Hector had told us had a lake with a rope swing. But it was also an old Boy Scout camp, and we were camping right by our cars instead of hiking in as we normally did and it was pretty disappointing. So when we got down to the last six-pack just as the mushrooms were peaking, we couldn't resist.

"Beer run," Nash yelled.

"Race!" Harry said as we all leaped to our feet.

We left the empty cans scattered around the smoldering campfire and ran toward the cars. Nash and Harry jumped into his Jeep, and Glenn and Hector and I got into my Volkswagen.

I cranked the engine and pushed my car as fast as it would go toward their taillights as we raced down the mountain toward town, now just a dull orange glow in the distance.

The roads were steep, full of turns and cutbacks. I raced up beside our friends in the opposite lane, not caring that there could be another car coming up the road, as the Misfits blared out over the stereo. My car's weak engine clanged behind the music, and the wind whipped in, blowing my hair in my face. Glenn threw his beer can out the window at Nash, and we howled with laughter when it hit the side of his Jeep with a thump.

"Direct hit," Hector shouted.

In retaliation, Harry turned on his flashlight and flashed the beam toward my eyes, trying to blind me as we squealed around the switchback turns.

We somehow made it home that night, but it was obvious that our good luck would not last forever. We were too reckless to remain wreck-less.

One day that summer, a bunch of us were hanging around my house, drinking beer and playing video games while my parents were at work. It was raining, and there wasn't nothing else to do. We started early, about 10:00 a.m., and by three it was just me and the two brothers, Glenn and Hector. I'd probably already had ten beers when the cordless phone rang that afternoon.

"Toss me that," I said. Glenn threw me the heavy white cordless phone.

"We had a wreck," Nash said when I answered, his words crumpled together like crashed cars as he gasped into the other end of the line. "We were driving down Paris Mountain and I lost control and we flipped off the side. I got thrown out. My ankle is broken. But Harry got pinned between the Jeep and a tree on the side of the mountain. It took forever for them to lift him out, and he's in ICU."

"We'll be right there," I said.

The brothers were already gathering up the clutter of empty beer cans sitting on the wicker chest that served as our coffee table when I hung up the phone.

"What happened?" Hector asked.

"Nash and Harry are in the hospital," I said. "We gotta go."

Glenn gulped the rest of his beer and handed me mine. I slammed it down. I stopped in the kitchen and scooped a spoonful of peanut butter into my mouth to obscure the smell of beer on my breath. We put all the cans in a plastic bag and ran out the door, then clambered into my rusted and leaking 1968 semiautomatic Volkswagen Bug with bad brakes and worn-down windshield wipers, and set out for the hospital through the downpour.

Our friends were in trouble, and we weren't going to let a little drunkenness stop us from seeing them. Hector handed the plastic bag of empty cans to Glenn from the back seat, and Glenn tossed them out the window. The cans clanged down the road as rain sprayed into the open window.

"I can't believe they flipped off the fucking mountain," I said.

"Maybe they didn't really," Hector said. "Maybe they're just fucking with us."

"Shut the fuck up, will you," Glenn snarled, turning back in his seat and swiping at Hector.

The brothers were two years apart and shared many of the same friends. But they also shared a bedroom in their mom's small apartment, so they fought a lot.

"I can't believe they fucking flipped off the mountain," I said again.

At the intersection in front of the bowling alley, the car in front of me stopped at a yellow light. I hit the brakes and my car careened, weightless, almost floating as it slid into the other car's rear end with a horrific crunch.

I looked up and the world was blurry. My prescription sunglasses had broken along with my nose on the windshield shattered in a spiderweb pattern in front of me.

My Bug was curled over on the bumper of the sedan. An elderly Black man with gray hair and a cane held on to his back as he got out of the car and then hobbled toward my door, flinching at the patter of raindrops landing on his skin. I was still in shock, trying to figure out what had happened.

I did a quick check to make sure Glenn and Hector weren't hurt before getting out. I used my shoulder to force open the door, which had crunched in and bent over as the hood curled, with a heavy heave against it. The metal squealed as it lurched open, and I staggered out into the rain, my Birkenstock sandals flooding with cold water.

"Are you all right?" the man asked, gesturing between my smashed nose and the shattered glass.

"Yeah," I said. "You?"

He didn't answer. A glop of blood fell from my nose into a puddle of water at my feet and floated there on top of it.

"What happened?" he asked instead.

I looked back at my crumpled car, where Glenn and Hector sat, looking stunned. I'd crashed my car on the way to see our friends who had crashed their car. It was almost funny.

"I just didn't expect—"

The whoop of a siren cut me off. The flashing blue light heralded the deputy sheriff, driving up through the median in one of the silver-and-black cars that we called storm troopers. The car stopped. The older Black man looked at me and I looked at him. We were both soaked, water running down our faces.

The deputy's door opened. He got out, squinting into the opposing head-lights. He walked up, white, stiff, and stern, moving as if his knees couldn't bend. The rain bounced off his plastic-wrapped Smokey Bear hat.

"What happened?" he asked.

"The light changed, and I stopped. And he just clobbered me," the old man said.

"I didn't expect him to stop on yellow," I shot back.

"Have you been drinking?" the deputy asked me.

With my long hair wild and plastered to my head, my nose smashed, and my white T-shirt soaked through with blood, I looked either out of my mind or drunk.

"No, sir," I said. There was a weed drought that summer, so I was momentarily relieved to realize that he wouldn't find drugs if he decided to search me.

"Why don't you come this way with me," he said, walking me to the storm trooper car. He opened the back door and gestured with his chin and I crouched in, shivering in the air-conditioning as the backs of my bare legs stuck to the vinyl seat. I pinched my bleeding nose. My hands were not cuffed. There was still hope.

"You can wait in your car and I'll be right with you, sir," I heard the deputy shout to the old man as he opened his door and ducked into the seat.

And now I was just sitting there, waiting, as the cop busied himself with paperwork on a hard aluminum folder, occasionally reading a numeric code into the radio. I strained my sight to see what he was writing. But my eyes were watering, and the back of my throat was filling up with blood. I gave up, leaned back, and pinched my nose shut again, hoping the coppery taste of blood would cover up the fetid booze on my breath. The adrenaline of the crash had surged through me, but it did not sober me up. Instead of being scared, I was restless and angry.

The police radio squawked. In my peripheral vision, I saw the dark mass of a person blocking the light through the steamy gray window. Knuckles rapped the glass.

The deputy rolled down his window—the rush of rubber tires on wet asphalt as the traffic struggled by and the claustrophobic smell of the summer storm shot into the car. Then a New York Yankees baseball cap moved toward me through the rain. Beneath it, my grandfather Summey's wrinkled, sunspotted face came into focus. He nodded toward me, his pale-gray mustache and rain-streaked glasses framing his long nose.

"Hey there, Tommy," Summey said to the cop. "Can I talk to you for a minute?"

I saw the deputy's eyes in the rearview as he looked me over. Several car horns dueled in angry protest against the delay our crash was causing.

"My grandson," Summey said, motioning toward me.

"Come on around and get in," the deputy said to Summey.

Then he turned around in his seat and faced me.

"Go wait with your friends a minute," he said. "Over at your car."

I stepped out of the police car and into the rain, puddles reflecting the flashing blue light in a pulsing rhythm. I looked over at the silhouette of the old Black man, who was about the same age as my grandfather but did not know the deputy. I limped on an injured knee over to my friends where they waited inside my smashed car. Glenn lit a smoke and handed it to me as I climbed in the crumpled driver's door that would no longer close. I took a big drag and then another. Hector handed me a piece of watermelon bubble gum for my breath and a handkerchief for my bleeding nose.

"What the fuck, dude?" Hector said, gesturing toward the police car. "What's happening?"

I shrugged.

"That's my grandfather," I said.

The sheriff's door opened. Summey climbed out of the car and strode toward us. He spit tobacco juice on the ground.

"I'm gonna tell your mother to pick you up," he said when Glenn, Hector, and I met him halfway between the cars. "And call a tow truck."

I nodded. We were less than a mile from his carpet store, where Mom was working.

"But the deputy's got some more questions for you first," he added, squirting a stream of brown tobacco juice into the rain. Then he turned to Glenn and Hector.

"I'll give you boys a ride," he said. "Get you out of this rain."

"Yessir," Hector said.

Summey waddled through the puddles in his Members Only jacket and baseball cap, followed by the drenched brothers. When he passed the deputy's car, he gave a quick, casual wave, flashing the fake Rolex on his wrist. The deputy approached me.

"I'm going to write this up, as you're at fault," he said. "But it's a minor infraction. You were driving too close for conditions."

That was the official word on what had happened. I never heard anything else about the crash until one evening a couple of months later.

"That man whose car you crashed into is trying to sue you," Mom said, going through mail on the counter, when I walked into the kitchen one day. I had pretty much forgotten the whole thing.

"Claims his back is hurt," Dad added from the table, where he was paying bills.

"He was fine," I said. "He's just faking it to get money."

I had no idea whether he was fine, and I didn't even care—to me, the only players in this drama were me and the law. I was the victim and the hero, and I had escaped. The old Black man just wanted to get something from us, I thought, but we'd won.

"You are so lucky that Daddy was able to talk to that deputy," Mom said, a sense of familiar relief in her voice. "That deputy wrote it up so that it was really the rain that caused the wreck."

"Insurance will pay," Dad said. "But that makes it real hard to sue you for being drunk."

"I wasn't drunk," I said, insisting on my lie.

Things had not gotten better between me and Dad. Whenever he was in town, the atmosphere was always volatile. A small exchange like this could easily blow up into a screaming match, each of us building toward blows with the other to prove his manhood: he needed to prove that he still had it, and I was desperate to show I had come into it. But today, Dad settled for a sarcastic quip.

"Just like Gary Hart wasn't on the *Monkey Business*," he said.

"We are so lucky that Daddy drove by," Mom said, directing us toward our common interest.

None of us questioned the source of my grandfather Summey's power. We called it the "good ol' boy system" when he used his connections to fix a ticket or otherwise help out someone who found himself in a bind. But even if such things were common, they were not exactly legit, and we knew it was best not to look too deeply into the source of his influence.

"Our lawyer made it pretty clear that it would be a lost cause," Dad added.

No one ever followed up about a lawsuit. That wreck demonstrated that the white solidarity of the good ol' boy system was at least as strong as the law, twisting the way the rules worked to provide me with privilege and protection. Good ol' white folks with power look out for other good ol' white folks with power. Whiteness is the belief that the freedom of white people is more important than the safety of people who are not white.

It is the freedom to deny race even as you use it.

Chapter 7

DAD GAVE ME A RIDE to the bank to cash a check when I got off work early one Friday afternoon. I was working as an assistant for a crew of carpet installers, but I was the boss's kid, so it hardly felt like a job. They worked me, but if I missed a day or something, they couldn't really say anything.

"The race to replace Reagan is shaping up. And on the Democratic side, it looks like Murderers' Row," the voice on the radio said.

Dad's office was in Charlotte, and he spent a lot of time on I-85 between there and Greenville. I'd noticed that the radio was always tuned to AM talk stations the few times I'd borrowed the car since my wreck. I thought it was entertaining. The rhythms that these men used, the rising cadence, the dismissive mockery, the rhetorical escalation, were intimately familiar to me from the arguments I heard from Dad and his brothers, who all had strong opinions and all felt it was their sacred duty as Americans to share those opinions with more volume than the next guy.

"Good thing Gary Hart is gone," the radio guy said. "Gary Hart is like some Weather Underground homosexual streetwalker who cheats on his wife and lies about it. I mean, that hair. What an arrogant sissy. But now they're left with Dukakis, who looks like an inept bookie. And then there's Jesse Jackson. Where do I even start? He was literally a Black Panther bank robber. He might say Rainbow Coalition, but make no mistake, he is the most racist man in America."

"He's got a point," Dad said, turning into the bank parking lot.

"What do you mean?"

"Jesse Jackson is a racist," he said, pulling into a parking spot.

I didn't say anything.

"He's from here, you know. From right here in Greenville. And he used to work as a waiter at the Palmetto Club, and he used to spit in white people's food," Dad said. "What do you think about that? Don't you think that's racist? He even brags about it, the same way he brags about being with Martin Luther King when he died."

He opened the car door and made as if to get out. Then he paused and turned.

"Except he was lying about that," he said, leaning toward me.

I opened my door and got out.

"He was King's rival, and he wasn't even with him," he said as we walked toward the bank. "When he got killed."

"If I could vote, I would vote for Jackson," I said, although I hadn't thought much about it. But I knew this declaration would outrage Dad.

"How can you say that?" he said.

I pulled open the glass doors, and we walked into the air-conditioned bank, which felt quiet despite the line of people waiting to cash their Friday paychecks.

"We should just cash it today and come back when it's not a Friday to talk about the account," I said.

I just wanted my money, but Dad wanted to see how much I would need in order to open my own account. He scanned the crowd and then looked at his gold watch.

"OK," he said. "But that is something you should do, now that you're working."

"Sure," I said.

We stood in silence.

When we left the bank fifteen minutes later, my pocket full of bills that I was going to spend on weed later that evening, Dad was shaking his head.

I could tell he wanted to make a point, but I didn't take the bait.

"That's why you're not allowed to vote until you're eighteen," Dad said finally.

"Why?" I sighed.

"Because you would be stupid enough to vote for Jesse Jackson," he said. "Even though you admitted he was racist."

"I didn't admit he was a racist. You said that," I said.

"You would say that's racist, wouldn't you?" he asked.

"I don't know," I said.

"What do you mean you don't know?" he asked as he opened his car door. "Something's either racist or not, right?"

I got in the passenger's side.

"I mean, it depends on what the white people were doing," I said.

"Well, he said he spit in their soup just because they were white," he said, putting his hand on my headrest and turning around in his seat to look behind him as he backed out of the spot.

"Well, then, I guess that would be racist," I said. "But not if, say, the white people had been beating him or something. Then spit would really be minor. An attempt to return fire, the best you can."

Dad threw his hands up in frustration at a car blocking him from pulling out.

"It's just racist," he said.

"Who are you going to vote for?" I asked after he made it around the car and turned onto Haywood Road.

"I wish we could just keep Reagan," he said. "Bush is OK. But I think I'm leaning toward Bob Dole. Either one of them would be better than any of the Democrats."

I remembered the arguments when Dad had voted for Reagan in 1980. Two of his younger brothers, Irvin and Gus, worked in the Carter administration, and it had seemed like a betrayal.

"You'd vote against your own damn brother?" Gus said to him once in anger at a family reunion. "I can't believe you."

"Our family has always been Democrats," Irvin chimed in. "All the way back to our grandfather who served in the legislature as a Democrat."

"The Democrats were different back then," Dad said. "Now it's just a bunch of union fat cats, Hollywood hotshots, civil rights frauds, and welfare queens. And Carter is just weak. Look at Reagan. We need a morning in America."

Dad voted for Reagan a second time, and he seemed to hate Democrats more every day.

"I'd definitely vote Democratic," I said. "But I'm really an anarchist."

"They all are," Dad said, tapping the steering wheel as he chuckled at his own wit. "That's the problem with Democrats. They're all secretly communists."

"I think Glenn's gonna spend the night tomorrow, if that's cool," I said to change the subject.

"That's fine with me," he said. "Are you two still seeing those scary-looking girls?"

"Come on. Damn, Dad," I said. "Why do you have to be such a—"

"They intentionally dress scary like that," he said. "That's the effect they're going for, right? So why shouldn't I say it? It's recognizing the artistry of their . . . costume design."

I just shook my head. His rhetorical questions drove me nuts. He was always needling, needling, needling. I never even knew anymore if he meant what he was saying or if he was just trying to piss me off.

But Glenn and I were dating two goth girls.

We drove along as the guy on the radio talked about baseball.

"Well, are you seeing those two nice girls still?" Dad asked finally.

"Yeah," I said. "Molly and Mindy. Sort of."

"Well, you be careful, Son," he said as we pulled into the driveway. "I know that she wasn't really going up the ladder to your room when I saw her that morning."

I spent a lot of time on the roof outside my window smoking cigarettes, and Dad let me put his ladder up so I could come and go that way. One Saturday morning he had been driving to the store and had seen my girlfriend coming down the ladder after staying in my room all night. She told him she was climbing up to see if I was awake.

"No, I didn't think you did," I said, and got out of the car. "Thanks for the ride."

The next night, I was sitting with Glenn on the roof. The blue smoke from my cigarette glowed in the streetlight filtering through the big old pine tree that partially blocked the view from the street.

We had planned to sneak out with Mindy and Molly, but they'd chickened out at the last minute. And the bag of weed I was supposed to get had fallen through. And because my car was crashed and Glenn didn't have one, we couldn't even manage to get any beer. We had nothing better to do than sit on the roof and smoke cigarettes as Bob Marley's *Legend* played on the turntable just inside the window.

"I went three places and applied for a job," Glenn said. "And not jack shit."

"I could probably get you on with one of the carpet installers who work for my mom. It sucks. My knees are always sore," I said. "But the guys are pretty funny."

"Three different places," Glenn said. "People are always talking about how oppressed Black people are. But white people are the ones who are really oppressed."

I laughed.

"Think about it," he said. "Blacks get welfare and affirmative action and they don't even work. What do I get? Shit. I won't get any scholarships or even welfare. Everything is set up for them and against us."

He lit another cigarette with his Zippo, his pink face glowing for a moment beneath his short black hair before he flicked the lighter shut. He reached into his leather jacket and pulled out a folded piece of paper.

What I'd thought of as an ordinary conversation with one of my best friends suddenly shifted.

"What is that?" I asked, looking at the xeroxed pamphlet.

"It's from David Duke," he said.

Duke was making a hopeless run for president that year, and I'd heard him described on the news as the former Grand Wizard of the KKK. I felt as if I were about to get buttonholed by one of those religious proselytizers on the street, as if this had all been leading somewhere.

"That's the KKK," I said.

"No, look," Glenn said, and handed me the trifold.

It was branded NAAWP—National Association for the Advancement of White People.

"Duke says it's a white rights lobby organization, a racialist movement, mainly middle-class people," Glenn said as if from a script.

There had always been skinheads around the punk scene that we hung out in, but I had never really thought about the ideas they had. I'd noticed Glenn hanging out with them more, but to me skinhead was just another subculture, a fashion statement.

"I'm for Jesse Jackson," I said, deciding to use the line that I had with Dad, and, saying it a second time, I felt as if it might be true.

"That's ridiculous," he said. "That's just betraying your race."

"Man, I'm happy to betray my race," I said. "My dad tried to follow the American dream and it almost fucking killed him. Fuck that. Not me, buddy."

Sitting there on the roof, I was surprised to find how easily I was able to say to Glenn the thing I didn't even know I needed to say to Dad.

Glenn shook his head, sadly, as if I were a lost cause, and put the pamphlet back in his pocket. A car drove by, and we sat still in case it was the cops. We weren't doing anything wrong, but it was a habit, and we didn't want to talk to them. The light swept through the pine needles. The sound of the car faded. The shingles dug into my palms.

"That's easy for you to say, in a place like this," he said.

"What do you mean by that?" I asked.

"You have a room to yourself," he said. "I share my room with my fucking brother. We share a wall with my mom. Maybe you aren't hearing me because *you* are getting the benefits that were promised to whites for building this country. But I am not."

"I don't want those benefits," I said.

In reality, I didn't think of my privilege as a benefit at all—only as a constraint. But there was something about this conversation that made me realize it was a luxury to feel that way.

"Well, that's good if you're for Jesse Jackson, because you'll sure as shit lose them," he said.

"Yeah," I said a little dismissively. "My dad just said the same thing."

"Just because he's your dad doesn't mean he is wrong about everything," Glenn said.

More lights flashed through the pine needles as a car approached. It slowed and stopped at the edge of the yard. We sat still on our perch: the sound of doors creaking open and then slamming closed.

"Hey, boys," Mindy said.

Glenn and I looked at each other and laughed. I turned around and shut my window, and we climbed down the ladder and scampered across the yard to Molly's old beige Buick waiting by the curb.

I felt uneasy as we rode around Greenville for the next hour, looking for somewhere that would sell us beer. I was in the front seat beside Molly, and Glenn was beside Mindy in the back. I was conflicted. I valued loyalty to friends. And Glenn was my friend. But I also thought that I shouldn't be friends with skinheads. I'd been around skinheads plenty—though I hadn't entirely realized until that night that Glenn had morphed into one—but this was the first time one had told me outright what he believed. And if Glenn and Dad agreed, did it mean that Dad was a racist? Instead of talking to Glenn about it, I got out of the car when Molly parked at Butler Springs Park, and she and I made out on one picnic table while Glenn and Mindy made out on the table beside us.

Whiteness is the freedom to ignore its threat.

Chapter 8

I STOOD BEFORE THE MASSIVE wall of neckties hanging at the back of Dad's walk-in closet at around eleven on a Tuesday morning. I'd spent plenty of time in the closet, rummaging around for porn or money I could swipe, and I had taken to stealing the old clothes he no longer wore, which were too big for me and communicated my disdain for social norms. But today was different. I needed a tie. I actually needed five of them.

I let my fingers linger a moment over the silken feel, appreciating the smoothness for the first time. I didn't particularly care about the pattern or the cut but tried to pick ties from the margins of the collection, ties I couldn't remember him wearing. I pulled down a red one with blue paisley patterns swimming across it. Then another red one, this one with white diamonds on it. Two blue ones and a black one.

I draped the ties over my forearm and walked back, otherwise naked, toward my room, my bouncing erection leading the way. Molly was also naked, lying back on my bed. She looked up at me from under her bangs and laughed. I walked toward the bed. She tried to kiss me, but I pulled my face away and took her right hand. I tied that arm to the bedpost, then the other.

Now it was time for the legs. She had just shaved her bush the night before—the first time I had ever seen such a thing in real life—and it was intoxicating to be able to clearly see that which had, for so long, been a mystery. As I took hold of the other leg, I could see the folds pull apart, and I thought that I should slow down.

I looked over at the brass pipe, still partially packed, sitting on my dresser. I took the final tie, the black one, and I wrapped it around Molly's head, pulling her hair as the knot caught her blond strands. Then I stepped away. She writhed a bit, the sun shining in through the pine tree onto her pale belly.

Instead of going to her, I stepped over to the dresser. The bowl was pretty much cashed, so I walked over to the window and dumped out the ashes. I opened my dresser and pulled out the sock I hid my bag of dry, crumbly weed in. I opened the bag and pulled out a small bud.

"What are you doing?" Molly asked, impatiently. "You aren't getting high again, are you?"

Sometimes she was like another parent, complaining about me getting stoned. She had already graduated and was going to the community college. Her friend Mindy had moved away and she was depressed and we were fighting a lot, sometimes about pot but also about all kinds of other dumb shit. I was supposed to be in school that day but we'd had a big argument on the phone the night before and we wanted to make up, so I had ditched class and she had shaved.

I held the lighter to the pipe and breathed in, just looking at her.

"You motherfucker," she said upon smelling my exhalation. But it was only pantomime, she was not really angry.

I put down the pipe and stepped toward her.

That's when Mom pushed the door open. I turned and looked at her, stunned. I saw her eyes dart from me to Molly, spread-eagled, splayed and shaved. And even worse, with the blindfold on, Molly didn't even know my mom was here yet. But she must have sensed something was going on.

She freed one hand and pulled off the blindfold.

Molly and Mom screamed at the same time.

"I'm running away," I cried, simply because there was nothing else I could possibly say. Molly tried to cover herself and extract her remaining limbs from Dad's ties.

I pushed past Mom and out of my bedroom into the hallway. I was still naked, so I ran back into Dad's closet and pulled on a faded old pair of Levi's. They hung low and I had no underwear, so my pubic hair showed when Mom came in, and when she looked at me, I grabbed a white V-neck undershirt of Dad's.

"I cannot believe you," Mom howled. "We did not raise you to be like this. Skipping school, smoking pot, and . . . this!"

I stepped out of the closet into Mom and Dad's room, where I could see Molly in the hallway busting it toward the steps, clothes bunched up in her hand.

"Well, I don't want to grow up to be like *this*," I said, gesturing not at a single object but at the entire edifice she had attempted to construct.

Tears started running down Mom's face, and I started to cry as well. We were screaming at each other through our tears as I ran down the stairs, following Molly.

"I can't believe after all we've done for you that you would disrespect our home in this way!"

"You just try to control my life—that's the only reason you do anything for me," I replied.

I ran to catch up with Molly. I caught a glimpse of her as she burst out the kitchen door and into the garage, her black eyeliner smeared by tears, her eyes full of horror.

"You cannot live like this," Mom cried. "Not under my roof."

"I'm running away," I said again, and ran out the door.

By the time I got to the driveway, Molly's beige Buick was backing out, fast, into the street, where she slammed on the brakes, put it in drive, and hit the gas so that the tires let out a little squeal like she'd run over a gerbil.

I got into my car and slammed the door. I turned the key and backed out of the driveway and drove in the other direction, away from Mom and away from Molly. I got to the stop sign and had no idea where to go. I lit a cigarette and turned up the Replacements song on the tape player and just sat there until another car came up behind me, forcing me to make a decision and turn.

I drove around from park to park that we hung out at—from Butler Springs Park to Cleveland Park to Gower Park—and walked around smoking cigarettes. Then I sat in my car listening to music until school was out and drove over to Glenn and Hector's. I didn't want to see their mom because I was angry and upset and had been crying and didn't know how to deal with an adult. I walked first to the place we had back in the woods behind the apartments, but no one was there. Finally I knocked on their door, but their mom said they hadn't come home from school yet and she didn't know where the boys were.

I drove downtown to my friend Bo's house. He was a tall, stringy, smart hippie kid. At his house, when we smoked pot, we'd usually talk about Hermann Hesse or the Beat poets, whom we had just discovered.

When I knocked, I heard some motion inside. I knocked again. When he opened the door, I could tell he'd been napping, as he often did after school. I told him what had happened—the need to tell the story to someone had been the prime motivation for my rounds of the city searching for friends, I realized, as the words poured out and Bo chuckled and shook his head in disbelief. But when I asked him if I could stay for a few days, he got kind of squirrelly.

"I don't know, man. Me and my moms have a lot going on, and I, I don't think it's a good time for it," he stammered, softly, as the sage incense he'd been burning in a seashell sent up a ropy, crisp white smoke against the afternoon sun.

"I understand," I said.

"You don't have any pot, do you?" he asked, drowsily.

"No," I said. "I forgot and left it in my sock drawer."

After I left Bo's house, I tried each of my friends in turn. No one would let me stay, so at 10:00 p.m., I drove my car back home. I sat in the driveway a long time before going inside, and there was no confrontation that night. That wouldn't come until Dad got back to town. Until then I'd do my best to avoid Mom, and it seemed she was trying to avoid me as well.

The night Dad came back from Charlotte, Glenn and I managed to get someone to sell us two twelve-packs of Milwaukee's Best, and we sat in the playground of an elementary school near my house and drank it all. Intoxication was a competitive sport for me and my friends, all of us bragging about how many beers we drank, how much pot we smoked, or how many hits of acid we took. Still, it was the first time I'd ever just sat down with a twelve-pack and determined to drink it all before I went home.

I was a little worried about what Dad was going to say about Mom catching Molly strapped to the bed with his neckties, and I figured this was an appropriate preparation. We plopped our asses on the rubber swing seats and started to drink.

"It's really done this time," I said.

"Yeah, that's what you said the last time you and Molly broke up," Glenn said.

"Fucking for real, this time," I said. I crunched my can, let out a loud burp, and dropped it in the sand. I reached into the damp cardboard box behind me and brought out another sweating can of now-warmish beer.

Glenn kicked his feet up on the swing, and the streetlight shimmered on the toes of his combat boots.

We hadn't talked about David Duke or the NAAWP in the weeks since our conversation on the roof, but I ended up in a confrontation with another of Glenn's skinhead friends. Some of the Grubs had just smoked a joint in the parking lot of a punk show when a guy everyone called Skinhead Steve walked up to us in his bomber jacket as we lit cigarettes.

Steve was the kind of freckle-faced, skinny-necked redhead who looked almost like a rodent. I think he was the one who'd first started preaching this shit to Glenn.

He looked at my Bob Marley *Uprising* T-shirt.

"He was a race traitor," Steve said.

"What?" I said, annoyed.

"Ask any of the Rastas. It's about Blackness. It's not for you," Steve said, condescendingly. "Bob Marley was half-white anyway, and he betrayed the Rastas to become popular with other race traitors like you."

Like most suburban white kids, all I knew about Rastafarianism was that it enthusiastically condoned the consumption of cannabis.

"Fuck off," I said.

"Oh yeah, race traitor?" he said, puffing out his chest beneath his bomber jacket. "Can't take the truth?"

"I said fuck you."

He pushed me, lightly, his fingertips pressing into my chest. I was skinny but surprisingly strong from skating, and I pushed him back and he stumbled and caught himself on his hands as he fell back onto the rough asphalt. He started to jump up, but Glenn grabbed him, and Hector and our friend Mike grabbed me and pulled me back. That was fine with me. I didn't really want to fight, but it was a fight that I was confident I would win.

The fucked-up thing was that I didn't know what side Glenn was on. Did he have my back or Steve's? He and I hung out all the time, and he rarely saw Steve, but in the parking lot at the show that night, it seemed that he had aligned himself with the skinhead.

Was he a skinhead or a Grub? Hanging out on the swing set that night, I thought he was a Grub, a member of our ragtag group whose only shared ideology was pissing off authorities and getting as fucked up as possible. But I couldn't shake the idea that he was also aligned with this other group of shitheads.

I was still brooding on this as we sat on the swings gulping down our beers in the queasy dusk. I watched as Glenn swung higher so that in my drunkenness all I could see was the top of his head when he reached the acme of his arc, where he paused a second before rushing backward toward me. I slid my feet back into my Birkenstock sandals lying in the sand in front of my swing and staggered to the woods behind us to take a leak.

As I pissed, I could hear the metal swing set moaning behind me and the last of the year's crickets chirping in the woods in front of me. The trees were barely visible, only vertical lines in the gloaming.

I don't know when Glenn left or how I got home, but I became a bit more cognizant as I stumbled in the door and saw Dad standing there in the kitchen, his arms crossed over his chest.

I tried to turn my stumble into swagger.

"Son," he said. "We need to talk."

"Son," I mocked.

"OK," he said as Mom walked in the kitchen. "It's clear you've been drinking—"

"He's been drinking?" Mom exclaimed, and immediately started to cry. This was not new, but she was shocked anew with every infraction.

"And we'll just wait until tomorrow," Dad finished.

"Why do you always think I've been drinking?" I slurred. "I haven't been fucking drinking."

"Watch your mouth," Dad said.

"Fuck you!" I screamed. "You're always telling me what to fucking do. Jesus Christ."

"You're drunk," Dad said. "Just go on up to bed and we'll talk about skipping school and all the rest of it in the morning."

"I can't believe he's drunk again," Mom cried. "Drunk. My son. My baby boy."

"I'm not fucking drunk! Why does everyone always try to say what I am?" I said. "You don't get to define me!"

My belligerence, and my belief in the veracity of my claims, increased with every articulation of this lie. Of course I was drunk. I had sucked down an entire twelve-pack over the course of two hours. I was smashed. But as I stood in the kitchen screaming at my parents, I convinced myself, if no one else, that I was absolutely sober.

"And he was with that girl," Mom cried.

Me and "that girl" were broken up, and Mom's words reminded me that I was pissed off about that too.

"God," I said. "Why are you such a bitch?"

That's when Dad punched me. I didn't see it coming, but at the moment his fist connected with my chin, it went all slow motion, like a movie, and I was aware of everything as spit flew out of my mouth, as my head turned. There was a roaring sound and the world went red, then black, and then I spun on Dad, adrenaline ripping through me.

He had hoped to knock me out, but I didn't go down. He stood there, fists cocked, wondering if we were going to have a real fight. I wondered too, fight or flight coursing through me. We both stepped forward, our fists raised.

And then I stopped. I looked at him dismissively. He was breathing hard. Mom was standing behind him, wailing.

I thought I could kick his ass. But I knew that if I did, if I punched my dad, I would be the one who lost. So I stood, waiting to see what he would do, and I knew I had won. Now I was the victim. My father had punched *me* for doing nothing more than sharing my side of the story and protesting my innocence. I could just walk away now, and I would be the winner, embattled, unjustly treated, and righteous.

I walked right past him toward the door into the dining room, which led to the stairway up to my room. When I reached the bottom of the stairs and looked back, I noticed my brother Christopher, who was fourteen and still skating every day, standing behind the dining room door. I could see he had been watching what was happening in the kitchen through the crack between the door and the jamb, and now he was left there in the dark holding an aluminum baseball bat in his hands.

Christopher and I had been close until I started hanging out with the Grubs. When he was born, he had a heart condition that the doctors told my parents would kill him. They were gone for months, leaving me with my grandparents while they went to Charleston and Birmingham for surgery. He survived and he thrived. I'd felt a deep affection and even tenderness for him when we were smaller. He was athletic and healthy, but he was less open and talkative than I, and for much of our lives he had hung out with my friends more than he did with anyone his own age. Once I started driving, he went everywhere with me as we found new places to skate around town. When I first started smoking weed, it didn't seem to bother him. I'd usually do it in the afternoon or at night, after we'd skated. Then I started smoking while we skated, and that made him nervous, since I was the one who would drive us home, and finally, when I pretty much quit skating and only smoked, we stopped spending time together. But as I looked at him standing there with the bat, a line of light from the kitchen cast on his face, I finally realized that the kid who had idolized me all my life now despised me. And it would only get worse.

A few days later, Glenn and I were hanging out at my house, working the telephone, looking for somebody who might sell us a joint.

"Call Molly," he said.

"Fuck you, man. She hated when I smoked weed," I said.

"But she usually had some stashed in that cigar box in her room," he said.

"I'm not calling her," I said.

"Then I guess we're not gonna get high today," he said. "I can't think of anyone else."

"Me either," I said.

Glenn and I were both realizing that we didn't enjoy hanging out with each other that much when we weren't fucked up.

"Let's go skating," I said, looking at one of the pictures of pro skaters now anachronistically hanging on my wall, relics from another era.

"Whatever," he said. "I guess."

Glenn was not a good skater; he looked stiff and awkward on a board. But it was a beautiful, bright, and crisp day and I hadn't skated in a long time, and if we weren't going to get high, I figured it would be fun to cruise around.

"We'll go over to the ramp by Stan's house," I said. "There's a dude who hangs out there who might have a bag too."

I was only half lying. My brother had started skating with a Black kid called Blaze. We'd hung out only once or twice, when he was over at my house, but I thought my brother might have mentioned that Blaze had gotten in trouble for smoking a joint behind the skate shop. I didn't know if he would have weed, but it was worth asking.

We got in my car and cruised over to the ramp, a half-pipe, which looked like the letter *U*, in some twins' backyard. The twins weren't very good skateboarders, but the ramp was nice, and a lot of good skaters hung out there.

As I pulled the car to the curb, I could see them—Blaze, the twins, and my brother—all standing on the platform at the top of the ramp, which loomed up above the ivy-covered fence at the back of the twins' driveway.

"Hey," I said as Glenn and I got out of the car.

"What the fuck you doing, Nazi?" Blaze snarled from the back of the ramp four feet above us as Glenn and I walked into the driveway and made our way toward the backyard. Glenn's head was shaved, and he had on combat boots with white laces and a leather jacket.

"Fucking n*****," Glenn said as he started to run toward Blaze. The back of the ramp was higher than the fence, and Blaze jumped down, easily clearing the chain-link and landing in the driveway. He darted toward Glenn.

I stood there stunned for a second. I hadn't expected this at all. But I had caused it. By the time this thought flashed through my mind, I was already running behind Glenn, hoping I could stop what was happening as these two bodies, one white and one Black, screamed toward each other, intent on collision.

Glenn was short and stocky, Blaze tall and lanky. Glenn hunched forward and burrowed his chin into his chest like he was going to tackle Blaze, but as soon as he was close enough, Blaze brought his fist down hard on the back of Glenn's stooped head. I could hear the sound of bone on bone as knuckles hit skull. Glenn swung wildly in reaction but barely made contact with Blaze's chest.

The rest of us stood there watching without a word until a few of us jumped in to pull them apart.

"The police are on the way!" I heard. I turned to see the twins' mom yelling. Glenn was already dashing toward my car.

That was when I caught my brother's disappointed and embarrassed eyes. I looked at him and at the twins and their mom. And then I looked at Blaze. He didn't know Glenn. But he'd been to my house and he had thought he knew me. His eyes showed both pain and fury as he stood there panting.

All of this was my fault. Even though Glenn had done everything possible to tell me what he was about, I had not taken his racism seriously.

I thought his David Duke talk was goofy and outdated, an embarrassing and unfortunate phase. But I had not recognized its danger.

I turned away from Blaze and my brother, unable to take their eyes any longer, and I realized they must have thought I was running to help Glenn rather than to stop him. I looked toward my car, where Glenn's bald head and angry flared eyes were framed by the window. Why wouldn't they think that I would help him? I paused. I could hear a police siren. "I'm sorry," I said quickly, quietly, before turning and sprinting toward my car. And I was sorry, but I couldn't articulate what I was sorry for.

"'Chase those crazy baldheads out of town,'" I heard Blaze yell, quoting a line from a Bob Marley song.

Glenn and I didn't talk as we drove back to his house. But I thought about it that night, sitting on my roof and smoking, and realized that all rebellion is not the same.

And though I didn't recognize it for a few weeks, I think Glenn learned that this skinhead shit wasn't worth it. He was mad at the world, sure. But he didn't want to get into a fight every time he saw a Black person. His hair grew out, and the white laces came out of the combat boots. But we never talked about what had happened that day with Blaze.

And though my brother looked at me with an even greater sense of hatred when we passed in the hall at home, he never mentioned it either.

Whiteness is a conspiracy of both silence and violence.

Chapter 9

DAD AND I WALKED THROUGH the parking lot of the Greenville County Detention Center, where I had been for the last nineteen hours, sometime just before midnight. We were silent. A gang of moths swarmed the flickering streetlight above his car. A silver-and-black storm trooper drove by. The cop lifted his left hand from the wheel and gave Dad a lazy wave, white guy to white guy, *blanco a blanco*.

Even though I was in deep shit, I was proud that I did not command such respect from cops. Quite the opposite.

"I hope you've learned something," Dad said.

"I did," I said. "The guys in my cell—"

"You were in a cell?" Dad asked, wincing a bit as he used the key to unlock his car.

"Drunk tank last night," I said as nonchalantly as possible, as if this were a world I now knew. "They moved me to a cell this morning with these two really cool guys, and when I told them what happened they both said there's no way the charge would stick because it was totally illegal."

"Your cellmates were *really cool guys?*" Dad said with a weary sense of wonder.

"Yeah," I said. "I learned so much and can't wait to get home and write it in my journal."

Dad shook his head. He turned down the talk radio station.

"So what exactly did happen?" Dad asked.

Another storm trooper pulled into the parking lot as we waited to pull out.

"Last week, we were all at my friend Tom's house after work," I started. "A cop stopped me in the apartment complex. Everyone else was drinking but I wasn't, and he searched me and I didn't have anything. He told me if he ever saw me on that side of town again, I was going to jail. So then tonight, uh, last night, we got hungry and went to the store—"

"Hold on," Dad said. "It was what, after two in the morning, and you go right to the place that a police officer warned you not to go?"

"He can't tell me to stay out of half the city," I said. "I don't even know what part of town he meant."

Dad sighed.

"We're allowed to get snacks," I said.

My friends, Glenn and Allen, were actually trying to buy more beer inside the store. But since they hadn't been successful, I didn't need to tell him that.

"Not if you have pot in the goddamn car," Dad said, his fury boiling over as headlights flashed across his face. "Or if you're drunk, then you stay away."

"But see, I was just sitting in the back of the car. I wasn't driving, and I didn't even get out. There was no way for him to know if I was drinking," I said. "One of the guys in my cell said it's called probable cause."

"But if you weren't there in the first place you wouldn't have been in a cell, and I wouldn't have to pay a damned lawyer to argue about probable cause," he said.

We drove in silence through the quiet city streets late that Sunday night.

"So he just pulled you out of the car?" Dad asked after a few minutes.

"Yes," I said, mimicking the action of grabbing someone by the collar. "I swear I was just sitting there, and all of a sudden, the door opened, and my face was pressed against the hot hood of the cop car with my arm twisted behind my back."

"Where was the pot?"

"In the car."

"Were you alone?"

"I was with Zooey," I said.

Zooey was my new girlfriend. When she started hanging around with us after her dad moved into an apartment complex between my house and Glenn's, everyone immediately fell in love with her. She had a smile that radiated like some kind of wild sunshine, illuminating her long, straight brown hair, her chestnut-brown eyes, and her coppery skin. She wore long, flowing dresses, wraps in her hair, and bells around her ankles that tinkled above her Birkenstocks everywhere she traipsed.

It seemed inevitable that someone would end up dating her, but for what felt like ages, she just hung around the Grubs as a friend, unattached to any guy. Zooey, Bo, and I would take acid and dance around naked to Grateful Dead songs. I'd never been around a naked girl in a nonsexual context and was impressed with myself when I didn't get an erection.

But I was even more impressed when I was the person she chose to be with. Knowing that the girl everyone wanted had chosen me allowed me to see myself for the first time as something other than an outcast even among outcasts. But it made me even more arrogant at home, certain that I was the only one with all the answers. I couldn't handle the self-confidence that being with her gave me. And it made me careless out in public, sitting there at 3:00 a.m., drunk and high, rambling on about how great Tom Wolfe's *The Electric Kool-Aid Acid Test* was, oblivious to my surroundings, even though, as Dad pointed out, I was less than a mile from the parking lot where the cop had said that if he ever saw me again, I would go to jail.

"And it was the other boy's car," Dad said as we drove toward home. I could see his mind working as he realized that my new jailhouse advisers might be right. And we both knew that I needed very much to call the arrest into question.

When we pulled into the driveway, he did not turn off the car. Neither of us moved.

"Remember when you were little and I'd spank you, and I'd tell you that it hurt me worse than it hurt you?" he asked. "Well, leaving you in jail all this time really was harder for me."

"I was the one in jail, remember?" I said.

"Sounds like you had a pretty good time," he said.

"It's not great when they make you bend over and spread your butt cheeks and shine a flashlight up your ass," I said.

Initially I had tried to downplay the experience of being locked up. But I didn't want him to do it.

"Or sleeping by somebody's vomit in the drunk tank," I added for extra effect. "There were like fifteen people crammed into one room with no beds, and it was cold."

"Well, wanna talk about cold. I was with your mother," he said. "She called me every name she could think of. She called me cruel and callous for keeping you in jail. She wanted to come and get you right then."

"She was right," I said with a touch of affection in my smile.

"It really was the most difficult decision I've ever had to make," he said. "But I had to try something. You could end up in prison. And you might have thought that a night in county was cool, but I'll guarantee you that prison is not. You don't want some big Black guy who's doing a life sentence to take out all his frustration on you."

He paused. I said nothing.

"This is your second drug arrest," he said. "You really could get sentenced to some serious time."

The first time, I'd gotten busted with a quarter bag at school. When they handcuffed me in the parking lot, with the whole school outside at lunch, one of the cops took out a megaphone. "Everyone, look at your friend. Look at your peer, see what drugs will do to you," he said as his partner pushed down my head and lowered me into the car. That should have clued me in that the deputies really wanted to turn my arrest at what was supposed to be one of the best high schools in town into something bigger, like some big-time Eastside Drug Ring or something.

No one put me in a cell that day. But I sat handcuffed at a desk while the deputy who'd arrested me asked me questions.

"Where'd you get the reefer?" he asked, leaning back in his chair and cleaning his eyeglasses with a handkerchief.

"I found it," I said.

"I don't believe you," he said, leaning forward, holding his glasses out between his fingers. "If you don't level with me, then I'm going to make this harder for you. People don't just find illicit substances—"

"Maybe someone threw it out when they saw you?" I said.

"Jim," the cop called to his colleague. "Let's just go ahead and put this guy in county. I think he was trying to sell that grass."

The colleague approached us. The first cop put his glasses back on.

"I wasn't trying to sell anything," I said.

"But you didn't find it," he said.

"No," I admitted.

"Who did you get it from?"

"Just some guy off the street."

I'd never bought weed off the street.

"What street?" he asked.

"I don't remember," I said. "On the Southside."

That was the Black part of town. I'd actually bought it from a preppy white kid at my school.

"Did you know the guy?"

"No," I said.

"What did he look like?"

"I don't know," I said. "He was just a Black guy."

I was not going to snitch on anyone real, and I was betting that they would not expect me to be able to distinguish one Black person from another and would stop asking me questions. I didn't see the role I was playing, giving them another excuse to target Black people on the Southside for selling weed to a "good white kid" like me.

The second deputy walked away. The one at whose desk I was sitting typed something on a form.

"You better be careful," he said after a minute. "You go over there messing around and you're gonna get robbed, or worse. You could be getting PCP. You don't know what you're getting. And if you think it's bad there, wait till you go to jail. You'll be some big Black buck's bitch."

After that arrest, I considered myself a victim of America's police state, and I thought I was as oppressed as any Black person could possibly be. I understood what Eazy-E was talking about. I told my friends I was going to demand to be treated as a prisoner of war according to the Geneva Convention since I had been captured as part of the war on drugs.

What actually happened was that I got diverted into pretrial intervention (PTI) and state-mandated drug counseling. And I hadn't finished it by the time of this second arrest, which could mean I'd be booted from the program and face both charges at the same time.

"What's the status of your PTI?" Dad asked as we slowly got out of the car, both reluctant to walk into Mom's emotional storm after our surprisingly quiet ride.

"I'm going to call first thing in the morning," I said. "They're supposed to sign off on my completion this week. So I think I can rush that through and they might not notice this."

"Good Lord, Son," Dad said. "How stupid can you be?"

I was stupid, but I was also lucky, and white.

"You should go in there in person," Dad said. "This is too serious for a phone call."

My PTI officer was a short Black man with light skin, a bald pate, and a thin mustache. As long as I passed my drug tests, he didn't show much interest in me or my case. I had passed one piss test, using someone else's urine in a travel-size shampoo bottle duct-taped to my leg. But I had also failed one. Someone had told me that if I put bleach on the cotton part of a Band-Aid and put it on my finger and then unwrapped it and peed on the cotton and into the cup, the pee would come up clean. It hadn't. And the officer had been, well, pissed.

"Do you want to go to jail?" he asked me. "Do you know what people will do to you with that long, pretty hair of yours if you end up in jail? Now you need to get it together, Son. You don't want to end up a blushing bride before you've even finished high school."

For community service, I was supposed to alphabetize the files of other people who had been through the program, but I spent most of my time reading over their cases. I'd thought PTI was supposed to destroy any records if you completed the program, but here they all were. I even managed to find a few friends. And after looking at hundreds of these files, I couldn't recall a single Black person who had been through PTI.

I had finally finished my hours and just needed someone to sign off—before they found out about my new arrest. The main requirement to get your record cleared was not getting in trouble again.

So the morning after Dad got me out of jail, I skipped school and walked into the PTI office with an exaggerated confidence as soon as it opened.

"Can I help you?" asked a Black woman wearing a purple dress as she looked up from her clipboard and over the tops of her reading glasses at me.

"I was supposed to come by and have y'all sign my final paperwork for release today," I said.

"Hold on," she said, and stood, still holding the clipboard from which she had been reading when I interrupted.

The office was cramped and hot. There were two wooden chairs in a small waiting area with brown carpet, and I sat down. The lights hummed. I started to sweat. Maybe my PTI officer was reading a report about this weekend's arrest right now and it would jeopardize my completion of the program and I would be facing two drug charges at once. Maybe Dad was right and I would go to prison. I wanted a cigarette. I put my hand in my pocket and fingered the opening at the top of the cigarette pack anxiously.

A few minutes later, the receptionist came back, still holding the clipboard. But nothing else.

"He is busy right now," she said.

I was stuck in a state of suspension there in the state office building, not knowing whether my first drug charge would be erased or my second discovered. Maybe the woman was stalling me while my PTI officer called a deputy to come arrest me right now.

"So he just went ahead and signed the papers," the woman said, pulling three sheets from the clipboard and handing them to me.

My hand lurched forward, hungry for the documents.

She looked at me, surprised, and then laughed.

"You're ready to be done," she said.

"Yes, ma'am," I said. "I've learned my lesson."

"Good luck to you," she said.

As I walked out the door, I felt like a free man, even though I was still facing a fresh charge of simple possession of marijuana.

I was a fuckup and I was oblivious to a lot, but even then it struck me how whenever authority figures, from the cops to my PTI officer to my parents, mentioned jail or prison, they always acted as if it was the Black men I would encounter who would be the worst part of the experience. Even if the PTI officer didn't actually use the word *Black*, it was implied. The culture insisted that my mind fill in the blank. I heard this trope all the time in the jokes that comedians told about dropping your soap in the shower or whatever. And it was always a big Black man on the other end of the assault.

The representatives of the state assumed that I was racist, that I feared imprisoned Black men, and they used that fear to make it seem as if the system were actually protecting me rather than taking away my freedom. In the day and a half that Dad had left me locked up, one of my cell mates had been Black and the other one white. And I'd learned that the inmates weren't the problem with jail, jail was the problem with jail.

The whole damn enterprise of "justice" felt duplicitous and cynical, but I *was* still afraid of being sent to prison and sexually assaulted—raped up the ass, as my friends usually put it—by a big Black guy, even if the guys I'd been in lockup with in the county were cool. They were not the kinds of murderers or rapists who went to prison. And I still thought of those people primarily as Black.

The close calls didn't make me adjust my attitude and conform. They pissed me off more and made the lie behind our world seem even more obvious and egregious. I felt as if dropping out of this hopeless and corrupt society really might be the best way to do it, as the hippies said. I'd tuned in and turned on. And I felt pretty goddamn ready to drop out.

My parents had always told me that success would allow me to be free—but I began to suspect that choosing failure was a far better route to freedom.

And time would show that my whiteness allowed me to fuck up without consequence.

Chapter 10

WHEN I WALKED IN THE door, I knew something was wrong. Dad was standing there, in front of the kitchen sink, just staring out the window. He turned when he heard the door close.

I'd just dropped off a woman at the strip club where she worked and bought a bottle of Jim Beam, and I was stopping by the house to steal a two-liter of Coke, and I hadn't expected anyone to be home, and something about the way Dad looked standing there staring, for the second before he heard me, was startling. It felt almost as if I'd walked in on someone about to jump out a window.

"You can't live here anymore," Dad said suddenly, but flatly and plainly, with no drama or affectation—just stating a fact.

"What?" I said, shocked.

For once, I had no idea what I had done wrong.

"Your mother walked into your room this morning to get a coat hanger and saw you lying there with some naked woman she'd never seen before," he said. "It was one thing when it was Molly or Zooey, someone we knew, but she'd never even seen this girl before. And I'm sorry, but it's going to kill her if you keep doing things like that."

Zooey had left me a couple of months earlier, shortly after I graduated high school, when she and Bo and a lot of my other friends bought a school bus together and went on the road with the Grateful Dead. I had no idea what I was going to do after graduation. Mom had filled out an application and even written an essay under my name and without my knowledge and somehow managed to get me a small journalism scholarship to USC, but I had turned it down and decided not to go. But just because I didn't want to go to college didn't mean that I could devote my life to following the Grateful Dead from town to town, seeing little of the country but gas stations and coliseums.

I felt as if the universe had swiftly rewarded my decision to reject both of these paths when I started hanging out with Blake, who was, I thought, the only really smart person I had ever known. She had studied literature and writing at USC but quit a semester before graduating because her professor had called poetry "the dung heap upon which the flower of literary criticism grows." Instead of taking a job in New York, which she said another teacher, James Dickey, had offered to get her, she had started stripping under the stage name Kali, after the Hindu goddess of destruction, in Greenville, the heart of South Carolina's Bible Belt.

We were both hanging around in Columbia and I had offered to give her a ride back to Greenville, where she shared an apartment with another dancer who had also moved up from Columbia. Instead of going to her place, she'd slept with me in my bed, and that's how Mom had evidently found us.

And now Dad was kicking me out—for that? I laughed. We hadn't even had sex, although she had given me a blow job, which was probably as bad in Mom's eyes.

"OK, I'll be back in a minute," I said to Dad. "Let me go get a few things, and I'll come back for the rest of my stuff later."

I went upstairs into my room, which still had posters of skateboarders hanging on the walls above the two double beds, and grabbed a couple of pairs of underwear, some pants, and a few T-shirts.

Just before I turned off the lights and walked out, I looked back at the room.

"I'll never live here again," I swore to myself. I turned off the light.

Blake and I had spent a nice day together, walking around downtown and shopping for books before I dropped her off at the club where she worked. She'd asked if I wanted to come pick her up, so I was confident I would have a place to stay that night.

I turned and walked down the stairs, away, I felt, from my childhood and into the world.

"I'm sorry, Son," Dad said when I stepped back into the kitchen. "Don't think that this means we don't love you. But Mom just can't keep living like this."

It looked as if he'd just wiped tears from his eyes. But it was hard to tell. His cheeks puffed up beneath his eyes, so it could have been sweat glimmering off his pink flesh.

"It's OK," I said as lightly as I could, as if moving out of my parents' house, with nowhere to go, were no big deal at all. "I'll see you around."

I told myself I was trying to spare his feelings, that this was something Mom's prudish Christianity had forced on him, but as I turned away from him and toward the door, I knew my indifference was intended as a final jab.

When I walked into the garage, I stood there a moment, taking in the oily, musty odor in what seemed to me the final act in the drama of my independence.

There were warm plastic bottles of soda stacked up by the kitchen door in the garage, and I grabbed one and walked back to my car. I got in and drove away from my parents' house.

When I went to pick Blake up from the strip club, I was drunk from the whiskey but took speed to counteract it, to make sure I could perform should she want to have sex. From the parking lot behind the club, I nervously glanced at the big tuxedoed bouncer who would stick his head out the door and scan the lot every few minutes. My pulse was enlivened when his head dipped back into the building and then from the cracked door Blake appeared and started walking toward my car, her long dirty-blond hair, parted in the middle, kissing her shoulders with each step. She wore a short purple velvet dress and a pair of thigh-high boots. The dress rose up as she crouched into the car.

"Hey, so, um, my mom came in and saw you in my bed this morning," I said as I pulled out of the parking lot, the bouncer watching my car to make sure she was safe.

"What?" she said.

Even beneath her thick makeup and the pale parking lot light—even after dancing almost naked for the last six hours—it seemed she was blushing.

"Why didn't you lock the door?"

"They caught me with girls too many times before and they took the lock off," I said with a shit-eating grin.

"You can stay with us," she said.

She directed me to the old mansion downtown that had been divided up into apartments.

"It used to be a brothel," Blake said as we walked up the stairs to the second-floor entrance of the place she shared with another dancer, Tammy, and Tammy's boyfriend, Vince. "There's a ghost of a whore in there—I feel like she's happy we're here."

Tammy and Vince weren't there that night, but over the coming weeks, I got to know them well. Tammy was a five-foot-tall petite white girl with thick black hair, and Vince was a morose Italian American motorcycle enthusiast with sunken cheeks and long stringy brown hair he wore tied in a ponytail. He usually kept a gun within reach: pistols, assault rifles, and shotguns were all placed strategically around the house in case of Tammy's ex-husband's return.

This was a bit scary because Vince liked acid and weed, and he loved to clean and study his guns when he was high.

"Man, check this shit out," he said, holding up what looked like a machine gun with a banana clip. "A fucking Kalashnikov."

Dad had always had guns, but he didn't fancy them. They were grim tools to remain mostly hidden. And I'd never seen one of these Russian rifles outside of movies. Vince and I were flying on acid as he waved this gun around like a recruit for the redneck Red Army.

"You wanna hold it?" he asked.

"Nah," I said, terrified. "But I would love to hear you sing 'Angeline.'"

It felt like the only time Vince wasn't gripping a gun was when he cradled his guitar on his knee and sang, and I was always trying to get him to play something for me.

Blake still had a boyfriend, Fred, in Columbia, but we were sleeping together in every sense of the word, sharing a bed and having sex, except on the weekends when Fred came up and I went to crash on a friend's couch. I knew I didn't have the right to be jealous, and I tried to treat it as a vacation from her voracious sexual demands, which required that I maintain a certain level of sobriety—at least enough to get it up—but something about the arrangement did bother me. I told myself the feeling in my gut was a vestige of the traditional uptight, white bourgeois relationship where one person thought they had to own or control somebody just because they slept together. I took more drugs.

I'd been staying with them for only a couple of weeks before Blake started talking about getting a place of our own—because Vince's guns and paranoia were just too much. I had really come to love both Tammy and Vince in that short time, but they were hard to live with. It finally came to a head when Vince came out of the shower holding a towel around his waist with one hand and a Glock in the other.

Blake grabbed my arm and pulled me into our room.

"I haven't told you this, but I am schizophrenic," she said. "Having these guns around is not a good thing. I can see bad things happening. The future. I can see the paranoia manifest into reality. We've got to find another place to live."

Her urgency freaked me out. The big volume of Percy Shelley's poetry that I'd stolen from the library lay by the open window, its red cover glowing in the light as the sounds of children playing outside drifted into the room. I knew she exaggerated a lot, and I wasn't sure if she actually had schizophrenia or if she was romanticizing mental illness as she did when she talked about Sylvia Plath and Syd Barrett, but I knew that she was right about the danger.

"When I saw my mom the other day, she said that my grandfather had an opening in the duplex he owns," I said. "She said I could live there if I enrolled in the community college."

"You have been so smart and strong to avoid school," she said. "College would kill your poetry. Especially the community college."

She had written part of a beautiful novel, which she said she was taking a break from, and in the meantime, she promised, she was going to help me become a poet.

"She said I had to enroll," I said. "Not that I had to go."

Blake looked at me for a moment before her mouth stretched into a tight smile.

"Let's do it," she said.

When I dropped her off at work later that afternoon, she peeled off one hundred singles that I'd counted out the night before.

"Try to get some weed and some pills," she said, handing it to me. "And talk to your mom."

I stuffed the money in my pocket. She kissed me on the mouth before she got out.

"And finish reading *A Season in Hell*," she said. "No more excuses. You need to know Rimbaud if we're going to achieve poetic insight through a derangement of our senses."

I'd been climbing a ladder of suburban rebellion, moving from skateboarding to punk rock to weed, and now with Blake I was setting out to use Rimbaud's "prolonged, vast, and systematic derangement of the senses" to destroy the vestiges my upbringing had left on my consciousness. I was trying to break down whiteness while only falling further into it. Whiteness is a power structure on whose refuse I was feasting. I could not get outside of it because I could not see it.

Then the bouncer walked into the parking lot, and Blake got out of the car and slammed the door. I thought about my luck again as I drove away, wheeling toward the carpet store.

I could smell the barbecue cooking at Little Pigs BBQ when I pulled into the shopping center, and the charcoal smoke in the air mixed with a hint of fall washed over me with a wave of roaming nostalgia—I'd been eating at that little barbecue joint with the smiling pig on its sign all my life, and I couldn't help being moved by its smell into some unbidden reverie of my childhood.

Summey was sitting in his rocking chair by the plate-glass windows at the front of the store.

"Goddamn worthless son of a bitch," he said as I walked in, and for a moment I thought he was talking to me. Then I realized he was cussing at someone on the other end of his cordless phone. His other hand gripped his spit cup so tightly that it looked as if his fingertips would puncture the foam, sending a mass of tobacco spit down the front of his pants.

His tirade stopped when he saw me looking at him, the rocking chair paused midrock. I kept walking to the back of the store, where Mom had her desk, with a space heater under it even in the summer and Bible verses hanging from the wall above it, along with a very bad poem I had written to her and illustrated with watercolor one year for Mother's Day.

"Hey, honey," she said, jumping up to give me a big hug. She looked older already than she had a couple of weeks earlier.

"I was thinking," I said. "And you know, maybe it would be a good idea to just take a couple classes at Tech this semester and move into Summey's duplex."

Her eyes lit up with delight and then clouded over with what looked like worry.

"Oh Lord," she said. "It is a mess over there. Jesse, the guy who is supposed to be painting it, he's a drunk and he got in a fight with this man who lives over there. Apparently the man was drunk and riding on a moped, and Jesse was drunk and almost ran over him with his van. When the man saw the van in front of the house, he picked up a big metal pipe and came in there at Jesse and made holes in all the walls and shattered the toilet."

"Oh my God," I said.

"I know," she said. "Those rednecks are a mess. But it should be ready for you by the end of the month if you're really going to go to Tech."

She paused a moment.

"But don't you regret not taking that scholarship and going to USC?" she asked.

"Regret," I laughed. "I've been living with two strippers who give me everything I need. We eat steak every day. And she is a great writer and is teaching me. I told you I am going to be a poet, and journalism would ruin that."

"What are you going to take, then?" Mom asked, hiding the pain in her eyes.

"Philosophy," I said, without having really thought about it.

"Well, as long as you're studying something," she said. "You better go by and enroll. School starts in a couple weeks."

"I will," I said. "And we'll plan to move in on September first."

"Move in where?" Summey asked as he walked into the room, followed by Jacob, a Kenyan student at Bob Jones University, who worked for him.

"To your duplex," I said.

Summey stared at me with his mouth agape just enough for me to see the brown tobacco spit swirl around the viscous pink of his tongue. The wrinkles around his eyes were amplified by his spectacles.

"He's going to Tech," Mom said.

"Well," he said. "If you're going to school, that's great. Maybe you'll turn yourself around. I was just talking to Jacob about what he needed to do over there to fix all the goddamn damage that lunatic caused."

"Hi, Jacob," I said.

Jacob waved and smiled but did not say hello.

Summey had used Bob Jones students as labor for as long as I could remember, but they were mostly anonymous, interchangeable white boys with bad haircuts and midwestern accents. Jacob was different; he had been working for Summey for two years now, and as a foreign student with no work visa, he had no other real options. And he was Black.

"School is very important," Jacob said. "That's how I'm able to be here."

"I know," I said.

I hated the idea that I was pleasing everyone, even if it was just a scam for room and board.

"I'm sure Jacob can get the place ready before September, can't you?" Summey said.

Jacob smiled and nodded.

There was something about the relationship that bothered me. It reminded me, perhaps, of the way Mom talked about Slim, the Black woman who'd raised the Summey children. To hear Mom tell it, she and Slim had loved each other, and I didn't necessarily doubt her, but I felt as if they must have had very different experiences of that relationship.

"When they tried to make her sit in the back of the bus," Mom said, "I tried to go with her, but she told me to sit my butt down in the front right now before I made things worse."

It seemed suspect, and something about the emotional part of Summey's relationship to Jacob bothered me in the same way. Jacob didn't just work for Summey doing odd jobs like helping fix the duplex. He also had to provide emotional support.

Beneath his bravado, Summey was a scared man. He could never be alone. He was terrified of silence and slept with the police scanner blaring by his bed at night. He was also petrified to travel and never went anywhere but Florida, for baseball spring training. But Nanny wanted to see the world, and she had started taking more trips, with my mom and dad or with my aunt Gaile—Mom, Nanny, and Gaile would go to three-day gospel music festivals the way Zooey went to Dead shows—and when Nanny was gone, Summey made Jacob spend the night with him. But then, he would always talk about how much he was helping Jacob, how much he did for Jacob, and how much Jacob loved him. I didn't know what to make of all this, or if there was anything to make of it, as I left the carpet store that day.

Later that night, when I mentioned it to Blake, she tilted her head when she looked at me, as she did when my naivete astonished her, as if the four years that separated us were an uncrossable frontier.

"Me and Candy, a white girl, and Syreeta, who, you know, is Black, were talking at work one night. Candy said her parents weren't racist, because her mom had been raised by a Black woman," Blake said. "Syreeta laughed so hard she spit out her drink. 'Your mama is just like the men who come in here and believe we love them.'"

I laughed, but I recognized something I'd not noticed before, something about how the strip club worked. The men who went in there weren't paying for a naked body, they were paying for a flattering fantasy. They wanted to believe the women would want to spend time with them even if they hadn't been working as strippers. It reminded me of Grandmother Woods's illusion that the Africans were happy to have been enslaved; she'd tell me how lucky they were to have been brought to America and how much they loved Ole Marse.

The fantasy of love in this sort of racism is not incidental, it is an essential feature. If we can tell ourselves that the people we oppress love us and are happy about it, then we can justify that oppression.

Chapter 11

BLAKE AND I'D BEEN UP for three days straight, taking acid and speed and watching the uprising in Los Angeles on the small television in our room, occasionally turning our attention toward sex. Whiteness allowed us the luxury of watching a riot on TV recreationally.

Because I'd had my run-ins with cops in this ultraconservative town, I felt an affinity with protesters. I thought I understood the frustration and the anger that was bursting into flames on the TV. It felt vital and heroic.

Blake's interest was more inscrutable, but also more intense. She rarely ever took acid but had demanded I buy a bunch for a "riot party" she insisted we would have. The flames had reflected nonstop off her eyes as she sat there, at one point naked except for a white fur coat, making cryptic pronouncements about the riot.

"These are the images of war they played on TV when I was a kid," she said. "The same images, the war is here. It stirs a primal emotion in me because of that resonance. Dead bodies on the news at dinner every night."

She talked about Nathanael West's novel *Day of the Locust*, which ends with a riot in LA, and insisted that I read the scene, right then, out loud.

My old skateboard buddy, Chuck, had been living with us since he'd dropped out of college a few months earlier, and he was lying in our big king-size bed with red velvet curtains hanging from its posts beside us as I read. Blake listened to me, watching the news with the sound down, until she fell asleep, just as the sun was coming up.

"Let's go out to the porch," I whispered to Chuck.

We walked outside and sat on the concrete porch to sip on final beers and watch the cars go by on their way to work. The big magnolia in the center of my yard sheltered us with its waxy leaves. A single white flower bloomed among them. The gravel driveway sparkled in the dawning light as the squat mill cottages across the street came into focus.

Summey had grown up in a mill village like this, back when the mills ran the town, and his father had been paid in company scrip. People mocked him growing up, calling him and other mill families "lintheads."

"Among the whites, that's the worst you could be," he told me one time when I asked him what a linthead was. "A linthead or a hillbilly."

So when he made money, he'd bought up this entire neighborhood. But he had a soft spot and let too many people slide on rent, the same way he was letting us and the woman and her four kids and truck-driving boyfriend who lived next door skip on rent month after month. Eventually he started losing money on the investment, so Nanny convinced him to sell most of the houses. Bit by bit he'd gotten rid of them all but this one little squat brick duplex in a swampy lot on Christopher Street.

Sitting out on the porch at times like this, I liked to think he kept it as some sort of reminder of where he came from, of all the things his rich old self had inherited from his poor younger self.

I lit a cigarette and handed Chuck the pack. We sat there a minute watching a cat skulking through the grass as the sound of cars on the highway filtered through the trees as the straight world raced to work. It was my favorite part of the day because, by sitting there, still drinking on the porch, I was rebelling against the role that had been prepared for me, rejecting my place as a responsible member of society.

"I gotta go to sleep after this," Chuck said, "if I'm going to make it to work by two."

"I don't think Blake is going to work today," I said. "So see if you can get some cash."

"I'll see," he said. "But it's getting harder."

We were either rolling in money—sometimes I'd count four hundred singles, plus the larger bills, in a night—or we were broke. Blake hadn't gone to work in several days, and we'd spent a lot on drugs and Chinese food for what she was calling the riot party. Our cash was all but gone.

Chuck and I had developed a little scam we'd run at the corporate bookstore where he worked when money got tight. He would bring in a new-looking book that we had on the shelf and fill out the paperwork to return it under an assumed name, pocketing the "refund." It wasn't especially lucrative, but it could get us ten or fifteen bucks—enough for some burgers and beers.

Chuck had grown from a fourteen-year-old skate kid into a sensitive, bookish twenty-year-old. We'd known each other for six years, which felt like an eternity to us, and it had bonded us like brothers. We'd even become literal blood brothers when we drank a half gallon of Rebel Yell whiskey camping out at Stone Mountain Park in Georgia, the night before a Lollapalooza concert, and cut the palms of our hands and clasped them together beneath the carved statues of Confederate generals.

But he was going to move back to Columbia soon, and I was going to try to buy a van with Blake and travel around the country, so we were simultaneously growing more emotionally distant with one another and romanticizing our friendship more.

"I really hope they don't call in the army to start shooting people," he said, referring to the Los Angeles uprising in protest of Rodney King's beating, as he dropped his cigarette butt into the mouth of his beer can and left it on the porch. He opened the screen door.

"Yeah," I said, following him inside.

Just as I closed the door, I heard something outside. I immediately ran to the window, fearing the police were about to raid us.

We were all increasingly paranoid, and this moment felt like a glimpse of the truth, of the rage that the era of Reagan and Bush had wrought.

I regularly spent hours high on acid or speed, imagining that CIA agents were on the roof ready to bust in and either arrest or assassinate me; watching footage of cops beating King on TV, followed by cops turning guns on residents, made it even worse. I was sure I was being persecuted, and so I naively felt that I could identify with the Black people in Los Angeles who refused to take it anymore. I thought we were all victims of a late-empire police state. I thought that I understood them and they understood me. It was an illusion of alliance that offered some validation to my romanticized sense of rebellion.

There was an infinite gap between my self-conception and my material reality. I saw myself as a radical revolutionary poet who was dangerous enough to surveil. In fact, I was a cliché: a nineteen-year-old white boy getting too high in a house his grandfather owned. Obviously, my connection to the Black protesters was some sort of wannabe-revolutionary white fantasy.

Whiteness is choosing to think we are something we are not while enjoying the very real privileges of the reality we deny. We think we are rebels when we are burghers; we consider ourselves radical when we are revanchist; we insist on our gentility at the very moment we engage in torture; we consider ourselves white when we are splotchy shades of pink; we think we are universal, irreducible individuals when we are white people, exhibiting a group characteristic.

Youthful rebellion, sowing wild oats, is not only accepted, it is expected among white men, a luxury Black male youth in this country haven't been able to indulge for fear for their safety. When white boys rebel we expand white freedom. Whiteness has always sent the outcasts out to colonize new territory. And Blake and I were ready to go. We had a plan. We were going to buy a 1972 Volkswagen van with a raised roof, a bed, a refrigerator, and a stove for $1,000. Then I would drive, and we would camp in national parks and go to cities where Blake would dance when we needed money.

Follow-through was not generally my strong suit at that point, but Blake and I managed to save some money, and a month later we drove home in our orange van with a pancake engine with two carburetors and two batteries. Dad was impressed despite himself as he and I stood in the driveway of the duplex looking into the engine. Blake had painted "Das Narrenschiff," German for "Ship of Fools," on the back.

Dad loved that.

"At least you two are honest about your endeavor," he said, laughing.

He loved to travel and was excited by the idea of our road trip, which terrified Mom. But he wasn't there on the day we left town. He must have been in Charlotte or working out of town. But Nanny and Summey weren't there either, or my brother. My exit, my escape, seemed particularly empty.

Mom and Aunt Gaile took me and Blake out to an uneventful dinner at the local steak house, and we were going to leave directly from there, hoping to make it to a campground in North Carolina before it was too dark.

All my life, Mom had dreamed of the day she would send me off to college like this. But instead of going to college, I was setting out at nineteen on a tour of the strip clubs on the seedy sides of cities throughout America, living in a VW bus as old as I was.

This was what she had saved and struggled and cried and prayed so hard for, this shaggy-haired son standing beside a stripper who was too old for him, too worldly. I could see all of that in her teary eyes as she held me one more moment, her thin fingers clasped around my forearms as I tried to break away. It was neither recrimination nor disappointment that I saw in her eyes. It was heartbreak.

"Please be safe," she said, and started weeping again.

I knew that from this moment on, she would not be able to imagine the scenery on which I enacted my life, and that was exactly what I wanted. When my parents could no longer envision me, I thought, I would be free. I would no longer be the son of John and Martha from South Carolina, I would just be me.

As I climbed up into the driver's seat, I caught a glimpse of myself in the mirror, and I liked what I saw. The young man in my reflection looked like someone who had made his own fate, who could live by his wits. I was my own heroic character, setting out to seek fame and fortune as a poet in the wide world, the mythical prince going out to conquer monsters.

I did not see myself as white when I looked in the mirror. But even if it was invisible to me then, whiteness would shield me and Blake on this reckless cross-country experiment. It would ensure some level of safety. We looked like hippies, but as long as we didn't have drugs on us, we would be fine anywhere we went. Cops might search us, but they weren't likely to shoot us or even jail us.

I looked in the rearview as we drove away and saw Mom fall into Aunt Gaile's arms as the van pulled out onto Greenville's streets and lurched toward the same mountains I used to race down. An hour later, when we crossed the state line into North Carolina, I realized that, for the first time in my life, I did not live in South Carolina, the state that had come to symbolize so much of what I hated and thought was wrong with the world.

From colonial ships crossing seas to the expansion of slave states and the covered wagons of manifest destiny to hippies hitting the road in vans, history has shown that whiteness demands expansion. The lie must be passed on, the fantasy enlarged.

In South Dakota the van was climbing a hill and just stopped. There was no smoke coming from the engine, no indication something was wrong, and suddenly the power was just gone. I barely had enough propulsion to ease off the road as motorcycles rumbled past, deafening us with their loud Harley mufflers.

It was the fiftieth-anniversary motorcycle rally in Sturgis, South Dakota, and for days these bikes had been everywhere. Since the Merry Pranksters and the Hells Angels hung out in the sixties there had been an outlaw affinity between hippies and bikers, so we'd felt generally safer around them, maybe, than we would around the average South Dakotan.

But when the van broke down and we reached an exit, where there was a restaurant filled with rowdy bikers, there were a lot of Confederate flags and iron crosses. I turned to Blake.

"I'm sure glad I'm white," I said.

I thought I had left home. But whiteness was a home I carried with me. A couple of months earlier, I might have identified with the people protesting the beating of Rodney King; broken down amid bikers in a strange state in the middle of nowhere, I accepted the conditions of racism and was happy to be on the safe side here.

I'd been calling Triple A—Dad had bought me a membership before we left—but because of all the bikers, every mechanic for a hundred miles was booked up for days. All the campgrounds and hotels were full. It looked as if we were going to be sleeping in the van on the side of the highway.

We each ate a buffalo burger and drank some coffee, and when we finally walked back to the van, preparing for a grim night, we saw a flashlight. Two kids who lived nearby had seen the broken-down van and thought they'd help. They had tools, and within a few minutes they fixed the car.

Blake mentioned that she sometimes worked as a stripper.

"My parents run the country club a couple miles over that way," one of the boys said. "You can follow us and park there and sleep for the night. And there's a restaurant. It's closed, but we could feed you. I work there in the day and know how to cook."

"Sure," we said in unison.

Whiteness moves quickly between bikers and country clubs, and it carries both—the law and the outlaw. The law establishes whiteness as the norm. The white outlaw, numbed by the privileges that norm affords, grows bored and rebels against it and expands the range of possibilities of white freedom, often while pushing Black and Indigenous people ever further from their freedom.

Whiteness is the ability to cast yourself as a hero in every story.

The next morning, we awoke to golf carts circling our van like wagons on the frontier. I peeked out the window, hurried to the driver's seat, cranked the van, and hit the gas, worried that the kids' parents would call the cops on the strange hippies sleeping in their parking lot, but in America whiteness is the ability to make a quick, if conspicuous, escape based on your proximity to that skin color.

We sputtered off through the dust, only vaguely aware of the massacres white people had committed on this arid land.

Chapter 12

BLAKE AND I EVENTUALLY ENDED up in Portland, where we were going to crash for a night with a guy I vaguely knew. He was having a going-away party, so it was no problem to sleep on the couch. But he'd be moving in two days, so we couldn't stay longer than that. At the party, he introduced me and his neighbor Oliver as fellow poets and our first instinct was to hate each other.

Oliver had sparkling blue eyes, a bespoke suit, slicked-back black hair, and an upper-crust whine that reminded me of the president, George H. W. Bush. He was equally unimpressed with my long, wild hair, stained cutoffs, and ripped T-shirt. We were at opposite poles of whiteness, but by the end of the night, we had all but fallen in love, the way borderline narcissistic young men do when they see a reflection of themselves in someone else. We convinced ourselves that our differences were like those between the orderly Apollo and the ecstatic Dionysus, or Percy Shelley and Lord Byron.

He wrote orderly, structured verse, and I wrote chaotic free verse, so there was no competition. But by each declaring the other the best at his chosen form, Oliver and I inflated our mutual arrogance tenfold. We got drunk and went to a poetry reading at a coffee shop and laughed at all the other poets. One of them said something. Oliver, wearing a suit and tie, jumped up on a chair.

"I hope George Bush wins the election and throws all you art f*gs into concentration camps," he screamed. The entire crowd descended on us, pushing us out the door. I don't remember much after that except that I got maced and then people were punching me. Poets were punching me. It was ludicrous. I hated George Bush and the homophobic slur, but the experience solidified the sense between Oliver and me that we were the superelite, misunderstood by everyone, even other poets.

Blake was a better writer than either of us, but because of the sexist element of our white-dude bromance, like Mary Shelley some 150 years earlier, the best of the bunch was seen as an afterthought. She was out dancing for our money when Oliver and I were disrupting poetry readings. But she also seemed like the unmoved mover of the whole thing. Often, when we were hanging out, she would sit silently while I spun speed-fueled monologues, but it felt as if she were dictating the terms of the conversation, the turns of my thought, always schooling me, quietly, behind the scenes.

Everything else about Portland sucked for us, but we stayed because of the big adventure we were having with Oliver and his girlfriend, Stacy. We alternated between sleeping on their floor and crashing in the van, which was parked on the street, where it was racking up parking tickets. The strip club scene was terrible. The clubs were far from where we were staying and seedy. They did not pay well. There were more gay clubs in town than straight, and Oliver and I talked about doing an Apollo-and-Dionysus act at a gay club for money, but we chickened out.

We were certain of nothing except our own privilege. We were smarter than everyone else, better in bed than everyone else, and more honest than everyone else. The world was full of shit, but we would exploit it.

When Blake and I left Portland and eventually ended up in Albuquerque, Oliver came to join us there, and we decided to study ancient Greek together.

"I'm going to learn all of the languages that make up English," I proclaimed. "That's the only way to be a poet."

It cost $300 for three credits, and you didn't have to apply to or be accepted into college to take a nondegree class. When I called my parents, I got exactly the response I had hoped for. They were delighted that I was going to school and agreed to pay the tuition and help me with rent, but they had no idea why I would want to study an ancient, dead language.

"Greek?" Dad said. "Ancient Greek?"

"It's what the New Testament is written in," I assured Mom.

"At least it's school," Dad said.

For me, that confusion was part of the charm. If I was going to college, it wouldn't be for the stupid reasons they had wanted me to go. With ancient Greek, I would not get a good job. It was perfect.

But when I started actually studying the ancient language, a change came over me, almost entirely unbidden. I was suddenly serious and studious, spending hours every day in the library going over verb conjugations. I loved studying, it turned out. But I also liked doing well.

At the same time, I quit smoking, and I all but gave up alcohol as well. When I wasn't studying Greek, I was reading about Buddhism—but Blake was moving in the opposite direction. She quit dancing when I started going to school and got into the Grateful Dead scene in town. She had mocked the Dead when we first met, but she had started making beaded necklaces and, as suddenly as I had transformed into a scholar, she was saying things that reminded me of Zooey and her Deadhead ambitions.

Late one Sunday afternoon at the end of the semester, I was in the library memorizing verb paradigms. I hadn't even noticed time passing, lost as I was in some transcendent space of the intellect that I'd never known before.

"Hey, *ese*," said Oliver, shaking me out of my trance with the exaggerated Spanish accent he sometimes employed, even though he was one of the whitest men on Earth with his blue eyes, black suits, Brylcreemed hair, nasal inflection, and aristocratic ways.

"You're still studying?" he asked, his voice an adolescent whine.

"Yeah," I said a little dismissively.

Oliver had started Ancient Greek 101 with me at the beginning of the semester and had, by now, quit coming to class after failing too many quizzes.

When I'd bumped into a mutual friend on the way to the library and told her I was going to study, she replied that Oliver had told her Greek was too easy and he knew it all already so he'd quit. That was how he was. If he wasn't good at something, he'd pretend he was too good at it and quit to avoid the feeling of failure. A few years earlier, he'd been rejected by St. John's College in Santa Fe, which had a Great Books program, and so he'd determined he was too smart for it and didn't really need teachers anyway. When he took a class, he used all his intelligence to find evidence that the professor was really dumb. He couldn't do that with Greek, where there were right answers and wrong answers and sophistry did not suffice. As a result, I hadn't seen Oliver much in the past few weeks.

It made me sad because when I'd met him in Portland, he had dazzled me with his learning and his intellect. He and Blake were the most erudite people I'd met. Now, after only a semester's study, I felt I was leaving them both behind—not because I was smarter but because I was willing to exert just a little effort. I had figured a back door into Dad's maxim about working hard and going to college and getting a good job. The world, or at least my family, would reward me for working hard, even if it was in a field it found completely useless. Studying Greek, I thought I had found a way to reap the privileges I had been promised while continuing to see myself as superior to them. Whiteness made it easy for me to recover my white inheritance, my privilege, no matter what path I took.

But it also made it easy to adopt the aristocratic attitude Oliver displayed, the one in which labor of any sort was beneath his brilliance.

"Let's go to the Frontier," he said. "My mom gave me some money."

I looked up at the clock on the wall, sad to abandon the hermetic enclosure of the library and the silent space of study. But I realized how hungry I was when he mentioned the all-night diner, with fresh tortillas rolling off a conveyor belt behind the counter and a big vat of steaming green chile and tomatoes, and I began to pack up my notes.

"Let's go," I said.

We walked down the winding stairway in the library and out into the bitter, blustery winter wind, talking as we walked across campus toward Central Avenue, where the long, low-slung, yellow barn-style roof of the Frontier took up an entire block across from the university's main entrance. Oliver never asked me how class was going but prattled on about the philosopher Bertrand Russell.

"He had chronic bad breath," he said as we crossed the wide, desolate desert street. "But he still fucked T. S. Eliot's wife."

When Oliver and I walked in, the restaurant was crowded with students studying for their exams over cheap coffee and cinnamon rolls. Oliver insisted that I get whatever I wanted as we waited in line. His family was rich—his grandfather had discovered a massive deposit of uranium and his mom was a well-known art dealer—but Oliver himself only sporadically had money. Every month he had to hit up his mom for rent anew, as if he hadn't done it the last month and wouldn't do it the next. Inheritance on the installment plan.

I ordered a bean-and-cheese burrito—a dollar ninety-nine—and loaded it down with green chile from the cast-iron vat near the counter. Then Oliver and I sat beneath a pointillistic portrait of John Wayne made with nails hammered into a white board.

"Eat your burrito, vato," Oliver said, again employing his stereotypical Speedy Gonzales accent. He had told me once that when his high school, which was mostly white, played a mostly Hispanic school in a football game, the white kids had thrown tortillas from the stands onto the field, and I could tell he had absorbed that kind of casual racism against Latinos, which was totally new to me.

There were almost no Black people in Albuquerque. At first I'd felt the absence, but I wasn't sure what was missing—it was like missing the trees or the humidity, things I saw every day in SC and had never noticed or cared about until they weren't there. Only after I had left home did I realize how entirely my whiteness was defined as "not Black" or even anti-Black. In South Carolina, in my mind, we became white people, noticed our whiteness, only when Black people were around. Whiteness existed for us in proximity to Blackness—which is to say Blackness threatened us with self-awareness.

Blackness made us see ourselves as white, and we didn't like that. We had been told not to see color. It was unpleasant to see it because we had some inkling that it would communicate something bad about us, insinuate a historical guilt or imply that maybe I wasn't what I thought I was, maybe I didn't deserve what I had.

In Albuquerque, without Black people, my whiteness became something different in my own eyes and in the eyes of those around me. There was a different set of social relations in New Mexico, where there were groups and ethnicities I'd hardly ever thought of before. As a result, I had to think more deeply about my whiteness.

Best I could tell, there were Hispanics, who identified with the Spanish, and Chicanos, who identified as mestizo, and then there were the American Indians, Navajo and Pueblo, whom everybody seemed to look down on. Racism, I realized, had many faces. And I'd never thought of any of that. Until I moved to Albuquerque, I hadn't even realized that half my skateboarding heroes—Mark Gonzalez, Tommy Guerrero, Steve Caballero—were not just plain old white dudes. As a result, I had no idea how to talk about race and ethnicity in New Mexico, and so I made mistakes. Once I pissed off a fellow student when I referred to Spanish as a foreign language.

"Spanish has been the language here for five hundred years," she said, her eyes flaring with anger. "English is the foreign language, and when you Anglos push that category on us, it is part of the colonial project."

This was new. I wasn't just white. Now I was "Anglo," which had a different weight to it altogether. Like *Hispanic* or *Latino*, *Anglo* is a label tied to a language rather than a skin color. And it is weighted with the infamy not of slavery but of US imperialism. All of this made me think more deeply about my identity, about what it means to be white.

Still, when Oliver said things like "ese" or "cholo," I thought I should correct him, until I realized I didn't even know what *cholo* really meant, so I didn't even know what I could say, and I'd started letting it go.

"Where's Blake?" Oliver asked.

"I don't know," I said. "I guess she's at home."

I think Oliver instinctually understood the way that I was ignoring Blake now because our white-dude pathology shared the same narrative structure. I saw myself as the hero of the story, just as I always had. And so whatever value Blake, or anyone else, had in my eyes was in direct relation to the story I was telling myself about myself. And at that moment, the story I was telling myself about myself was that I was a scholar and a spiritual seeker. Because I no longer had my parents to rebel against, I was rebelling against Blake, showing I could move beyond her world as well.

I was constantly reinforcing that narrative structure with books like Joseph Campbell's *The Hero with a Thousand Faces* and Robert Graves's *The White Goddess*, stories that told me that I was fulfilling the world's archetypes, that I was the center of the story, that the world revolved around my inspired actions.

Sitting there in his disheveled suit with bags under his eyes, Oliver had more meaning in my mind than Blake did. Each of us was on his hero's journey and saw the other as the helper. I had seen Blake as the prize. But I had already won it, and now my journey was moving on. The *Argo* was sailing.

"Are you going to take the exam?" I asked him about our Greek class.

"I don't think so," he said.

I waited for his excuse.

"Are you going back to the library now?" he asked as I pushed my plate away from me.

"No," I said. "I should walk home."

"I'll walk with you," he said. "At least as far as my house."

We stepped out of the warm fluorescence of the Frontier onto a blustery Stanford Drive and passed by the Living Batch Bookstore, meandering slowly down the wide street lined with pebbles and prickly pears toward Oliver's house a couple of blocks away.

"See you, Woods," Oliver said from his porch.

When I got home, Blake was in the kitchen, stooped over a beaded necklace she was making at an old desk against the wall in the kitchen, where the light was best. She was wearing a tie-dyed T-shirt and her hair was stringy and clinging around her cheeks.

"I'm going to see a few Dead shows in Arizona in March," she said.

"I don't think I can," I said. "I have school."

"I know," she said, and went back to staring at her beads.

A roach ran across the floor by my feet. Under the influence of Buddhism, I did not stomp it.

"I thought you used to make fun of the Dead," I said.

"And you used to make fun of college," she said.

I should have known then that this was the end of our relationship. Instead, I did the best I could to ignore her over the next three months, and it seemed sometimes that we only talked when we argued about the shows she was going to.

Her friends thought I was a monster, an awful boyfriend, she told me. I wasn't surprised. It was true. We'd almost quit having sex altogether, and I had started sleeping on the hardwood floor. I had become an ascetic, and she was an obstacle on my path to enlightenment.

I believed that if the Buddha could sit down under a tree and get enlightened, then so could I.

"I'm headed out for class," I said on the day she left for the Dead shows.

"They're gonna come by and get me around eleven," she said. "So I'll probably be gone when you get home."

We gave each other a cold hug, and I walked off toward the university, beneath the blooming elm trees on Silver Street.

She was gone when I came home that day. She was supposed to be away for four days. On the fifth, I called her friends. They had all come home. She had not, but they would not tell me where she was. They said she was safe, but I still imagined the worst as my emotions swung between anger and self-pity.

It was another week after that when she finally called.

"Hello," I said, after rushing toward the phone hanging on the wall in the kitchen.

"Bay?" she said, her voice timid, yet full of distaste and dread.

My mind flooded with relief, and then it went blind with anger.

"Where are you?" I yelled. "Where have you been? How could you not have called me? You are so cruel."

"I'm coming to get my stuff. Tomorrow," she said. "Can you get it ready so we don't have to spend too much time—"

"You are with a man, aren't you?" I screamed. I was crying. I couldn't contain my rage.

She told me, tersely, that she had fallen in love. He was a forty-year-old with a school bus.

"I'm tired of being the one to take care," she said. "I need to be taken care of."

When she came the next day, the guy was not with her, but she had her pack of girlfriends. Whenever I tried to talk to her, one of them would follow and shut me down. I finally just walked back into the bedroom and closed the door.

Lying facedown on the futon on the floor, I heard the four women rummaging through the house. And then I heard the screen door slam shut, and it was silent in the shadow-dark room, and I wept. I had done everything possible to drive Blake away, and now that she was gone, I could wallow in an aggrieved innocence that cast me as the victim of a cruel and heartless woman who had left me and not even bothered to call.

As I indulged this sense of righteous indignation over the coming months, I grew increasingly antisocial and distant and even more paranoid than I'd been at the height of my acid phase. Maybe it was residual, I sometimes thought. "PTSD from the drug war," I told my old friend Chuck about my mental state when I called to complain about Blake.

Oliver and I both dabbled around the edges of the occult, and one day at the new age bookstore he bought a book called *Behold a Pale Horse*. The author, William Cooper, purported to be former military intelligence, and he had bad news for us.

"FEMA has concentration camps waiting for us," Oliver said, waving the book so that its cover flapped. "There hasn't been a real democratic government or a republic in ages. The Bilderberg Group decided it all in 1954."

I looked at the ugly cover, a childish painting of the apocalypse.

"I'm serious," he said, and he left the book.

As I sat on my porch reading that evening, the book confirmed my general view of the world. The only constant belief I'd had since I started puberty was that the system was full of shit. So when I read that politics was all a sham and the Illuminati were working to form a New World Order with the aliens, it sorta made sense. More sense than the muddled mess the world usually presented. There was a reason that my parents, and everyone else, was full of shit.

Bill Clinton had been elected president, ending a twelve-year Republican reign that had dominated most of my life, but the massacre at Waco, where, after a standoff of several days, the ATF set fire to the compound of a religious group called the Branch Davidians, had proved to me that nothing much had changed.

"They're burning the heretics on live TV," I declared as we watched the conflagration unfold, just as we had the LA riots. It seemed to me that it proved my point that white rebels like me, white people who didn't do what was expected of them, were as likely to be victims of the police state as Black people were. I was oppressed. *Behold a Pale Horse* had put a framework around all of that for me, building an elaborate schema for my white victimhood.

When I flew home that Christmas, my family laughed at my new ideas, just as they'd worried about me in my hippie phase.

"Tell them what you told me," Dad said as the family gathered around the table at Capri's, the Italian restaurant we'd always gone to for special occasions, the first night I got back.

Summey sat at one end of the table, looking older, the skin hanging looser under his eyes in the shadow of his Yankees cap. He slapped the server's ass when she walked by, even though Nanny sat grimly beside him. Across from her my brother, a senior in high school now, sat eating a mozzarella stick, uninterested in anything I had to say. I was between Nanny and Mom, with Dad on the other end and Eric and Gaile beside him.

"What?" I said.

I had no idea what he was talking about. But I knew he was about to make a joke at my expense.

"He told me he was worried that when they put him under to take his wisdom teeth out that the government was going to put mind-control implants in his head," Dad said, and started cracking up. Everyone joined the laughter.

"Implants?" Summey said. "Boy, you are crazier than—"

"They do it with fillings already," I said. "What is a filling except an antenna?"

"Oh my God," my brother said, cutting his eyes at me.

My cousin Eric, across from me, just looked down, confused, his bangs hanging over his eyes. They were both still dressed like skaters. The gulf between us was incalculable, and it struck me as infinite. I was among the enlightened. My family, sitting here in the flickering red light of the candle on our table, shoving pasta into their mouths before going home to watch TV, they were sheep. I was special.

The following semester, I started school as a full-time student. My high SAT scores and the straight A's I'd earned as a nondegree student had made up for my horrendous high school record. Again, it seemed the whole spiel had been false. My parents and teachers had always told me that I could never recover from bad grades in high school, that my failures would somehow end up on a permanent record. But with a few nondegree classes, the system embraced me as if I had never strayed. I had to enroll in English 102. But after a week, the teacher asked to see me after class.

"You seemed way too smart to be in this class," she said. "I checked your records and your SAT was high enough to skip it. You need to transfer out."

My performance on a single test had negated all my fuckery. Whiteness is immediate forgiveness and even assistance. I expected the grad student teaching my class to check my records for me and help me advance. Whiteness is accommodating.

I thought of Shakespeare's *Henry IV* plays, where Hal, the son of King Henry IV, goes off and parties with Falstaff and a band of robbers. He flouts the law, squanders money. But upon his father's death, when he is to become king, Hal coolly rejects all his old wastrel friends, and the kingdom rejoices in him, as he assumes power as the brutal Henry V. That was a story of my whiteness.

I was in my third semester of Greek, and we were actually starting to read literature in the language. I also took a course on Schopenhauer's philosophy, and, since I no longer took English, I enrolled in a linguistics class. I started hanging out with people, going out for drinks occasionally and dating again—I was twenty-two now—and as a result I grew less paranoid and started to break through the morass of conspiracy that had been flooding my brain. The hooey in *Behold a Pale Horse* was too easy, too badly written and poorly argued. Friedrich Nietzsche was much better at pointing out the bullshit I experienced. I spent my time typing up insanely complicated attempts at experimental literature, obsessed now by the modernists, who held me in their sway.

A group of kids from Colby College had all moved in two doors down. Before them, a bunch of punks had lived there. The punks had had a big old car that had "fuck art, drink beer" painted down its side. The Colby kids, to the contrary, were the first people I ever knew who used email. I'd still never been online and had no interest in it.

"I'm an English major," one of them said. "But I'm just working on my thesis now. That's why we all came on the exchange here. To work on our theses. But I'm mostly reading."

He was a tall, amiable, and athletic white guy with glasses and curly hair.

"What are you reading?" I asked.

"Right now, I decided to only read Black women," he said. "To get that perspective."

"What?" I said. "You are reading people only because of their sex and their race?"

"I mean, isn't that what we all do?" asked his friend, a woman with freckles and stark black hair. "The canon is what it is because it only included white men."

"I'm in a class on Greek lyric poetry," I said. "And we're translating Sappho right now."

"Yeah, that's cool," she said. "But she's like literally the only one."

"That's true," I said, and laughed. "There's no way to argue that."

They laughed too, and we all said our goodbyes, confident we would be fine as neighbors and maybe even friends.

But when I went home, I wrote in my journal about the idea of a white guy only reading Black women. I railed against "political correctness." There was nothing new in my critique. It was the same bullshit Dad listened to on the radio—feminazis controlling what we could say, Afrocentrists making it look as if the Greeks had stolen everything from Africa, and a queer agenda to make straight people feel bad—and I knew it was bullshit, this straw-man version of liberal elite political correctness, but something about the conversation with my new fancy-school neighbors made me embrace it anyway.

Scrawling away in my notebook, I indulged in the pleasures of being retrograde, reactionary, and unreconstructed. But then I stopped and sat up for a minute and looked at the books piled up all around my apartment. Joyce, Faulkner, Proust, and Céline were my prose passions. I adored Greek poetry. And I loved Ezra Pound, who, I believed, had died at the same moment I was born, on Día de los Muertos in 1972. People told me I looked like him. I thought sometimes that maybe his soul had passed into me. I knew he had been arrested for making fascist broadcasts and had been in a psychiatric prison for his final years. I hoped I got only the good parts. But the fascism didn't bother me that much.

Walking around and looking at my books, I realized that I'd read only white men my entire life. The closest I had come to Black literature was the Public Enemy and KRS-One records I'd listened to as a teenager.

I thought I read books solely because I loved them. But because my entire identity rested on being a writer in the white modernist model, I also had to tell myself that they were the best things that had ever been written. "And it's not that I don't like Black women authors or anything," I wrote in my journal. "I just like what I like. And I love Sappho. I spend like ten hours on each poem. I love her more than any of them love any writer. They don't understand literature at all. They care more about political correctness than writing. I'm really the only one that gets it."

The idea of reading only Black women offended me precisely because it pushed me toward recognizing the racial nature of my reading, which forced me to see myself not as a universal human or a unique hero but as part of a group—the same way I already saw everybody else. And that made me resentful.

Instead of going to the library to pick up a book by a Black author, I dove even deeper into the white men I idolized, not only reading their books but leaving their biographies lying on the bathroom floor so that I could read about the life of Balzac or Flaubert or Joyce in order to justify myself to myself. I clung with a fury to writers in whom I could see myself. And I was angry that other people also wanted to see themselves in the works they read.

Chapter 13

THE PHONE RANG. I WAS reading and let the call go to the machine. "I have spoken too long for a writer," the voice of Ernest Hemingway said as my outgoing message. "A writer should write what he has to say and not speak it." *Beep.*

"Baseball," Dad said, using an affectionate but ultimately mocking nickname from my childhood. "When you get this—"

I stepped over to the phone and picked it up.

"Dad," I said.

"I want to run something by you," he said. "Mother is not doing well."

"Oh no," I said.

"My mother, I mean," he clarified. "I don't mean to worry you, she's OK now. But she was saying how much she would love to spend some time with you. And I was thinking what if you came and spent a couple weeks with her this summer? You could help her be able to stay home and be independent a bit longer. We're not sure how safe it is for her to be alone."

"That sounds great," I said.

"I've always wanted to canoe down the Edisto," Dad added. "Maybe I can come for a couple days and we could take a canoe trip."

A few years earlier, when I had announced to the family that I wanted to be a poet, most everyone had rolled their eyes or mocked me. But Grandmother Woods had said, "Why, that's wonderful. We haven't had a poet in the family in hundreds of years." I still cherished that, and now, I knew from our occasional letters, she was proud I was studying ancient Greek and Latin, and I wanted to spend time with her.

I was living with a new girlfriend by that time, and things were not going well, so I was happy to have an excuse to leave Albuquerque for the summer. We'd met in French class. She was only eighteen. Soon she moved in with me, to the same apartment where Blake and I had lived on Coal Avenue. I used my broken heart as an excuse to maintain a distance while also having the warmth of another person lying beside me. She really loved me, but I couldn't return the affection, and our relationship had become acrimonious.

"Maybe I'll call Chuck and try to go spend a few weeks with him in West Virginia," I said to Dad.

"He's living there now?" he said. "I thought he was in Columbia."

"He moved into an old hunting cabin that his grandfather owned down in a hollow. He works the 'hoot owl' shift, as he calls it, at the nearest truck stop."

"Well, good," Dad said. "This sounds like a plan."

Over the coming weeks, Dad and I worked out the details, and as soon as I finished my last exam, I got into the Isuzu Trooper he had bought me after I sold the van and cranked it up. I drove a few blocks down Lead, which was parallel to Coal, and merged onto I-40, which I stayed on for the next three days.

I'd hoped to make it in two, but on my last night, I finally gave up and stopped at a small motel between Nashville and Knoxville and slept a weary sleep in which I felt as if I were still rolling forward, exhausted, restless, and nearly feral. I woke up and left around ten the next morning, starving. I saw the yellow sign of a Waffle House and pulled off the highway and into the parking lot. I'd eat some breakfast, hit the road, and make it to Greenville by dinner.

After days alone, walking into the chain restaurant was a sensory overload. The crackling of bacon, the smell of brewing coffee and cooking eggs and toasting toast and frying hash browns all blended with the bright-yellow decor and neon lights and the country songs playing on the jukebox as people sat chewing at their tables. As much as I hated to admit it, I felt as if I were home when I sat on one of the round stools at the counter.

When the waitress brought my coffee, I ordered eggs, grits, hash browns, and toast. When someone played David Allan Coe on the jukebox and everyone in the restaurant sang along, I almost thought I could like the South.

Mom and Dad were living at Summey's house again while they built one in a new subdivision about a mile from where I'd last lived with them, and as I pulled into the driveway later that afternoon, the flower beds in front of the house were exploding in a slow profusion of color. Pale-orange tiger lilies regally drooped between purple irises beside the garage. Woody Guthrie's "Pretty Boy Floyd" drifted out my open windows and through the yard, where I noticed Summey, crouching down pulling weeds. I turned off the car and opened the door.

The air was thick, the humidity pulsing with the thrum of insects and the emergent, occasional flashes of evening's fireflies.

"Hey," I said.

"Hey, boy," he said, straightening up slowly and wiping his palm on his cheap Kmart chinos. He spit a squirt of tobacco on the ground and started to walk, tottering, toward me. He had had a relatively minor stroke and had aged more than the time that had elapsed since I'd last seen him the previous winter would suggest, his movements halting, his eyes rheumy, and his skin splotched and dry, hanging from his skull like a grease-stained paper sack.

"What was that you were listening to?" he asked as we walked toward one another, where the gray driveway met the lush green yard.

"Woody Guthrie," I said. "I listened to his Smithsonian recordings half the way home."

"I used to love him," he said. "Back when I was young. 'This Land Is Your Land,' 'Pretty Boy Floyd,' but then he became a goddamn communist—"

I wanted to talk to Summey about music. He'd instilled a deep love of country music in me that had been reborn over recent years.

"Once he went Red, I wished that sumbitch was dead," Summey said as Mom stepped around him to see me, pressing her hair, a brighter brassy shade of middle age than it had been, against my face.

"Baseball," Dad exclaimed, his big Woods voice booming out over the hill as he wrapped his arms around me.

For the last few years I had been surrounded by people I'd known only for brief periods, and it was strange to be embraced, surrounded, by so much shared history.

"Come here and give me some sugar," Nanny said as she shuffled out in the biggest rush she could muster. "Let me hug your neck."

This was the same party of people who'd assembled in this same place just after my birth, when they released Mom and me from the hospital twenty-two years earlier and we moved into the basement here. After the long days on the road, little sleep, and constant motion, sunstruck, I was overwhelmed with emotion, and that feeling annoyed me. I didn't know what to do with it.

I kissed Nanny's cheek and wrapped my arm around her.

"You need a beer?" Dad asked.

"I'd love one," I said, and we all walked inside.

I was going to rest up there for a few days and then drive down to Edisto, where I'd stay for two weeks. After the first week, Dad would come, and we'd go on the canoe trip. And when he left, my cousin Michael was going to spend a few days with me and stay another week to take care of Grandmother after I drove to Chuck's in West Virginia.

On my second day in Greenville, Summey wanted to go to the Jockey Lot—a giant flea market—in Anderson, South Carolina. We all got up early and piled into his burgundy, wood-paneled station wagon. Mom drove and Summey sat shotgun beside her in the front, while Nanny sat beside me in the back. Behind us was a wheelchair that Summey used sometimes since the stroke.

We were on some small rural road, trees and fields passing in a thick green blur outside the window, when the lights of a patrol car started to flash behind us. I felt the familiar thudding dread in my chest, even though I didn't have anything illegal on me.

"How fast were you going?" Summey asked.

"I don't know, Daddy," Mom said.

"I'll take care of it," Summey said as she pulled off the road.

"Daddy," Mom said.

"I got it," he said.

A red pickup rattled past. Summey opened his door at the same time the deputy, parked thirty feet behind us on the side of the road, opened his.

"Hey there, buddy," Summey said, tottering forward on the road's narrow shoulder, pocked with weeds and trash, his Yankees cap perched lopsided on his head and Levi Garrett dripping from his lips.

"Get back in the car, sir," the deputy said, insistently.

"But hey," Summey said.

"Daddy!" Mom yelled from the car window.

"Sir, get back in the car," the deputy said, his hand hovering by his hip above his gun.

"Buddy," Summey said, his voice desperate, pleading.

"Sir."

"Goddamn it, Daddy," Mom said, starting to open the driver's door.

"Ma'am!" the patrolman yelled. "Stay in the car!"

Summey finally turned and tottered back to the car, the bill of his Yankees hat pointed straight at the ground as he studied the motion of his feet through the sand on the road's narrow shoulder. When he sidled back into the seat in front of me and the door slammed shut, I looked down, pretending I hadn't seen anything, as the deputy approached Mom's window, wary.

In the end, the cop only gave Mom a warning. As the deputy walked, straight legged and stiff, back to his car, and Mom eased onto the two-lane road, Summey muttered, "Goddamn it," over and over again, almost under his breath but entirely audible, and my heart broke for him. I realized that being part of the good ol' boy system—that loose network of the white men who controlled these towns—was essential to his identity.

When he had bailed me out of trouble, it was about him as much as it was about me. He wanted to prove that he could do it. It was a demonstration of his power as a white man in white America. He'd been insulted as a mill-village linthead kid and he never wanted to stand for that again. He needed to be singled out for being powerful and special rather than for being poor and powerless.

But as we made our way in relative silence toward what was dubbed "the South's biggest and the world's biggest flea market," he grappled with this realization that his power had slipped.

"Goddamn it," he snarled. "I can't believe you were speeding like that. Could have killed us all."

"Daddy, we only got a warning," Mom said.

"You were driving like a goddamn maniac," he said. "Women should never be allowed to drive."

"Carl," Nanny said from beside me. "You're just mad that the deputy didn't know you."

"Oh, shut up," he said. "I don't give a damn. Times have changed. Can't fix no tickets anymore. To be a homegrown white man just don't mean what it once did around here."

"Like I said, you're just mad that he didn't know you," Nanny said.

"He was only Bay's age," Mom said. "How would you expect him to know you?"

"Goddamn it, I said shut up," Summey said.

When we got to the Jockey Lot, Mom and I traded off pushing Summey's wheelchair, and as he perused baseball cards, bonsai trees, orchids, and various of his other obsessions, it was as if he was determined to prove, through his pugnacious haggling, that he still had the power and the juice to get what he wanted.

I remembered that whenever he used to take me to see country concerts at the Carolina Coliseum when I was little, he'd always walk up to an usher at a side door in order to avoid the line. But he'd talk so long with the usher before the guy would finally say, "Oh, just come on in here," that it would have been much quicker to wait in the line like everybody else.

And though he never showed our tickets, he'd always bought them long in advance. It just made him feel good to know he could get in free if he wanted to.

"None of the same old vendors are here anymore," he said. "The ones with the good stuff. They been replaced by so many of these Chinese and all kinds of other people."

Summey saw his own decline as universal. It was not that he was failing the world. The world was failing him. It had gone to shit, and for the next couple of days, he stumbled around, muttering angrily and yelling at Nanny for no reason.

Sitting out on his back porch, looking over the city, I asked him one afternoon about when he was stationed in Nashville during World War II.

"Did you ever go see any country concerts then?" I asked him.

"Oh, hell no," he said. "People would ridicule you. The *country* in *country music* was meant as an insult. Back then, they didn't even call it that yet. They just called it hillbilly music, and being called a hillbilly was even worse than being called a linthead. Only thing socially lower than a hillbilly was a colored person. They didn't have signs hanging up that kept hillbillies out, but boy you could tell by their attitudes that most fancy whites didn't want no goddamn hillbillies around. If I'd listened to that music, they probably would have sent me off to war instead of keeping me in the office."

"What did you listen to?"

"I told you I listened to some Woody Guthrie before he became a goddamn commie, because he kinda had that country sound but was accepted by everyone," he said. "But mostly we'd just listen to the big band stuff that they had at army dances and that sort of thing."

"I've been listening to a lot of Hank Williams Sr. now," I told him. "And you remember I loved Junior when I was growing up. But what I notice now is that Hank Senior just sang country songs. But all of Hank Junior's songs are meta—"

"Are what, college boy?" he said.

Summey had not gone to college, but he'd ended up in Nashville during the war because when the army created a new air force division, he had aced the test, and he was always a little resentful of college people, including his grandson.

"Junior's songs are songs about country music," I said. "It's something that he's mad about, that disdain we both felt. Something he wants to fight about."

"Goddamn right," he said. "We need more fight like that."

His own sense of fight had become more pugnacious even as it became less effective.

I felt bad watching Summey's decline, but by the time I left Greenville to drive to Edisto two days later, I couldn't wait to escape the atmosphere of resentment that filled the house. In his fury at his failing life, he was determined to fight against something all the time, and usually the target turned out to be Nanny or Mom. That was the way white men rolled, I was learning—at war with the world, until you start to lose. Then at war with women, especially those closest to you.

On Edisto, a barrier island whose purpose is to protect the mainland from storms, it had always seemed as if the world were declining, crumbling under the weight of the waves of time. But unlike Summey, Grandmother Woods could surf those waves, happily advancing toward the time when her body would find itself in the earth beside her parents and her grandparents, and, she believed, her soul would be reunited with them in heaven.

A decade earlier, she'd had a heart attack and been declared legally dead. Dad was the only one of the brothers at the hospital, and she said that as her spirit rose from her body toward the most peaceful white light imaginable, she could see Dad sitting alone in the waiting room and decided to come back into her body. Now she faced her own demise with grace.

It was a balmy, hot afternoon when I arrived at her house at the beach.

"I hope you don't mind if we leave the windows open instead of using the air conditioner," Grandmother said, her bent body hunched like a question mark in a loose-fitting blue shirt, as she pointed at the window unit, as soon as I walked into the kitchen. "I want to get as much ocean air as I can before I die."

There was something bracing about her breezy embrace of mortality, something not unlike the desire to keep the windows open despite the heat and the humidity, an acceptance of reality that I admired. And since I had become increasingly interested in environmental issues, I was happy to forego the Freon.

"My friend Sally just dropped off a whole basket of tomatoes," she said. "And a loaf of John Derst bread. Would you be interested in a tomato sandwich?"

"Yes, ma'am," I said, looking at the bowl of globular red tomatoes on the counter and the picture of a Confederate officer on the brown plastic wrapper of the Captain John Derst bread, which was hard to find outside the Lowcountry and was best for tomato sandwiches.

"I'll make two for us if you'd like," I said.

She smiled her crooked, lopsided smile.

"Why, I'd love that," she said. "And there are some beers that Irvin left. We can have one of those with the sandwich and it will be grand."

"Edisto has the best tomatoes in the world," I said as I walked over to the bowl.

I picked one out to slice; heavy and warm in my hands, it felt alive. I washed it in the sink and then opened the drawer beneath the cabinet and pulled out a knife.

"Do you like your tomatoes peeled?" Grandmother asked.

"I can peel it for you if you'd like," I said.

"That would be nice."

She turned on the TV.

I slid the silver blade of the knife as gingerly as I could beneath the skin of the tomato, trying to separate it from the flesh without gouging out chunks of good meat.

"Do you think he did it?" Grandmother asked.

"What?" I asked, looking up from my lip-biting concentration on the tomato, as its juice dripped off the cutting board and onto the counter.

"O. J. Simpson," she said. "I assume you've been following the trial."

"No," I said. "I really haven't."

I prided myself on not watching TV, remaining separate from the cultural moment, and I was disappointed by how closely Grandmother seemed to be following the trial of a famous Black football player accused of killing his white ex-wife and her lover.

"I don't know if he did it," she said as the blade of my knife passed through the tomato's pink flesh. "But I watched the entire prosecution and I don't think they have the evidence to prove he did it. There are still too many questions."

"I really haven't watched it," I said, slathering a thick layer of mayonnaise across the slices of yellow bread.

"If they find him guilty after this case," she said, "I'm afraid the Blacks everywhere will riot like they did in Los Angeles."

Sweat dripped down my face, and I noticed that the air outside had stilled, taking away our breeze.

"I definitely think in that case, with Rodney King, that they had a right to be mad," I said, bringing both sandwiches over to the table.

"We've always had good relationships with the Blacks here," she said. "There are many more Blacks than whites on the island, and so there was always a certain respect. Growing up, I learned to speak Gullah, but I didn't think anything of it. But now I'm proud of being able to speak it."

I walked to the refrigerator and came back to the table with two cans of Olympia Beer.

"In fact, I have a lovely idea," she said. "I can say the blessing in Gullah and you can say it in Greek."

"I don't know if I can think of a blessing," I said. "Because it's not a spoken language anymore, what I study, and we just translate literature. But I do know a couple brief passages from the Bible."

"Well, we'll each do that," she said, delighted. "I'll recite a Biblical passage in Gullah and you can say one in Greek."

"OK," I said, sitting down.

She recited a Bible verse in Gullah-Geechee, which was musical and lilting and also sounded like what was being discussed at the time as "Ebonics." I'd later learn that Gullah applied an English vocabulary to various West African grammatical structures. But back then, I just reveled in the juxtaposition of this little old white lady speaking in a dialect that seemed to me so "Black."

The only Greek verse I had memorized was 1 John—"in the beginning was the Word, and the Word was with God, and the Word was God"— and I thought it was an appropriate prayer, but as I finished, I imagined Grandmother saying, "Word up" instead of "Amen," and I laughed out loud. She didn't know what I thought was funny, but she seemed delighted and joined in my mirth, allowing her chirping laugh to flutter from her lungs like a beautiful, erratic bird.

"That was lovely," she said. "We have a new tradition."

The sandwich was divine. When I took my first bite, the tomato juice mixed with the mayonnaise and ran down my chin.

"Let me get us napkins," I said, rising from the table and catching a drop of tomato juice in the palm of my hand as it fell from my chin.

"We have always had good relations here," Grandmother said, evidently needing to unburden herself of something. "I would never judge a colored person for being colored. But there have always been so many more of them than us down here on the island—in the Lowcountry in general—that we always had to be worried about outsiders coming in and turning them against us like they did in the horrible days of Reconstruction. That's why I'm so worried about what is happening with this trial."

Her use of the word *colored* was antiquated and discomforting. But who was I to judge? I loved her as much as I loved anyone and, whatever she said, she seemed far more comfortable around Black people than anyone else in my family did. She even knew Gullah. There was no way she was racist.

Still, it seemed strange what she was saying, about Black people vastly outnumbering white. That was clear in the center of the island, I guessed, away from the shore, where it was sparsely populated and there were small houses and shacks tucked back amid overgrown patches of vine-wrapped trees. Those houses were entirely populated by Black people. But I realized I'd never seen a Black person on the beach here. Maybe at the pavilion, but hardly even there and never on the beach itself. She'd told me once that Black people didn't like the water, but that story seemed even more puzzling if they lived here in vast numbers. And I saw plenty of Black people at the lake in Columbia. So something about the way the population of the island worked didn't make any sense to me. But I didn't follow the thought very far—because my whiteness meant I didn't have to. It wasn't in my interest to consider how the whites seemed to have gotten all the wealth and how they managed to keep it. That's the way whiteness works. Brutal interventions create circumstances that appear natural to the next generation.

There was no reason for me to think about why there weren't Black people on the beach and why Black people didn't own any of these beach houses. I could just go swimming. And after my years in the desert, I couldn't wait to run into the ocean and dive into a crashing wave.

The day after Dad arrived, we woke up early to go to the river. We had packed a cooler full of beer and sandwiches. We put it in the back of the car and drove an hour inland, stopping to buy five pounds of boiled peanuts at a roadside stand before we reached a recreational outfitter on the Edisto River, where we rented a canoe.

Dad had been in the Coast Guard during Vietnam and had owned a boat when I was a kid, and he was comfortable on the water and confident as we set out. I was a good swimmer but did not have much experience rowing canoes, and as we shoved off into the tea-black water, life jackets draped over our necks, I had a hard time paddling so that we went straight.

"Serpentine," Dad yelled, laughing as I sent the boat slithering over the water like a snake. He was making fun of my physical limitations the way he had all my life, but I had been away from home long enough that I could laugh along now.

"Oh, shit," I said, a couple of hours later as I noticed the first drops from the heavy rain cloud that had been advancing toward us all morning.

We could see the I-95 overpass up ahead.

"Let's try to reach it before it gets too bad," Dad said. "It's just a summer storm, it shouldn't last long."

We dug our oars into the thick water made dark by the tannin in all the cypress knees growing up from the surface like the Gothic spires of sand-castles, and we paddled hard through the rain for five minutes. We reached the bridge just before the sky erupted in torrents of water. I stepped off the front of the boat into the shallow water off the bank and pulled it ashore.

Dad opened the cooler and handed me a beer. He cracked one open for himself.

"You want your sandwich?" he asked.

"Might as well," I replied.

We sat there a few minutes eating our sandwiches and sipping our beers, listening only to the sound of the rain in the water around us and above us as the tires on the bridge sloshed through it.

When I finished my sandwich, I leaned forward and pulled out the damp paper bag of boiled peanuts. I took one out and cracked the shell with my thumbs, then slurped out the salty brine before I ate the purplish flesh of the nuts ensconced within it. I dropped the shell into the water, where it drifted like a canoe in a naval battle, bombarded by giant drops as the rain started coming down even harder just as the sun cut through bloated clouds. Balls of water bounced up off the surface of the river and caught the light like pearls.

"How did your dad end up with the name Hernando?" I asked Dad, idly.

It had always seemed odd to me that his father, a white guy from Clarendon County, South Carolina, was named Hernando Jennings Woods, even though everybody called him Jenks, a shortened form of his middle name, but I'd never asked about it. Since I lived in New Mexico, where Spanish names were the norm, I'd been meaning to inquire.

"We don't have any Hispanic blood, do we?"

Dad smiled and leaned toward me, the tight life jacket hugging his Falstaffian belly as the weight in the beached canoe shifted dramatically starboard.

"The story is that his father, my grandfather Dr. Irvin McSwain Woods, had to go hide out in Texas," he said, leaning back so that his weight settled our boat once more. "Somehow he got into trouble there or on the way there. And, as my daddy told me, a woman saved his life. He promised to name a son after her husband, who was named Hernando."

"Your granddad was an outlaw," I quipped, putting a cold, wet peanut shell between my lips, extracting the meat, and tossing the shell into the black water, where it floated, bobbing for a moment, before it was lost.

"After the Wo-ah," he said, as if that explained the man's story all in three words. Like many people in our region, Dad pronounced *war* in two syllables, and for most that made it clear which war they were referring to. *The Wo-ah* always meant the War between the States.

"Why did he have to hide out after the war?" I asked.

"He killed a man," Dad said, looking away.

I knew my great-grandfather had fought in the Civil War, but this was the first time I'd heard this story. A gust of wind swept over the water, and we remained silent for a while. The storm had cooled the air, and the dark cypress knees looked less hazy around the edges than they had earlier, despite the raindrops rushing down to the river. I washed down the peanut brine with my warming beer.

"Who did he kill? And why?"

Dad paused, thinking. The smell of rain cut through the odor of over-ripe vegetation and the swampy, alluvial rot at the edge of the rolling river. A car above us blew its horn.

"Because the man was Black, I guess," Dad said. "There was a lot of that in those years, I think, when people returned from the Wo-ah. They couldn't accept that it was over. I don't know if it was a lynching or a murder or...."

He trailed off, staring hard at the peanut he was picking at with his thumbnail. The shell dropped from his hand and fell into the shallow puddle of water sloshing in the bottom of the canoe, then floated there.

I didn't know how to respond. I had always heard my great-grandfather had served in the state legislature, and these two pieces—outlaw and lawmaker—didn't seem to fit together.

"So he killed somebody and then came back and was elected to the legislature?" I asked.

"I think so," Dad said. "But nobody really talked about it. The killing."

"And what was his name again?"

"Dr. Irvin McSwain Woods," he said. "I. M. Woods."

"And he fought in the Civil War, right?" I asked.

"He was in the military academy in Camden when it broke out and joined and was shot in the knee at Gettysburg," Dad said. "It's rare that someone my age has a grandfather who fought in the Wo-ah, but Daddy was so much older than Mother that we sort of gained a generation. Or lost one."

He dug his hand into the cooler and scooped up a Pabst Blue Ribbon and offered it to me. His gold St. Christopher pendant swung out from under his T-shirt as he handed it to me. I leaned back onto my bench and looked at him fishing out a beer for himself as I pulled my old can from the foam koozie, crushed it, and put it in the plastic bag tied to my bench.

Maybe we both wanted to talk about the deep history of white supremacy underlying that murder, underlying our shared history, but neither of us had the courage or the language. We did not know how. Instead, I took a slug of my beer, wanting more answers, even if I didn't yet understand my questions.

It's difficult for white people to think about whiteness; it is like walking in a hall of mirrors where each lie reflects all the others. At the center there is horror. I knew this murder was only the tip of what whiteness hides. Behind it lay enslavement, rape, torture. To think such thoughts feels overwhelming, and so, most of the time, we quickly quit.

We sat there in silence listening to the rain and sipping on our beers.

He used the bottom of his T-shirt to wipe the rain from the lenses of his glasses. I did the same with mine.

"Once we regained control, Granddaddy was a hero," Dad said. "He had redeemed the state."

I realized that the *we* Dad used here meant white people. Or southern white people, as opposed to the Yankees.

I'd heard the word *redemption* in my South Carolina history classes in the third and eighth grades, but I couldn't remember what it meant, and here it seemed nefarious, associated with this murder.

But more than I felt any moral opprobrium, I was taken with the narrative of the story, which was like something out of William Faulkner or Cormac McCarthy. I was excited more than horrified. I could identify with Dr. Woods's flight into the desert to escape South Carolina, whatever its cause.

"What happened in Texas that he had to be saved by the woman?" I asked, imagining writing a novel about the whole thing.

"I don't know," Dad said. "Maybe he got shot. Some kind of physical injury where she had to nurse him."

He took a sip of beer and looked away. We sat like that for a few minutes.

"The rain has let up," he finally said.

A pale sheet of golden sunlight ran across the surface of the now-steaming water. A black snake slithered by our craft and disappeared as we pulled our oars off the rails. Like a couple of adventurers, we pushed ourselves out into the current. We steered toward a bend of knotted cypress knees and an overhang of old live oak as the sound of the highway and human life grew distant, replaced by the insistent hum of frogs and insects as we moved away from the overpass toward a less traveled part of the river.

We didn't talk about the murder as we drove back to the house or later that night, and I never asked Grandmother about it. But I kept thinking about the crime, possibly a lynching, and it came up again a few nights later, after Dad had left the island and returned to Greenville, when my cousin Michael and I were drinking.

We were sitting at Coot's Lounge, the only bar on the beach. It was humid, and the spinning fan swirled cigarette smoke around in the thick air. The band had just quit playing, and now its members gathered around the other end of the bar, accepting shots from a crowd of tourists. Michael and I sat sipping beer from plastic cups, and I kept bumming cigarettes from him. A breeze blew in the open windows and scattered our smoke as the sound of balls on the pool table clamored across the room.

"Did you ever hear much about our great-granddad when you were a kid?" I asked.

Michael was four years older than I, and when he was a kid he had lived in Manning, where my murderous great-grandfather Dr. Woods had also lived.

"He fought in the Wo-ah, I think," Michael said, his voice resonant and slow. "Was a doctor maybe."

"My dad told me that he lynched somebody," I said.

Michael squinted weirdly at me, and I assumed he couldn't hear me, despite the generally loud volume of my voice.

"Yeah," I said, even louder. "He had to go hide out in Texas after he lynched someone after the War. Isn't that crazy?"

Michael cut his eyes at me more forcefully this time.

"Chill," he hissed, barely moving his lips.

I had been sitting sideways on my stool, one elbow on the stained blue bar, facing Michael. I turned to look in the mirror behind the bar to take in the scene. There was a Black man sitting two stools down on the other side of me. He was older, probably sixtyish, with a bald head and thin white whiskers etched across his mouth.

He was also looking straight into the mirror, where he held my reflection. I turned and smiled.

He directed his gaze toward me but did not smile back. He picked up his watery drink, took a sip, and squinted at me with what looked like disgust.

I flushed, feeling a bit flummoxed and confused. I was just talking about history.

I did not look away.

"How's it going?" I asked the man. He barely lifted his chin in acknowledgment.

I spun slowly on my stool toward Michael. There were fresh beers in front of him. I took the last sip from my cup and set it on the bar, then picked up the new one.

"Thanks," I said.

"Let's walk outside and have a smoke," he said, already standing up. "Check out the ocean."

We palmed our plastic cups and got up and ambled out of the bar.

"What was up with that dude?" I asked.

"Man, you can't go around talking about lynchings and shit," Michael said, laughing and shaking his head a little. "He was fucking pissed."

"What?" I said. "What's there to be pissed about? None of us were around then."

"I know," said Michael, who still lived in South Carolina. "But I could see him over your shoulder when you were talking, and his eyes kind of lit up and his shoulders tightened. It's the kind of look you see someone get a few minutes before a fight starts. With the trial and all, things are tense."

"Free O. J., those cops are definitely racist," I said. "But a murder our great-granddad committed a hundred and fifty years ago doesn't have anything to do with that."

The surf crashed against the sand in the distance.

"I heard that the Klan burned a church in Manning a couple weeks ago," Michael said. "They caught some dudes, I think."

"Yeah, that's terrible too," I said. "But what does that have to do with us or with our great-grandfather?"

"I told you my idea," Michael said as the sea breeze ruffled his hair. "We need to bring back the Confederate flag, as a sign of rebellion, but put a Black Power fist in the center—or maybe instead of the stars—because that's also a sign of rebellion, and together it would be a sign of unity. We have more in common down here, Black people and white people, than any of us have with Yankees, whatever race they are."

That was the kind of clever but meaninglessly abstract argument that passed for iconoclastic with a certain sort of Gen X white boy raised on David Letterman's sarcasm and music ranging from the Clash to Public Enemy. White boys like me. We'd smoke weed and snort coke or Ritalin or take Xanax and drink liquor and riff, endlessly entertaining ourselves and each other with this idle bullshit. Such proposals were our version of baseball statistics, more smoke to keep us from having to really look at the world.

"Something both Strom Thurmond and Louis Farrakhan could get behind," I said, and snuffed out my cigarette on top of the trash can, still feeling uneasy about the allegation that I was somehow responsible for the deeds of my ancestors.

"Exactly," Michael said. "If you can get the extremes, you get the middle."

We stood and looked out into the darkness for a minute, contemplating this sophomoric profundity with no intention of ever following through on any of it.

"You want another beer before we go?" he asked.

I wasn't going to leave because some old guy had gotten pissed off at me.

"Yeah," I said, and we turned toward the door. "This round's on me. You want a shot?"

"Just chill, though," Michael said.

I nodded.

"I mean, it's not like we killed the man," I muttered as we walked back inside, taking up stools a bit farther down the bar from the Black man who had scowled at me.

I was deeply invested in the freedom my whiteness granted me to see history as story, invested in my insulation from the horrors of my inheritance. But the story I'd heard from my father would stick with me in ways that I could have never predicted at the time, leaving me feeling uneasy, as if there was something just beneath the surface of myself I could not see. It would not be too much to say that whiteness was a ghost that began to actively haunt me, even if it disappeared whenever I tried to get a good look at it. Eventually I would come to see that each of my evasions, every insistence on my innocence, every deflection of responsibility, was an echo, not of the earlier crime, but of its cover-up.

The cover-up that constitutes the contemporary sense of whiteness has whitewashed the crimes of our history and the privileges of our present, so we are able to think of ourselves as victims.

Chapter 14

I DROVE BACK TO GREENVILLE the next day, and from there to West Virginia, where I was planning to spend two weeks in Chuck's cabin, helping him chop wood for the winter. He'd told me to call him from the truck stop off the highway and he would come and meet me, and I could follow him into the holler where he lived in his grandfather's old hunting cabin.

As I waited for him in the truck stop parking lot, I marveled at the depth of green in the rolling range, which somehow combined the smaller hills we'd grown up tramping around in with the wildness and the fury of the western mountains I was only learning about living out West.

I saw the old two-tone blue truck pull up in my rearview. Then he drove up beside me, windows down, Bob Dylan coming from the radio.

"Let's go," he said, and I followed him down some wildly winding roads, around whose curves he went faster than I was comfortable going, until we reached a long, shadow-covered gravel road that led us deep down into the holler, toward the river at the bottom of the valley.

When Chuck got out of the car, I noticed the big, dirty-looking bandage hanging off his pinkie. He'd told me the story about how late one night he was trying to make a bong from a coffee pot and when he pulled hard on the plastic handle, the glass carafe came apart, creating a sharp shard that sliced through his pinkie's tendons and clear to the bone. Blood was everywhere, he said, and he had no gas in his truck. He also had a motorcycle, but he couldn't hold the handlebars or use the throttle with his hand like that. He had no phone at the time, and he was worried he was going to bleed out and somehow managed to siphon enough gas from the motorcycle into the truck to get to the house of a neighbor who was a nurse, and she helped him stop the bleeding enough to get him to the hospital.

But now he couldn't work, and, as importantly, he couldn't chop wood, which he needed if he was going to make it through the winter in the small, two-room cabin, and I was ostensibly here to help him, although we both probably knew we would do very little chopping.

"This is amazing," I said as I walked in and set my bag on the couch. The walls were a bright, unfinished wood that still smelled alive, despite the many years now they had been holding up the cabin's tin roof.

I'd been hearing about this cabin on Chuck's grandfather's farm, and his neighbors up here, ever since I'd first met him a decade earlier, when he'd moved down the mountain to Columbia as a teenager and we'd gone skateboarding downtown. The best thing he'd ever written was a story about driving between West Virginia and South Carolina as a kid and seeing lights burning in cabins like this and wondering what people were doing in there and then, years later, meeting his neighbor Dale and realizing they had been listening to bluegrass music and smoking homegrown marijuana.

"Let's go to the river," Chuck said.

He was bigger now, around the waist at least, after working in kitchens in the years since he'd lived with me and Blake, but there was something else different about him. Chuck moved with a kind of practiced certainty as he walked out the door into the bright-green field surrounding the small wooden cabin on his grandfather's farm, just up the hill from a pond whose brown surface sparkled in the sun. His gait displayed a sense of being at home as he let the fingertips of his good hand run across the slick black coat of his dog, Jack.

Chuck stepped wide over the seat and sat down on his three-wheeler and cranked the engine so that it belched out a big cloud of petrol smoke.

"Hop on," he said.

I'd been expecting some kind of Thoreauvian idyll, but the loud clanking of the engine assured me that I'd been wrong about that. Because we were in the wilderness, we would use more obvious, if not just more, machines.

Nervously I got on the back and wrapped my arms around Chuck's chest, and he tore through the woods, small branches bouncing back, slapping my arms and my face. My heart pounded, and I felt certain I would fall off or that we would crash. But I realized that to Chuck, this was now as ordinary as driving to the store in a car.

When we got to a clearing by the river, bluegrass music seeped out above the squeals and splashes of delighted children playing in the running water and the laughter of adults watching them.

Chuck introduced me to Dale, a tall, thin, shirtless man with cutoff jeans and dirty-blond hair hanging over his shoulders and a light mustache, and his two brothers, Bob and Steve. Dale introduced his wife and his kids, but the segregation of the sexes began when the conversation really started rolling, and it quickly became clear that the three brothers were going to test me while the women tended to drying and feeding the children on the banks of the river.

"We rassle for brown eye around here," Dale said, looking me dead in the eye.

Chuck had warned me about this. His neighbors were very aware of Appalachian stereotypes, especially from the 1972 Burt Reynolds movie *Deliverance*, where inbred and isolated mountain men torment and rape the interloping city guys who end up stuck in their holler.

"Why do you think I'm here?" I said.

They laughed, and it seemed I had passed the first test, though many more would come.

As we stood there talking for the next hour as the sun cut through the tops of the trees to mottle the rock-ripped river, I learned that the three brothers sometimes built fences for other folks but that Dale had gone without a real job for years. He hunted for meat, chopped wood to heat their house, and grew vegetables. And, Chuck explained when we got back to his cabin a little later, for cash, Dale grew and sold pot.

"We're in business together now," Chuck said.

A little later, just after dark, we saw lights cut through the windows and heard the rumbling of tires on the gravel. Dale's brother Bob knocked on the door. He was a big guy, with a broad head and a haircut that went straight across his brow in a way that seemed almost childish.

Chuck had told me that Dale didn't drink, but Bob did. He had a twelve-pack in his hand as he walked in. He cracked open a can and tossed one to each of us. Then he sat down and crushed up pain meds and snorted a line.

"Want one?" he said.

Sure.

"Let's go driving," Bob said as soon as the crushed pharmaceuticals had flown up into our nasal cavities.

I thought it was a terrible idea, especially since they had been talking about how "Ole Ernie," a friend who seemed to have been better than everyone else at everything, had recently died while driving over the mountain.

We walked out into the incredibly dark night and piled into a busted-up old Mustang 5.0, all carrying beers. Bob looked around the headrest at me in the back seat, his eyes gleaming in a way that struck me as demonic, just before he cranked the car and hit the gas, sending a spray of gravel up at Chuck's cabin.

"Watch the dog," Chuck said as Bob skidded off for the beginning of the most terrifying drive I'd ever been on, jumping hills and gullies, real-life *Dukes of Hazzard* shit on the dark mountain roads. I closed my eyes in terror as they laughed at me.

"Ole Ernie could jump this better than anyone," Bob howled as he hit the gas and roared up a hill, resulting in one of those awful airborne moments when your stomach flies up into your throat.

"That's where he got killed, right there," Bob said after his tires crashed back down onto the earth.

Amazingly, we made it back to the farm unscathed, with a new case of beer.

"I'm hungry," Chuck said.

"Me too," Bob said.

I was also hungry, but I'd rather have starved than get back in that car right then. As it turned out, they had something worse in mind.

"Let's gig some frogs," Bob said.

"Frog giggin'!" Chuck exclaimed. "Hell yeah."

Gigging frogs means going out in a boat with a lamp strapped to your brow and a silver, five-pronged spear in your hand and using the light to freeze big bullfrogs long enough to bring the spear down through their heads and then pull them up into the boat.

We were wasted, and I didn't like the idea of being in a boat like this, and I hoped they would abandon the idea when they realized that the boat was down at the river. Instead, we got in Chuck's truck to go and fetch it. But the truck got stuck in the mud. My Isuzu was a four-wheel drive, so they made me drive it over, where they tied it to Chuck's truck so I could pull it out, and then, finally, an hour after the idea came to them, we were sloshing around in our boat on the primeval pond, scanning the scum at its edge, looking for the big bullfrogs making their deep, riveting ribbits roar up through the night.

After seeing Chuck use the spear a few times, I was ready. We paddled slowly up toward the bank, where he had a frog frozen in his beam. I could see the eyes glowing orange above the submerged green skin. And then like lightning my silver spear came into the beam of light and straight down so that its pronged spikes went right through its head. I pulled it up and scraped it from the spear and into the bucket and I felt kind of sick.

When finally we'd caught enough for a snack, we ran the boat ashore and went back to Chuck's porch, where we cut the skinny long legs off the big plump bodies of these amphibious beasts the size of baseballs.

"It feels bad to waste so much of them," Chuck said, slicing off the legs. "But there's nothing you can do with the bodies."

"That's right," Bob said, heaving the bleeding, legless body of a frog down toward the pond. "No meat, just guts."

Then Chuck battered up the legs and fried them in a skillet on his stove. We each ate four legs and ended the endeavor a lot hungrier and drunker than we had been when they'd decided we should go frog gigging.

The whole scene was impossibly exotic to me. On a census form, we looked the same: Gen X white men. But the lives of Chuck's rural neighbors were worlds apart from mine. My romanticism was flecked with what was probably some obvious condescension—but it went both ways.

"Man, you're city," they said so often during the short time I was there that they finally just started calling me City.

For Dale and his brothers, *city* was the worst insult, a nearly fatal and insurmountable flaw. In my case it meant that I was physically weak and didn't know how to fend for myself or survive without the massive modern infrastructure, which they hated almost as much as they hated Bill Clinton and the ATF.

"They've got assault rifles disassembled and stored away in PVC pipes buried all throughout the hills so Clinton can't come and take them away," Chuck explained one morning. "Anybody comes to fuck around up here is gonna have a real bad time. In whiskey days, when the revenuers came up, they didn't come back down."

I looked up at the shotgun hanging on the wall above the fireplace.

"My great-grandfather apparently killed someone," I said. "A Black guy, after the Civil War, and had to go hide out in Texas."

"Really?" Chuck asked.

I was rolling a joint on an album cover as Chuck flipped through his collection looking for something to play.

I recounted to him the story my dad had told me. I'd not been able to stop thinking of it since I had left Edisto. I'd begun to use the Greek mythology in which I'd been immersed for the past couple of years to try to make sense of it.

"In Greek tragedy there's an idea of miasma," I said. "It's an inherited curse that comes down for generations. Like Tantalus cooked his child

Pelops and fed him to the gods, and the curse stayed with the family, causing increasing grief, including the Trojan War, for four generations, until Orestes, who had killed his own mom, went and made peace with the Furies—the deities who avenge shit like that—for all of the crimes of his family."

"And you think your family is cursed because of your great-grandfather?" he asked, pulling a flat black vinyl disc out of its cardboard sleeve and setting it on the player.

I brought the joint to my mouth and licked the paper, giving it a final twist as the first deep, resonant bass notes of Peter Tosh's "Legalize It" blared out of the speakers. Chuck turned down the volume a notch or two and tossed me a lighter.

"I don't know," I said. "But I feel like the Furies might be demanding something."

Chuck laughed.

These thoughts sounded ridiculous as I spoke them. I was always dramatizing my life, my mind a self-mythologizing machine. But I was getting high, in a cabin in the woods, with one of my oldest friends, and this seemed like the time to indulge in such speculation.

I passed the joint to Chuck, who took it between his thumb and forefinger and took a big hit.

"Why did he kill the guy?" Chuck asked, his voice scratchy and faint from the smoke filling his lungs.

"My dad didn't really know," I said. "But he thought it was *because* the guy was Black."

Chuck took another hit and handed me back the joint. He picked up the album cover lying on the top of the stack in front of him. On the cover Tosh was standing shirtless, with dreadlocks and a pipe, in a field of cannabis.

"I love my neighbors," Chuck said. "I mean, I couldn't survive up here without them. They help me in so many ways. And they're mostly cool as hell. But they are also super-racist. And I don't think they mean it. It's just like they've never been around Black people before."

I inhaled from the joint, the pot inside of which Dale and Chuck had grown.

"I thought that Dale especially is such a cool guy that he'd understand if I explained it to him," Chuck said. "So one day, we were getting stoned and I was playing this album and I showed him the cover, and you know what he said?"

"What?" I asked.

"He said, 'I'd like to kill that n***** and take his pot.'"

"Damn," I said, feeling a bit less certain about where Dale's taunting of me might eventually lead.

"It really shook me," Chuck said. "It made me question what I'm even doing up here."

"What did you say?" I asked.

"I tried to say something about how we were all the same and treated by the government the same," Chuck said. "You know, about how we were playing into what the government wants if we let them separate poor white folks from poor Black folks."

He took the joint back from me and took a hit. I got up and walked over to his coffee maker and poured myself a refill.

"But he said, 'That n***** is rich and I ain't,'" Chuck said, dropping his voice to a whisper when he said the offensive word, even though we were in the middle of the woods, evidently surrounded by racists.

"Fucking A," I said. "I imagine that's something like what motivated my great-grandfather, but I don't know. I always heard people in my family talk about how they lost everything after the 'Wo-ah,' as they call it. I guess he thought that was who took it from him."

"I remember when we first met in Columbia arguing about the Civil War," Chuck said. "You were kind of into it."

"I wouldn't say I was into it," I said. "At least not then. But when I was a little kid, totally. All my heroes were Civil War generals and shit. My mom used to read to me from a little red biography of Robert E. Lee, and I loved that book. I can still smell it in my mind."

"The small farmers up here didn't want any part of helping the plantation owners," he said. "But if anyone is gonna rebel against the government now—it's gonna be some hill people."

We both started laughing, but it was a dry, uneasy laugh.

"You want to go see the plants today?" Chuck asked.

He had a field of pot plants hidden in the wild, and when we tramped out to look at them, I didn't think to put on long pants. Two days later, my skin was oozing and weeping a yellow pus, with enormous blisters swelling up until they burst. I had never gotten poison ivy in South Carolina and had assumed I was immune to it. But the West Virginia variety kicked my ass.

Finally, after a few days of constant misery, I asked Chuck to take me to the emergency room. They drained the poison from my legs and gave me a cortisone shot. On the way home, we stopped by Dale's house.

After he smoked two joints with us, he started asking what they'd given me at the hospital.

"Cortisone," I said.

"Oh, shit," he said.

"What?" I asked.

"I had this friend who took that, fucked him up. They use it to control your mind," he said. He went on like that, telling me increasingly grim horror stories about my medication and the untrustworthy doctors at the ER.

"Then his nuts swelled up so big they was like cantaloupes," he said.

"I gotta go," I said to Chuck, feeling light-headed and nauseated and paranoid and doomed. My heart was pounding, my ears ringing. I wouldn't know that these were all symptoms of a panic attack until years later.

"He's just fucking with you," Chuck said.

"I can't stand up," I said. "I need to go."

We got in Chuck's truck. I buried my face in my arms as Chuck drove down the winding path to his cabin. I got out and staggered over to the deck, where I lay down flat on my back, barely able to breathe, and stared up into the infinite blue of the sky.

After a few minutes, Chuck was standing over me looking down.

"You OK, dude?" he asked.

"I think so," I said.

"Your mom is on the phone," he said.

"Tell her I'm asleep," I said.

"She said it's important," he said. "Something about your grandmother."

I went into the cabin, still feeling as if I could barely breathe, my lungs constricted, struggling.

I picked up the black phone receiver.

"Grandmother Woods has to have an emergency surgery," Mom said. "Your Dad is on the way there now. You need to come home."

I left first thing the next morning. Grandmother died before I made it to Greenville, and so a few days later I was standing there in the Edisto Island churchyard where hundreds of years of Baileys were buried, my skin weeping yellow pus beneath my thick black wool suit, wiping sweat from my face with a handkerchief and trying not to scratch my legs as they laid her body in the ground beside her husband, Hernando Jennings Woods, and her parents.

Dad stood there in his black suit in the shadow of the Spanish moss hanging from the live oak trees, and he looked wrecked, his face somehow both ruddy and ashen all at once. He told me he'd driven around in Grandmother's burgundy Plymouth that day listening to oldies with the windows open, and by his eyes I could tell he had been weeping. He was an orphan now, and though it was weird to think of my own father in that way, it seemed to fit the forlorn way he carried himself.

In the service, the minister had remarked on Grandmother's love of the word *pusillanimous*, which, he confessed, he hadn't known until she taught it to him. But now, as he reflected on its meaning of stingy cowardice, he could clearly say that Gertrude Woods had been in no way pusillanimous. She had faced death magnanimously, with an open heart.

I watched clumps of the porous gray dirt fall onto her casket. Dad walked up and put his arm around me.

Back at the house, Dad and his five brothers sat around the kitchen table playing cards and gambling for items that weren't included in the will.

They were all drinking and were louder than normal, and I could see that they were working out their remaining issues, orphans all, but still a band of brothers, "my little Woods men," as Grandmother liked to say.

"Hell no, you're not getting that," Irvin said. "She always promised that to me."

"She promised it to me too," Bully said.

"She promised that painting to everyone," Richard said.

Laughter rippled around the table.

"Deal," someone said.

"Oh, look," my aunt Alice said, holding up a stack of papers. "Here's a short story she wrote in high school. 'A Dark Romance,' it's called."

"She got an A on it," another aunt, Susan, said from beside her.

I noticed Michael slip out the kitchen door, and I followed him down under the house. We went into the small room and he lit up a joint.

"I imagine this will be the last time we're all here together," Michael said.

The whole family used to gather for a few days every winter that culminated in a big New Year's oyster roast. Once we'd awakened to an alligator under the house next door and stood around watching as rangers lassoed it and wrestled it onto a truck.

"The will says to keep the house for the use of the family," I said, trying not to scratch the blisters filling up again with yellow liquid on my legs.

"Come on," Michael said. "They'll sell it."

"The family used to own most of this island," I said. "And soon we'll have nothing."

"Nothing," he said. "But some cash—and of course we won't see any of that."

"Tragic," I said, without any real sense of the real tragedy of my family's history on the island, the infamy that was my true inheritance.

I knew that Grandmother had experienced an increasingly urgent sense of guilt for the Edisto, or Oristo, people who had lived on the island when the Europeans arrived in 1666 and were all gone by 1700.

"They destroyed a whole world," she'd said of her ancestors. "Even if they didn't know it."

That destruction was only the beginning of what we had wrought, but in this moment of confusion and grief I was reverting to the sense of familial pride that had been instilled in me.

A few days later, I said goodbye to Mom and Dad, Nanny and Summey, in the driveway of the house they all shared again, eager to get back home to Albuquerque.

"I'm so glad you got to spend that time with Mother," Dad said.

"Me too," I said, wrapping my arms around him.

I got into the car, cranked it, and backed out of the driveway up on Piney Mountain. I drove toward Ashville, where I got on I-40 headed west, and for two days I sat there, lost in a kind of meditation as the flat landscape rolled by. When I finally crossed from Oklahoma into Texas, I thought about the story of my great-grandfather's flight from South Carolina into the desert, about how much harder such a trip would have been in those days, of how many things could go wrong, requiring the assistance of a woman who was married to a man named Hernando. I thought about the crime he had committed and what might have prompted it. Why had he killed a Black man? And how had he managed to return? What had it meant for him to have redeemed the state?

I knew I couldn't answer any of those questions, but I let them ride with me as I passed the panhandle stockyards and then went through Amarillo with its signs advertising a free seventy-two-ounce steak to anyone who could eat it in a single sitting. I allowed my mind to bounce around the mystery of Dr. I. M. Woods and what kind of inheritance, miasma or hidden treasure, he might have left me.

But I was thinking about it wrong from the start, and that error guided all my subsequent thinking. When Dad told the story to me, and when I passed it on to Michael and to Chuck, we'd framed it as if Dr. Woods had killed the man because the man was Black. But that line of thinking ultimately blamed the Black man for his own death. We could have said that it was because Dr. Woods was white that he'd killed the Black man. But then we would have been forced to ask what part of that whiteness we had inherited.

When I got home, Dad sent me a photocopy of "A Dark Romance," the short story Grandmother had written. I held the gray, lined paper in my hands and looked at the title, at the way she'd looped the script, and at the phrase *cullud gal*, which the teacher had underlined, writing, "Very good" beside it.

I folded the story and put it back in the envelope and put it in a drawer with my writing. I thought that whatever she had written about a "dark romance" would not reflect well on her, and I did not want to see it.

Whiteness is the freedom to forget, the ability to look away, that we might see our families the way we want to see them, the way that best reflects the way we want to see ourselves, whether as rebels or as scions.

Chapter 15

I WAS STANDING WITH FIVE other people in the desert-dusty backyard of a small stucco house with a big garden, looking up into a towering elm tree, where Darren, a thin, muscular guy, was hanging our radio antenna. The ragtag group assembled here ran a pirate radio station, and because the station was illegal and the FCC had targeted similar operations, we changed our location every week, and the area that our signal could cover was proportional to how high someone could climb in a tree, and Darren, a train-hopping Earth First! environmentalist radical, could climb higher than anyone else.

A lot of people I knew in college were online by this point, but I had never been on the internet, and most of the Luddites gathered around in that yard hadn't either. We were engaged in an old-school form of media sabotage—or "taking back the commons" as Bruce, one of the guys who ran the station, put it. Our crew was made up of seed savers, foragers, Earth Firsters, and other refugees from mainstream white America. And we were all white except for one American Indian named Roger, who came around sometimes.

Most of the band of rebels just wanted to play punk rock and say cuss words on the air. *The Drunk & Stoned Hour*, from midnight until 1:00 a.m., when we went off the air, was probably the most popular show.

I occasionally played sets of free jazz and other "out" music, but I was trying to get us to do political programming more like *Democracy Now!*, which I listened to on public radio.

That's where I'd heard about Mumia Abu-Jamal, the Black Philadelphia journalist who had been convicted of murdering a white cop and sentenced to death in 1982. Philadelphia's governor had recently signed Abu-Jamal's death warrant, and there was an intense and concerted push to stop the execution that was, as far as I could tell, led by a woman named Pam Africa, who was part of the MOVE family, whose house the Philadelphia police had bombed, killing eleven people and burning sixty-four houses, in 1985. I wanted to get her on our station.

Darren climbed down the tree, his pink face sweating with the effort. He had started the station, learning how to broadcast and getting a transmitter from Free Radio Berkeley, a group that was trying to spread the movement and had given a transmitter like ours to the Zapatista revolutionaries in Chiapas, Mexico.

"Hey, man, what's up?" he said when he saw me.

He'd just come back from Mexico on a freight train he'd hopped, explaining that he went somewhere every spring because his allergies were too bad in New Mexico during April.

"I was thinking that I might try to call up Pam Africa, from MOVE, and ask her about the Mumia case," I said. "You think it would be cool to play something like that?"

"It would be great," he said. "Some of the people might not love it. But we'll cut it up with some Public Enemy and Last Poets and it will be cool. We should have a regular segment of stuff like that."

The next day, I rode my bicycle to a RadioShack and bought a suction cup I could put on the headset of my phone to record a call. I set it up and did a test call to Dad.

"Hey," I said.

"Baseball," he said. "Good to hear from you."

"I'm recording you," I said.

"What?" he said.

"I bought a thing to record calls because I'm going to do some interviews for the radio, and I want to test it."

"Radio! That's great," he said. "What station?"

"Ninety point nine," I said, deciding not to tell him it was an illegal station.

"Who are you interviewing?" he asked.

"Pam Africa, from a group called MOVE—"

"Those damn radicals in Philadelphia," he said. "I remember all that. Why would you interview them? I thought they were all dead or in jail."

"There's a journalist who covered their earlier standoff with police, and the cops framed him for a murder, and the governor just signed his death warrant," I said.

"Oh Lord," he said. "And you're going on the radio with all that?"

"You know it's true," I said, "if you remember seeing it. They dropped a bomb on those people's house. How is that different than Ruby Ridge or Waco or those things you complain about?"

"Because Bill Clinton killed the people in Ruby Ridge and Waco," he said.

As I moved further left, embracing the antiglobalization movement, Dad kept moving to the right. He loved Newt Gingrich, the radical-right Georgia Republican who had taken over as Speaker of the House after the 1994 election, and his Contract with America. For Dad, Bill and Hillary Clinton symbolized everything that was wrong with America, even as they moved to end the welfare system that he had spent a lot of the last fifteen years complaining about.

"I'm sure you think O. J. is innocent too," he said.

"Everybody was focused on O. J. because he was a famous athlete, but we should be focusing on Mumia," I said.

I stood, frustrated by Dad's stubbornness, watching a skateboarder glide by on the street outside my window.

"I gotta go," I said. "It's long distance and I have to do an interview."

"I'll call you soon," he said. "I wanted to see if you wanted to go with me and get anything from Mother's house at Edisto this Christmas, before we sell it."

"So you are selling it," I said. "Michael knew it. I guess greed is good."
I hung up the phone.

I was annoyed with Dad and all his brothers. They cared more about money than family, I thought. My great-grandparents had owned hundreds of acres, but because male children had inherited all the real wealth, Grandmother hadn't gotten anything but that beach house to start with. And now that would be gone too. I felt that I had, somehow, been cheated out of my inheritance. But it also seemed that losing this last little piece of land, the beach house where the Woods brothers congregated, would mean the end of the extended Woods family as a unit.

At least if the family was over, I didn't need to worry about going back home to visit too often, and I could continue with my life out here in the desert. Things were going well. I had gotten a great job at the university tutoring Greek and Latin, where I was available in the library for twenty hours a week and got paid whether anyone came to be tutored or not, and so I mostly wandered the stacks. I also ran the campus Green Party and was involved in various forms of activism.

I dialed the number I had for Pam Africa in the Free Mumia campaign.
"Hello," she said.

"Hi, my name is Bay Woods, and I'm with Rebel Radio 90.9 in Albuquerque, and I was hoping to interview you about new developments in the case," I said.

"I'm busy," she said. "You can hear the kids in the background. But I can give you a minute. What's your question?"

"What should people be aware of in the fight for Mumia Abu-Jamal's freedom?"

That was the only question I got to ask. For the next ninety minutes, Africa schooled me, going through nearly every detail of the case, from 1981, when a police officer named Faulkner was shot and Mumia was arrested, up to the appeal of his death warrant in the Pennsylvania Supreme Court.

As she spoke, I jotted down notes and watched as the tape rolled from left to right. When the tape ran out, I flipped it over to the other side and hit record again, as fast as I could.

Now Africa was explaining the MOVE family and why the police in Philadelphia had been so frightened of the group's self-reliance that they'd bombed them. Mumia and the bombing were all tied together, and that's why she and the rest of the MOVE family were fighting to free Mumia.

"Is that enough?" she asked as the second side of my tape wound down.

"Yes, ma'am," I said. "That was amazing."

She hung up the phone and I sat there, stunned. It was the first interview I'd ever conducted, and even if I'd only gotten in one question, that was all I needed. I had made the call. I was learning about the world directly. By asking the people involved, instead of, like Dad, hearing it from Rush Limbaugh. And I had recorded it and would play it on the radio, counteracting Limbaugh even if we could transmit only in the area we called the "student ghetto" surrounding the university.

The next Tuesday—we only broadcast once a week, because of the logistical difficulties caused by the illegality of the station—we aired the interview, cut up, as Darren had suggested, with Public Enemy and the Last Poets. I was kind of annoyed at this concession to music and, in the kitchen of the house we were using that week, I mentioned it to him.

"Why do we have to dumb it down with music?" I asked.

"Well, look," he said, his hair newly shaved into something sort of like a mohawk. "It's a really long conversation, and, you know, people are coming on to get a variety of stuff and mostly to hear music. You can contextualize it, and we'll keep playing the tunes, and it's cool. I'd love to see more like this. But also, if I'm gonna tell you the truth, the audio quality just sucks, and it's gotta get better to air."

I hadn't even thought about how it sounded. I'd just known there was knowledge there, wisdom, and I'd wanted to share it. But as soon as he said it, I realized that the interview was obviously almost inaudible over the airwaves. I felt the shame that comes with a lack of skill.

But it didn't matter. That feeling passed. We were all learning at our makeshift station. But something more permanent had clicked in me, something that would later prove formative.

The interview with Pam Africa had made me reconsider my views on racism and its prevalence in society, which I had always considered minimal and limited to people like Glenn, my old skinhead friend, or his hero David Duke. But listening to Africa talk, I could see how deeply racism affected the world, especially when it came to police. They were able to bomb a Black neighborhood and I'd never even heard of it? With a real bomb? That was crazy.

I didn't wonder so much if I would have done time in Greenville if I'd been Black—the answer to that was most certainly yes—but whether I would have survived at all.

As I thought about my conversation with Pam Africa, my whiteness began to eat at me. I hadn't felt this way since I began reading feminist writers who filled me with a deep sense of uneasiness about my masculinity.

I could see how much violence and coercion were required to make me masculine, and I figured the same was true of my whiteness. I wanted to be anything but a straight white man.

One cold night, furtive and nervous, I went to the only gay bar I knew of in the city. I walked in and ordered a drink and stood at the bar. It was dark, and there were purple neon strips along the bar. A few men moved around the dance floor. No one spoke to me, and I left after that first drink.

I told a few friends that I thought I might be bi and one of them, a redheaded woman named Nora, who started photographing me in dresses, said she knew of a great guy I should meet. He was a graphic artist and he was also from South Carolina, one of two queer brothers from the small town of Seneca, which was near Greenville, so we met up one night for a drink.

We had a couple gin and tonics at a place on Central called the Anodyne where I often drank, but our conversation was stilted and slow. He was very shy, with long, straight brown hair parted in the middle so that sometimes it fell forward and covered his face. He wasn't my type, if I even had a type of guy, but after the second drink, we were walking down Central, holding hands.

"I hate South Carolina," I said. "Except for Edisto. And my family has betrayed its connection to the island, so I don't know if I'll ever go there again."

"I really love Seneca," he said. "There were the rednecks and stuff, but mostly people were nice and it was beautiful. I miss the green."

He sounded so sweet, his voice soft and lilting with a real rural up-country accent, but he was naive. How could he love a place like Seneca, South Carolina, which, except for being named after a Roman philosopher, was even shittier than Greenville?

We went to his apartment, which he shared with his brother, and we stood in the poorly lit living room until he said, "Why don't you kiss me?"

I did. I'd drunkenly kissed guys a few times before, and I was always stunned by the roughness of the male face; even with this guy who seemed to barely have a trace of a beard, I felt it scratching me. We fell into a fever in his bed and jerked and sucked each other off quickly. I got up and got dressed.

"You're not staying?" he asked.

"No," I said.

I walked out the door, my face burning. It had been kind of fun but very forced, and I was worse to this sweet kid than I was to any of the women I went out with. Mainly, as I left, I felt good because my dick was much bigger than his. Objectification didn't really have to do with who I was fucking, I realized, it had to do with me.

I had confirmed, to my disappointment, that I wasn't queer, and I was no closer to solving the problem of how to deal with sex and relationships than I had been before I'd put the dude's dick in my mouth.

I was, I had confirmed, a straight white man, a fact that presented itself now as an ethical problem. I would have to learn to deal with that—even though I had no idea of how to even start.

A few nights later, I went over to Nora's house, where she lived with my old roommate and classics classmate Uli. She had an old friend in from out of town. We'd been drinking and talking and arguing, and it seemed to be going well. Nora and her friend went back into the bedroom and were catching up, I reckoned, as Uli and I sat in the living room.

"Can I see you outside?" Nora asked, coming in from the back of the house.

She had red hair parted starkly to one side and was wearing a surplus green army jacket. I felt a hint of exhilaration walking out the door because I thought she was going to tell me her friend liked me.

We stepped outside into the windy spring night and stood under the green light bulb on the porch.

"The way you treated me when we were talking in there is not OK," she said.

"What?" I said, stunned.

A big gray moth fluttered toward the light behind us, flapping drunkenly between us.

"We were talking about something I know about, and you wouldn't even let me finish a sentence and just kept going on and on, even though you don't know anything about it," she said, her green eyes gleaming. "It really upset me, and I don't want to do it anymore, and I don't think we can be friends if you don't change that."

"I'm really sorry," I said.

I didn't know what else to say. I didn't go back inside but just turned away and walked down the steps. I twisted to look at her just as the door slammed. The moth flittered around the light.

I knew she was right. I had gotten into that same old argumentative endgame mode that clicked and made me ready to rhetorically annihilate anyone for anything, for the "sake of the argument," but it was so common, had become such a part of my wiring, that I hadn't even noticed it. I believed the world should listen to me.

As I kicked along through the dusty, unpaved alley in the wind, I felt all the confusion and despair about trying to be a better person well up around me and erupt in a sandstorm inside my brain.

It wasn't so much that I had been a dick to Nora as that I had not had any idea I was being a dick. I had been so clueless about my own appearance to others, so wrapped up in myself, that I'd thought she was asking me on the porch to tell me her friend liked me instead of seeing that she was so hurt she no longer wanted to be friends with me. I had no idea how I could be so clueless, and I started to cry, small, dry little desert tears, lamenting the human condition, the impossibility of actually knowing ourselves as others know us, as much as I bemoaned my own idiocy.

I thought about my interview with Pam Africa. I hadn't had to argue back with her. I hadn't had to say anything for the sake of the argument. All I'd had to do was listen and she'd opened up the world as it appeared to her, so different from how it had appeared to me.

I realized then that was also what Socrates had tried to do. Despite my turn toward left-wing politics, I was still deeply involved in the study of classics and philosophy. I began to think I should do more interviews, engage with people in order to see how the world appeared to them. Maybe that would be a way to save myself from myself.

But not long after that, the FCC raided the house where we were broadcasting and fined everyone there $10,000. I'd just left and wasn't caught up in the snare, but I hadn't done any more interviews yet, and I realized Rebel Radio was not the right platform for what I had in mind.

I wondered if the FCC had let the broadcasts go on until I started airing MOVE and then decided to raid us, indulging my old taste for paranoia. Even if that wasn't true, I thought, why risk it when no one really liked my interview anyway? I wasn't going to get arrested so a crust punk could say *fuck* on the radio, so I drifted away from that group and started writing a political column for the school paper, where I attacked corporations on campus, the ROTC and other forms of militarization, and the fraternity system.

The tutoring center in the library offered me a fellowship to run the language program as a grad student, and the Classics Department said if I stayed and got a master's in comparative literature, I could teach intro Greek and Latin courses. So my graduation was definitely, as the etymology suggests, a step up, rather than a radical departure.

I'd been in college for six years already, and it was finally time to graduate. Mom, Dad, and Nanny all flew out to Albuquerque to watch me walk, since I had not been allowed to attend my high school graduation. It was a small December graduation, which made it all easier, with fewer students and less pomp and circumstance.

"It's unbelievable," Dad said as I drove them to the motel from the airport. "You go from getting all F's to summa cum laude."

"I always told you how smart you were," Mom said.

I laughed because I felt as if they were trying to ruin it for me by forcing me to feel as if I had finally come around to their side, when I didn't care much about the honor or even about graduating. But I was looking forward to making more money and getting entirely off the family dole. College there had been cheap—about a thousand a semester when I started—and Pell Grants had gone a long way toward tuition and books, but Mom and Dad had helped round that out and covered my rent. And Nanny had put away money every year since I had been born for a college fund, which I had burned through. I'd never thought any further than "from my family" when considering where that money came from. My critiques of capitalism never went quite far enough to see how inherited wealth and privilege had made their way down to me. But I did feel that between teaching and running the tutoring program, I would get out from under my family's weight.

I drove them to the hotel near the airport. A sign we passed had the words *white water* on it, and Dad made a joke about Bill Clinton, who had been under what seemed like an eternal investigation over a real estate deal that bore the same name.

"I don't know why you always act like I'm a fan of Bill Clinton," I said. "I am a Green. I don't believe in the two-party system. I hate both of the corporate-controlled parties. And Clinton is dropping bombs on Iraq right now."

"That's the only good thing he has done," Dad said. "Why have a no-fly zone if you're not going to enforce it?"

"OK," Mom said. "Enough, you two. It's a happy occasion. It's your graduation and it's Christmastime and we're here."

"All right, all right," Dad said.

"I'll pick y'all up at noon," I said. "For the ceremony."

"You got your cap and gown?" Mom asked.

"Yes," I said, exasperated.

"We will be so proud," she said.

That night I cut a piece of poster board so that it fit the top of my red satin cap. On it I wrote "Peace on Earth?"

I kept it hidden beneath my robes the next day, until just before we walked into the auditorium. Then I taped it to the top of my hat as a hundred or so students filed into the basketball auditorium, surrounded by friends and family looking down from the stadium seating. I heard the blond girl walking behind me in the honors section give out a little huff when she saw it, but otherwise I couldn't sense any response to my query, which I intended as a protest against Clinton's bombing campaign and a rejoinder to Mom and Dad in our discussion of it the night before.

We all sat down. And then something happened that I had not taken into account. The announcer asked us to rise for the national anthem. I hadn't been to a big event like this in so long that I'd almost forgotten the national anthem was a thing. But I couldn't just stand up while we were bombing. And even if we hadn't been, I fully believed that America was an imperialist power and was not going to stand up for some jingoistic song.

As the red robes rustled and straightened around me with a soft, rolling swoosh, I remained seated.

"O say can you see," the singer started as the graduates removed their caps. Mine, with its sign, was the only one that remained on, and it felt as if every eye in the place were on me, and the seconds ticked away with the rhythm of the horrible song and seemed to slow with each beat so that I blushed the color of my robe until the tune was done and everyone finally sat down, joining me. I could feel the hatred all around me still, but the moment was over, and I felt proud.

"I can't believe you did that," Dad said when I met them in front of the auditorium after the ceremony.

"Did what?" I asked. "Graduated summa cum laude?"

"Didn't stand during the anthem," Mom said.

"With that sign on your hat," Dad said.

Nanny was silent.

"What was that supposed to mean?" Mom asked.

"What?"

"The sign," Nanny said.

"We're saying 'goodwill and peace on Earth' and celebrating the pacifist Jesus at a time when we are bombing other people, and we just pretend it's not happening," I said. "To me that seems hypocritical."

"No," Dad said. "Hypocritical is Al Gore preaching about the environment while flying around on Air Force Two."

"I wish you didn't have to make that point right then," Mom said. "The people in front of us were talking about you, and I wanted to bop them— even if I would have felt the same way if it was someone else doing it."

"You always told me to stand up for what I believed in," I said. "Even if it wasn't popular."

"Right," Dad said. "We taught you to stand up. And you stayed seated."

"Ha ha," I said sarcastically.

I had a small party that night, and Mom and Dad met a few of my other friends. I heard Dad telling Uli that he was going to go to Key West and win the Ernest Hemingway look-alike contest next year.

"You really should enter it, Papa," I said, walking up to them.

"I was just telling Uli that I'm going to win it next year," he said.

"The beard is a lot better than your mustache was," I said.

"Hemingway had a mustache when he was younger too," he said.

"That's the writing of his I like," I said. "The early short stories."

"I tried to listen to one of his books recently, and the sentences were just too long to follow," Dad said.

Dad listened to a lot of books on tape, but he didn't really like Hemingway the writer; he liked Hemingway the image. But whether Dad had read Hemingway or just absorbed the spirit of it, the ethos the author had created through his characters defined some of the qualities that Dad and I shared. Hemingway, I thought, had framed white masculinity for several generations of American men, including Dad and me.

For all our differences, Dad and I both thought we had the inside scoop on things, knowing either the cheapest or the best or the rarest options; we both thought we could handle ourselves well in a variety of situations, especially emergencies; and we both thought we deserved to be heard, and that whatever we had to say was not only important, but more important than what the other person had to say. We believed we had experienced the world; believed we could hold our liquor; thought ourselves above average in bed; and took a certain pleasure in noticing the mistakes of others, while refusing to see the most obvious in ourselves. These attitudes were not just idiosyncrasies but our cultural inheritance as twentieth-century white men on the cusp of the twenty-first.

Our differences, I realized with some horror, amounted to matters of style. In terms of our basic engagement with the world, the way we moved through it and interacted with other people, we were, without a doubt, both white dudes.

Chapter 16

THERE WAS A KNOCK ON the door. The sun had just set, and my apartment was dark. I got up and turned on the light and walked to the door.

"Hi, Bay," my old friend Oliver said, his voice nasal and dragging. He had just moved back to town, for about the fifteenth time, a month or so earlier. And I had just decided to move away that day.

"This is Nicole. She's from South Carolina too," he said, introducing his date.

In my eyes, the woman standing there in the doorway looked nothing like South Carolina. She had giant, stunning brown eyes in the middle of a compact, pale, and powdered white face with an upturned Irish nose and small narrow lips. Extremely thin, wearing a jean jacket and black pants, she had a long, gorgeous neck like Virginia Woolf in the photograph I had hanging by my bed, but with the Beatles haircut of Anna Akhmatova, the Russian poet, whose picture also hung on my wall.

But when she said, "Hi," there was no hiding the fact that she was from South Carolina. Even in that single word, I could hear the full-on twang.

"You don't sound like you're from South Carolina," she said, as I loaded up a bong and she sat on a tottering pile of books.

"I've been gone a long time," I said.

She said she had just moved here from her hometown near Myrtle Beach a few months earlier, at the beginning of the school year.

"You'd think I was from another country. When I ask for water at the Frontier," she said, "they say, 'An order of what?' So I have to say *wa-ter*."

Sure enough, she said *warder*—and she drank whiskey. We smoked some pot at my house and then walked out to her silver Ford Taurus and drove the few blocks down to the Anodyne, on Central Avenue downtown.

When we walked in and climbed the stairs to the long, wide barroom with black walls, exposed ductwork, and red pool tables, I saw a half a dozen people I knew. It was chaotic and we crowded around the bar, but, however newcomers to our loose party redistributed the energy of the group, Nicole and I kept ending up beside each other.

That morning I had accepted an offer to go to graduate school in Pittsburgh, where I would study philosophy with a fellowship to work as the assistant book review editor of the journal *Ancient Philosophy*, and so this would be my last semester here. I looked on the bar with a future nostalgia, knowing I would miss it one day.

"To ancient philosophy," my friend Torres said, hoisting high one of the shots he'd just bought for the group.

"Cheers," everyone said.

We took our shots.

"Oh no, she's here," Oliver said, pointing at his ex who wanted to look like Bettie Page. She had just walked in the door and hadn't seen us yet.

"Pretend you're talking to each other," Oliver said to me and Nicole.

"That's easy enough," I said, since we were already talking. She had instantly dissolved my hatred for South Carolina, or at least made it a lot more complex.

"That girl said she was going to kick my ass," Nicole whispered. "Really threatened to fight me at a party. Look at me. I barely weigh a hundred pounds. I'm not fighting anyone."

"That table just opened up," I said. "Let's go snag it."

We sidled deep into the dark booth and sat across from each other as the candle on the table flashed shadows across our faces. For a moment we watched out for Oliver and his threatening ex, but soon we were oblivious to everyone else in the bar except the waitress, who kept bringing us whiskey.

We discovered that in addition to sharing a home state, we were in the same comparative literature program—although she was studying pop culture and I did Greek and Latin and we had never had classes together. Still, the effect of this juxtaposition of academic learning and our shared culture was electrifying as our conversation drifted between southern foodways and French theory.

Whiteness is the assumption of a universal, shared identity. But it is also a series of loosely related cultural traits and practices that are subject to regional and national differences. Our whiteness allowed us to be universal individuals, practitioners of deconstruction, cosmopolitan. But our southernness marked us as a particular kind of white, sharing a separate, smaller group of cultural referents and associations. White southern, I realized only in talking to Nicole, wasn't just the same thing as white. There was a deep historical shame, but there was also, burgeoning in us both over the course of this conversation, a recalcitrant pride.

"Do you ever watch NASCAR?" she asked after a while, shyly, as if she were asking about a sexual kink, the thin bony fingers of her right hand falling from her glass to absently clasp the left.

"My dad is a fanatic," I said. "He and all his brothers worshipped Richard Petty."

"Who's that?" she asked.

"One of the old-school drivers," I said. "Growing up, I went to races all the time. From the big Winston Cup races down to small ones on local dirt tracks. Those were my favorite because it was so dirty and close. I mainly remember that the air was a deep red under the big spotlights with clay and exhaust hanging there over us. But I never liked it like he did. I enjoyed napping to the sound of a race on Sunday most of all, I think."

"My dad was a teacher and later a principal, and he didn't ever watch NASCAR at all," she said. "I just started watching it with my friend from home Jan, who moved to Tucumcari the same time I moved here. She's really into it, and it's fun to watch with her because she knows what's happening and what it means. And neither of us know a lot of people out here, so it gives us something to do."

She pulled a cigarette from the blue-and-white pack.

I'd been on and off them for the past couple of years, and I bummed one.

"There's a race this Sunday, isn't there?" I said as she struck a match and the sulfur flared up in front of her face and turned the tip of her cigarette orange. We both leaned forward, the match dangling between her fingers, until its flame enveloped the end of my cigarette before burning out and slumping over in an exhausted string of cinder.

We left the bar together that night. I walked her outside, and we drunkenly wandered the streets for another half hour, vaguely looking for a car, but after a few minutes we'd get distracted and lost in the pleasure of our conversation and forget about the search until we found ourselves at the same intersection three or four times.

I recited from memory the circular beginning and end of James Joyce's *Finnegans Wake*, in which the same long dream sentence loops around like a racetrack. I'd tried that move with a lot of women, but she was the first to seem really impressed.

We finally stumbled upon the car, parked on a side street, and Nicole drove me home. We talked some more in my apartment at my little table surrounded by tottering piles of books until she announced it was time for her to go. I walked her out, and in the parking lot we finally fell into each other and started kissing and stood there by her car making out until 4:00 a.m. When she pulled away, we agreed to watch the race in Bristol, Tennessee, at her house on Sunday.

I was waiting outside when her silver car pulled into my parking lot at noon to pick me up for our date.

"We should get Miller Lite," I said a few moments later as we browsed the cooler at Smith's grocery store. "It's the only major beer that's still union made."

"Sure," she said. "That's fine with me."

When we pulled up to her apartment complex with our case of beer and some cigarettes and Doritos, I was disappointed. I had always lived in the small houses surrounding the university and thought of Albuquerque as a very walkable city. But this apartment complex, over a bridge from the university, surrounded by highways, seemed as if it could be anywhere, despite its bullshit flamingo-pink stucco. Why would you move to a city that had such cool old adobe houses and old historical buildings like the one I lived in downtown and stay somewhere like this? I wondered.

She seemed to sense my disappointment.

"My parents rented this place," she said. "Before I moved here. And then we loaded up a truck and my mom, dad, brother, sister, and nephews all came with me to move."

"That's amazing," I said.

"We're all really close right now," she said. "My parents, my grandparents, my sister and her family, and my brother all live in a field around a big pond."

"I was trying to escape my family. I just drove as far as I could from them, I sometimes think," I said.

I liked her place better when we got inside. It was a small one-bedroom loft where the main room was dominated by a beautiful orange couch the color of fire.

"I didn't really think anything about the South before I left," she said as we sat down and turned on the TV. "Now I'm fascinated by it. I notice how many cultural things are really distinct that I'd never even noticed before. Like me and my friends made a short movie called *The Chicken Biscuit Killer* about a woman who loves Bojangles. When I tell people about it here, they don't even know what I'm talking about."

I opened a beer and handed her one.

"Do you like Bojangles?" she asked, pulling a Parliament Light from the pack.

"I love biscuits, but I'm a vegetarian," I said.

She lit her cigarette.

"Can I have one?" I asked.

She nodded.

"I'm not vegetarian. Not at all," she said. "I was vegan in high school, but I love me some bacon and some barbecue. That's another weird thing here. I ordered barbecue and I got beef."

The cigarette was too harsh, and I put it out to finish later.

"Totally," I said. "I still ate meat when I first got here, and the same thing happened to me. My family is really into Clarendon County barbecue from my dad's hometown of Manning. My uncle Bully is a pitmaster kind of guy. In contests and stuff."

Especially when it comes to food, southerners, regardless of race, share more with each other than a white southerner and a white New Mexican might. But other referents, such as NASCAR and country music, were almost entirely white in their appeal, even if they were trying to push beyond that. And as we turned on the TV, I didn't really see that as wrong. It was better, perhaps, than trying to glom on to Black culture or Chicano culture and act as if you weren't white.

"The race is about to start," she said, turning toward the TV. "Who's your driver?"

"I don't know. My whole family pulled for Richard Petty. And they liked his son Kyle, but he was no good."

"I pull for Bobby Labonte," she said. "He's number eighteen, in the green-and-black car. You have to pick someone."

"I'm going to go with the number two Miller Lite car—"

"Because it's union beer," she said, taking a sip of hers and looking at me over the can with those big brown eyes.

"Unions are important," I said. "With globalization and corporate irresponsibility, pretty much everything we wear or use is made overseas, and it all hurts workers, and we need to—"

"OK, OK," she said, laughing. "Look, there's your guy in his union-made-beer car."

"Oh, Rusty Wallace drives that car," I said. "I feel like I remember him from when I was a kid."

A few minutes into the race, we began to kiss, pressing our faces and bodies against each other's, desperately searching for something in the friction of flesh, marveling at our own corporality as the sound of cars driving in circles droned on behind us.

"They're running door to door," one of the announcers was saying. "This early in the race, with the tires cold, you do not want to be outside on the track."

"You need to be patient, especially in these early laps," another sports-caster said.

The voices became blurs as we pressed denim against denim.

"They're pushing for position," the TV said as our clothes came off and I looked at her naked body against the orange couch. The drone around us. The blood racing through our veins. The announcers' thick southern accents, blending with the roar, and our flesh-on-flesh sensation.

When it was all over, Rusty Wallace had won the race and Bobby Labonte had come in sixth, which was enough to put him in the lead for the season.

"We both won," Nicole said as we sat, naked and sweating, smoking cigarettes on the couch. A breeze came in the open window, where a cherry tree was blooming.

"I have to go to work," she said, getting up off the couch. "But I dread it. I'm the worst waitress in the world."

"I'm sure you're not," I said.

"I don't even know any of the dishes. They all have melted cheese on top. I pronounced the double *l* in *relleno* and someone complained to my boss," she said. "The best tip I ever got was when I spilled a beer in a guy's food. He said it was fine. He'd eat the food if I'd just bring another beer. Then I spilled that one into his food too. It was a serious pity tip."

I followed her up the stairs to her loft bedroom. I sat on the bed and watched her put on a white shirt and black pants. Then I followed her to the bathroom, where she touched up her makeup and brushed her teeth.

"Do you want to drive me to work and keep my car and come back and pick me up?" she asked.

"That sounds great," I said.

I spent the night at her apartment after I picked her up from work, and we stayed together every night after for the next two months. The sense of our impending separation gave everything that spring a romantic flair. We conspired to spend as much time together as possible before I started the PhD program in the fall, and we decided to drive across the country together and meet each other's families.

When Dad found out that Nicole watched NASCAR, he invited us to come see the Memorial Day race with him and his old Coast Guard buddy Larry. So after a leisurely drive across the country we were going to spend one night in Greenville and then ride up with Dad to Charlotte, where we'd camp out in a field near the track. Then, when we left there, we were going to go and spend a few weeks with Nicole's family in Conway.

We set out from Albuquerque with a spirit of high adventure that shielded me from the sadness of leaving this city I had loved. The fact that she would still live here for another year also gave me a kind of anchor, the ability and the desire to return.

Three days into our trip, we were standing in a small honky-tonk in Fayetteville, Arkansas, on a fiercely stormy night, watching Hank III, the grandson of country great Hank Williams. When the first Hank died in 1953, everyone had expected his young son, Hank Williams Jr., to be just like him. But around the time I started to love country music as a kid, Junior rebelled against the image that was expected of him. He grew a beard and long hair and began playing music influenced by southern rock. I saw him when I was in the fourth grade, and the entire thing was a display of angry southern white masculinity, full of rebel flags, whiskey, and insults hurled at New York City.

I'd loved it as a ten-year-old. But now, while I still liked a few of his songs, I found Junior bombastic and ridiculous. But sitting there in that little Fayetteville bar, we were stunned by how much Hank III, the grandson, looked and sounded like his grandfather, skinny, with wild mean eyes and a sneer across his hairless face out of which emerged a haunting high and lonesome twang. We'd read that his band did a second set that brought in punk and death metal, but it didn't seem he was going to play it here, where nearly everyone in the crowd was wearing a cowboy hat.

Nicole and I danced the two-step through much of the set, regularly walking up to the bar to order more beers and shots. At some point I got the idea that I would interview the singer that night. "That's a great idea," Nicole said, as drunk as I was.

We thought there was something really important about what was happening up there on the bandstand. Our musical tastes had come together in what was called alt-country or Americana. It was our generation's attempt to fuse punk and country and find what was authentic in the white South that we had tried to escape, to purge it of the negative and own it for ourselves.

With his duct-taped cowboy boots and old-timey sound, Hank III represented to me what was cool in the generation of our grandparents. Growing up in Tennessee, he would have listened to the same amalgam of music as I did, and he had found some way to synthesize that identity into a whole.

I'd be a poseur to pretend to be a beret-wearing poet in Paris, but I found something real in the poetry of country music, something that moved me deeply, and I wanted to explore that as some kind of authentic poetic expression of the world I'd grown up in.

"Goddamn, he looks like his granddad, don't he?" an old cowboy said as he walked up to the bar beside me.

"That's exactly right," I said. I ordered three shots. I brought one to Nicole and set one at the foot of the stage. She and I held ours up and gulped them down. I danced and drank and cheered throughout the show. It felt to me as if there was a real push to create a positive sense of authentic white identity that wasn't built on the history of racism, oppression, and uptight corporate bullshit—but that didn't address it either. It was as if we could just ignore the horrors of the southern past as we waxed poetic about screen doors and South Carolina pines and the smell of a pork shoulder smoking.

Whiteness was the ability to bracket the unpleasant, to overlook the cost of our culture, treating the world like a cafeteria where we could choose to pay for only those aspects of our inheritance that we liked.

A few days later, at the NASCAR race with Dad and Larry, such a bracketing of history and politics, for me at least, wasn't optional. It was a requirement.

When we pulled up to the campsite in Dad's SUV, Larry was standing outside a modest trailer in a polo shirt and shorts, smoking a cigarette, his white hair pushed back, thinning over his sunburned scalp. He and Dad had been in the Coast Guard together, roomed together, and had remained friends all of their lives. Larry had sold ceiling fans for a while and then log cabins.

"Hey, Baseball," he said when I got out of the car.

"Hey, Larry," I said. "This is Nicole."

She looked longingly at the fresh cigarette Larry lit. I'd just started back up and assumed I'd quit again soon, so I didn't smoke around my parents, and that had become a point of contention.

"I'm smoking," she said to me quietly as we started to set up camp.

"That's cool," I said. "It will give me cover too, and it's mainly Mom who freaks out."

We cracked open a beer and stood there looking at the bright flags flapping against the trees in the late-spring sky. Flags for drivers like Jeff Gordon, Dale Earnhardt, and Rusty Wallace, as well as American flags and rebel flags.

"I can't believe people are seriously flying rebel flags," Nicole said, "while the NAACP is boycotting South Carolina over flying it at the statehouse. My friends said they're planning a party for us that is themed 'bring down the flag, bring home Nicole,' where we're going to burn rebel flags."

"That's awesome," I said. "I am totally for the boycott. But the American flag is pretty much as bad, though. It's purely imperialistic, and even in the Civil War, America didn't care about the slaves. They just wanted to keep the union together."

"It's so wild to walk around here and be having a really good time and then start thinking about all these flags in terms of semiotics," Nicole said as we wandered around the camp into the woods to smoke a cigarette. "They all mean something to the person who flies them. Something they are trying to communicate to everyone else. But we can't tell what that something is unless we consider their particular sign in the entire system of signs, the economy of images. Sometimes it's obvious—like a flag supporting the driver you like. But even that, what does it really say? And is a Confederate flag different here, among all these other symbols, than it would be somewhere like the statehouse?"

I loved that Nicole could fit in perfectly with Dad and Larry and all these NASCAR fans and that she could also offer a semiotic analysis. But I also felt a deep sense of internal conflict—as if I were betraying something about myself by being here.

By the time we got back, Larry had the steaks cooking on a grill laid across a fire he'd built in a pit. Beside their sizzle lay the sad round cap of a portobello mushroom.

"I can't believe you'd want to eat this when we're having that," Larry said to me through a cloud of cigarette smoke.

Like NASCAR, steaks symbolized all true, red-blooded Americans.

"When we were in Oklahoma, at a diner last week, he ordered eggs," Nicole said. "The waitress brought him a plate with bacon. 'I'm a vegetarian,' he said. 'I ordered this without bacon.' 'Well, honey,' she said, 'they were cooked on the same grill.'"

Everyone laughed, including me. I could stand a few jokes at my expense if it meant that Nicole and Dad were bonding. That was why we were all there. It was why people waved flags and wore hats and shirts for their favorite drivers. We were all trying to bond, to be a part of a community, by focusing on some spectacle we had in common, the apotheosis of car culture and capitalism and consumption. And at that NASCAR race, in the year 2000, whiteness was a big part of the common denominator. Racing was about race.

As much as I had worked my entire life to escape and be different from all of this, I couldn't help but think of it as my culture. But I still believed I could just leave the bad parts behind. I could accept my southernness and my whiteness while also looking with superiority upon all the southern whites who could not distance themselves from parts of that past, who could not see it ironically—or so I thought.

The next day Dad and Nicole and I walked up the long gravel road from the campground to the speedway with hundreds of other people decked out in swag for their favorite drivers and the corporations that sponsored them. Larry had gone up earlier and was already in his seat.

We showed our tickets and walked through the hallways and past concession stands with thousands of people also looking for seats. The sounds of trash talk, merchandise vendors, and excited families echoed through the open-air passageway. We found our section and climbed up above the massive speedway below.

On the inside of the circular track, in what was called the infield, there were hundreds of vehicles where people had camped, ready to watch the race from the doughnut hole so that the cars would be roaring around them, riding up high on the banked track above them instead of below, as they appeared to us up in the stands.

"When we were young, we used to watch from the infield," Dad said. "Camp out for a couple days. That's where it would get rowdy."

"Lot of rebel flags down there," I said.

"Used to be a lot worse," Dad said.

From the 1960s on, the rebel flag had been the semiofficial emblem of the track in Darlington, the closest one to the town where Dad grew up. I recalled how he'd bought me little toy flags when I was a kid, and I realized he had probably been one of those redneck rebel-flag wavers you could see in pictures of old races. But I didn't want to think about that right now.

"It's offensive," I said. "But the corporate signs everywhere here are also offensive. They use slave labor overseas, not just in the past but at this very moment."

My politics, like those of so many white leftists in the nineties, were predominantly anticorporate. To me, corporations were a worse threat and a worse problem than racism. I was concerned with what was happening to the people in East Timor while ignoring both the past and current oppression of people of color in my own state. But it was harder to ignore now, thinking about how, back when Dad had been down in the infield with all those flags, they'd actively signaled resistance to integration, and it troubled me to imagine him as a young man on the infield telling drunken racist jokes.

Then, as if to stop this line of thinking and underscore my point about corporations and American imperialism, the air began to swoosh and thrum as a military helicopter came from overhead, sending rustling waves of sound and wind across the stands as it landed on the track, its blades thwapping the air, which seemed to rip apart further as four military jets made black silhouettes against the crisp blue sky.

"Please rise for the national anthem," a voice boomed from the PA.

Oh, fuck. Refusing to stand for the national anthem at a college gradua-tion in Albuquerque was one thing. But here, with a giant cadre of soldiers standing at attention and this rowdy crowd of rednecks on Memorial Day, it was another matter altogether.

I didn't know what to do. I decided to take a half measure. I did not take off the Rusty Wallace Miller Lite hat that I had been wearing so I would fit in. I kind of stood up while leaving my knee in my seat. Nicole stood up beside me. She did not put her hand over her heart.

I wondered if anyone noticed—and this time I also wondered if they would come and punch me out as soon as the song ended, these drunken race fans with their corporate logo hats pressed tight against their man-boobs.

The war planes flew overhead again when the song ended, and the engines of the cars combusted, converting the air into a cacophonous explosion of carbon.

The pride in the stadium rang through the mostly white audience like a bass note, and the smell of the exhaust, the bright colors of the corporate logos, the overall sensational display made it hard not to feel something, and for me that something echoed back to childhood. If this noise and roar and white fellowship were overwhelming now, they must have done some serious work on my five-year-old brain. Despite everything, this was a place where I belonged, even if I didn't want to. And I could tell Nicole felt the same. In order to experience the emotion, I had to bracket my feelings about my belief that the sport existed to glorify the military-industrial complex. It had a racist history. But I couldn't deny the hazy nostalgia circling me. This is how roots work: even when we want to resist their pull, they are still there, tethering us to a place—and a version of ourselves—we want to escape.

After the race, we started talking to the folks camping next to us, and they were partying.

"Y'all want any of these?" asked a shirtless guy with a cowboy hat. "It's strawberries soaked in moonshine."

"Sure," I said.

"Definitely," Nicole said.

Dad and Larry said they were going to turn in.

"Y'all are welcome to come over and have some more," the guy said to me and Nicole, and we walked over to their camper.

With her charm, her good looks, and her accent, Nicole fit right in. I tried to prove myself by talking about country music, but our new friends seemed suspicious of me.

"You like Merle Haggard?" one guy asked, a note of surprise coloring his voice.

"Hell, I saw him in concert when I was five years old," I said.

Soon we were singing along to old country songs by the fire, sharing our common language.

"You ever heard this?" one of the guys asked.

It was a bluegrass version of Snoop Dogg's "Gin and Juice." One of the women, wearing jeans and a Jeff Gordon shirt, started clog dancing in a traditional flat-footed style, the soles of her feet slapping against the dust. The shirtless guy did stereotypical "rapper's hand gestures" every time Snoop said, "Laid back." Everyone laughed. More drinks, more music.

Finally, about three in the morning, we were all singing along to David Allan Coe songs. I gleefully joined in the choir, but when the song "If That Ain't Country" came on, I paused. I swallowed anxiously as I hummed along, anticipating what my southern white brothers and sisters would do with a troublesome lyric I knew was coming, the line where he sang, "Workin' like a n***** for my room and board." I sat there in my cutoff jeans, swatting at insects and dreading it.

I looked at Nicole, but she didn't seem to recognize the significance of my glance, even though she had told me that once when her dad was driving, the song had come up on a tape of her brother's, and her dad had stopped the car and thrown the tape out the window. I reckoned that I wasn't that kind of guy as I sat there waiting.

The song has a long talky part at the beginning. I lit a cigarette. Nicole asked me for a light. Then the refrain came, and everyone started singing, louder than ever.

"Trying like the devil just to find the Lord," they sang.

It was about five of them and two of us, all sitting around in camp chairs. There was no stopping it now.

"Workin' like a n***** for my room and board," everyone but Nicole and me roared.

We didn't sing along, but we didn't say anything either or even look at each other.

We'd been drinking all day, and somehow Nicole and I ended up in our first fight that night. When I woke up the next morning I felt as if I made an ass of myself and said some stupid things. Though I had made it my life's mission to rebel against that culture, my dad's culture, what he and Mom had tried to groom me to become, a homegrown white man, the night before I'd felt somehow threatened by the other campers' approval of Nicole. I was jealous that she fit in and I didn't. Something in me had surfaced that I hadn't known was there, a need to belong. I had no control over it, as if my DNA had been brewing inside me under a closed lid and now it had finally overflowed with a strong craving for what I had thought I had unlearned by reading books and studying and philosophizing with like minds. Yet I could not deny it was still there. In my essence, I still wanted their approval.

Chapter 17

MOM TOOK THE RING OFF her finger, a small diamond set in rose gold that had rubbed against her wedding band for nearly thirty years.

We were standing in the kitchen, and she held the ring up to the light streaming in through the window above the sink.

"I've always loved how imperfect the cut of the diamond is," she said.

She handed it to me, and I held it up in the same way, the light refracting off the odd angles of the jewel.

"Grandmother Woods told me that it had been in the family for seven generations," she said. "They had to cut the diamonds by hand back then."

I did the math in my head. So the ring I was holding had been in my family—had in some ways created my family, bringing two disparate lines together to form a new generation—for something like 210 years, or since 1791. This ring was roughly as old as the United States Constitution.

"And Grandmother gave it to Dad to give to you?" I asked.

"And I'm giving it to you," she said. "To give to Nicole."

My first year of graduate school in Pittsburgh had passed like a dream where I sat in a grim and dusty, cold apartment that I'd sublet, reading and pining for Nicole. She was still two thousand miles away, and we had seen each other only twice that year. But it was going to be easier the next year, though we would still be apart, because she had been accepted into a PhD program in Maryland, which was much closer to Pittsburgh. So the minute school was out, I caught a plane to Albuquerque, from which we would make a couple of trips back and forth to South Carolina before her move.

We had been about to drive back to Albuquerque from South Carolina to finish moving Nicole's stuff when I told Mom and Dad that I was going to ask her to marry me, and now, just before we left, Mom had pulled me aside.

"When are you going to ask her?" she asked after she gave me the ring.

"I think I'm going to do it when we're on the road at some really cool place," I said.

"Don't lose it," she said, pointing to the ring.

"I'm terrified of that," I said. "I kind of just want to give it to her now."

"You will do it at the right time," she said.

She hugged me again.

"I'm delighted for you to marry her," she said.

"Thanks," I said.

She got a little box for the ring, and I put it in my pocket.

"We better hit the road," I said.

We walked out into the early-summer morning, where Dad and Nicole were standing by her Ford Taurus, whose silver paint job reflected the blue Carolina sky.

"Another great year at the rock," Dad said. The pull of belonging was strong and Dad and Nicole and I had camped out for the race with Larry again that Memorial Day weekend at the same campsite and ended up drinking with the same people as the year before. "We'll have to make it a tradition."

I noticed Dad look down at Mom's ring finger as we walked up. They must have talked about it.

"I'm so glad you go to the race so I don't have to," Mom said to Nicole.

"Boy," Dad said, looking at me knowingly, "it's been good."

"Yessir," I said. "We'll call you when we get there."

We got in the car, pulled out of their driveway, and headed toward Ashville, where we'd hit I-40.

Two nights later, a tornado warning forced us off I-40 in Arkansas. It was pouring rain, and we pulled into a little motor court.

"We have one room left," the woman said as I dashed, drenched, into the office. The neon sign on the window magnified the drops on the window and painted them a spectral orange.

"We'll take it," I said.

Country music drifted from the radio behind the counter, and I knew I would give Nicole this ring that had been in my family for seven generations that night, in this motor court.

The weather was muted on the TV.

"Are you worried about a tornado?" I asked the woman behind the counter.

"Nah," the woman said. "It's just a bad thunderstorm here. But up ahead, in Oklahoma, it's looking bad."

When we walked into the room a few minutes later, I was certain I'd propose there. There was a black leather couch. An old-school TV that was a piece of furniture as much as an electronic device. A rotary phone. Rain beat against the windows, and it was the perfect place to be.

"I love this place," she said. She had written her master's thesis on South of the Border, a roadside attraction/sleazy motel, and this motor court had exactly the kind of trashy aesthetic that would appeal to her.

Lightning crashed outside the window.

"Let's check the weather, just to make sure," she said, and turned on the TV.

"The woman at the desk said it shouldn't be too bad here," I said.

"Oh, look," Nicole said as the television flickered on. "*The Jeffersons.*"

Every time George Jefferson, a wealthy Black man, would insult Florence, his Black maid, the network would flash a score card on the screen with some kind of special effect. And it would do the same thing every time Florence insulted George, as if it were a boxing match.

Nicole was sucked in. She forgot the weather report as the storm raged outside. That would give me a chance to pull the ring from the bag where I'd hidden it and put it in my pocket.

"What are you doing?" she asked as I dug through the luggage, panicking when I could not find the ring.

Then I felt its cool metal, palmed it, and relaxed.

"Here's a beer," I said, slipping the ring in my pocket and reaching toward the cooler.

I handed her an ice-cold Miller High Life.

"The champagne of beers," she said, opening the bottle.

This was perfect.

"Cheers," I said, popping the top of another beer and holding its mouth toward her.

"Oh, look," she said. "Another episode. It's a George and Florence insult marathon."

Thunder crashed again, a flash of blue, and then the room was black. The power had blown. The lights flickered. I reached in my pocket. The lights came back on.

"Will you marry me?" I asked.

"Yes," she said, immediately, but I could tell she was genuinely surprised. Neither of us had really seemed to ourselves like the marrying kind, but our year apart had affected her the same way it had me—it had filled us both with a longing to be together.

We kissed and toasted with Miller High Life and whiskey. Eventually we had cheap-motel-room sex, one of our favorites. Then we watched a few more episodes of *The Jeffersons*, lying in bed, the world still moving from our long drive.

"You didn't watch this growing up?" she asked.

"Of course I did," I said. "Every afternoon, in reruns, *The Jeffersons* came on at five, I think. Right after *Good Times*."

"Totally," she said.

In the same way that many whites in our parents' generation knew Black people primarily through domestic workers, my generation of white latchkey kids had spent more time with syndicated Black TV characters than we ever had with real Black people, and we could see ourselves and our families in them. It was through these shows that we first identified with Black people in any personal way. The imperfections of George Jefferson and Fred Sanford gave me a framework with which to view the cantankerous and paranoid behavior of my grandfather Summey, humanizing both the Black characters on TV and the man who had raised my mother. Each gave the other some context in my mind.

Summey had suffered from another series of strokes and was now a holy terror to Mom and Nanny. One day he'd tried to take his van, which he no longer had a license to drive, and told people his family had kidnapped him. He ended up crashing through the back of his garage because he couldn't control the vehicle.

I thought of him as we lay there sipping beer. I knew he wouldn't make it long now. When I went to see him he could barely talk, which was, in some ways, a relief, because he had lost all the charm his words used to carry, and now it was as if his life had become an insult marathon without humor or heart. He was scared and bitter.

That was what happened, I thought, when we repressed reality, attempting to see only the world we wanted, the world we made, whiteness. Whatever we refused to look at came back unbidden to haunt us, either stripping us of memory altogether or overwhelming our thoughts with paranoid delusions. We always learned too late that our fantasies have consequences.

Nicole held up the ring to admire it on her finger.

"It really is interesting," she said.

"Mom said it has been in my family for like seven generations," I said.

"It's beautiful," she said as it sparkled on her finger. "Were they here in America or did they bring it over?"

"I think they were here," I said. "Grandmother's family came to Edisto in the sixteen hundreds, she always said, and my dad's family had people who fought in the Revolution, I think."

"I have no idea where my family was back then," she said.

"I know that on my dad's side, my great-grandfather fought in the

Civil War and later killed someone, a Black man, I heard, and had to flee the state and hide out in Texas," I said. "He came back and was in the legislature and died I think around the turn of the century. So that ring is even three generations before that. I'm guessing around the late seventeen hundreds."

"Back when things were real good for the women who wore it, huh?" she said sarcastically. "And the slaves who polished it."

"Yeah," I said. "Pretty shitty. I think that's about when Mary Wollstonecraft wrote *A Vindication of the Rights of Woman*. If you're not into the institution or whatever—"

"No. I love you. Let's just be better than the past," she said. "Is this the right hand to put it on?"

"I don't know," I said. "Maybe."

We'd thought so little about marriage and tradition that we had no idea what hand to put the ring on, but as we lay there watching TV as the bluster of the storm outside began to subside, it felt right.

"Who do you think should perform the ceremony?" she asked, drowsy now beside me. "Dad would love for it to be Catholic, but we're not doing that."

"I was thinking maybe the judge who Summey was friends with," I said. "Judge Dobbs."

"I definitely want to do it in my parents' yard, though," she said.

"Definitely," I said.

Her parents' house had become a kind of holy place to us. When we visited, we stayed in a small room that had once been her grandmother's beauty parlor and spent our days out by the pool playing with her nephews and drinking beer or reading. It was the one place I felt fully relaxed.

Another episode of *The Jeffersons* came on, and I got up and got the last two bottles of beer. We lay there on the bed, holding hands and lazily watching the sitcom, and I thought of Summey and of Grandmother Woods and of what I had inherited from them. This ring was a physical embodiment of that inheritance, a stone-and-mineral-alloy reminder of generations passing. It was also a reminder of the patriarchy that marriage represented and the racist regime it was part of. But I hoped it was also something else. Was I continuing a legacy, or breaking with it? I wondered, and which was the right answer? I pondered the relationship of the past and the present as I drifted off to sleep.

A year later, Nicole and I were standing under a tent in the pouring rain by her parents' pool, getting married. My uncle Bully had cooked the hog for the rehearsal dinner the night before and was now performing the ceremony, his thick white hair feathered back, his litigator's voice booming out above the storm that had severely curtailed our plans.

Standing there in a black suit, looking at Nicole, her hair back tight against her gorgeous forehead, a white lace veil draped over it, I repeated the vows we had hastily compiled, adding only one real tweak to the traditional version. "For better or worse," Bully said and I repeated.

"For poor or poorer," he said.

"For poor or poorer," I said.

Everyone laughed as we continued. But afterward, at the reception, when the rain had let up, one of Dad's cousins approached me with the severe look of an offended dowager upon her face.

"You should not have said that," she said.

"Said what?" I asked, a bit annoyed. This was my wedding, after all.

"The Woodses have always been a proud family," she said. "The king granted us land in 1775. You should not say 'poor or poorer.' It does not do justice to your family. The Woodses have always been a proud family."

"Maybe," I said. "But if they had any money, it didn't come to me. And I'm trying to be a writer with philosopher as a backup job, so I'm just being realistic."

"You are from a proud family, and I know you will do perfectly well," she said. "Whether or not you inherited any money. Family lineage means something."

"Thank you," I said, for lack of anything better to say. I thought of the diamond that had been in our family for seven generations, and I wondered what proud deeds anyone had accomplished other than murdering a Black man and hiding out in Texas before returning to an active life in politics.

"Are you still working on the PhD?" she asked.

"I am, but I am done with my coursework. I moved to Maryland about a month ago, and I start a new job teaching literacy classes at all levels in different places all around the region on Monday morning," I said, explaining my situation for what felt like the ten thousandth time that day. "While I do that, I'll be reading for my comprehensive exams, and then I'll just have to write a dissertation."

"And where will you be living?" she asked.

"Nicole and I just bought a house," I said. "Or a co-op, actually, in the historic town of Greenbelt. It started as a New Deal project in public housing and public works."

We were extremely excited about our little row house in Greenbelt, which had a stop on Washington, D.C.'s Metro system. It cost $72,000, and we'd put $30,000 down. Nicole had gotten the money by selling a piece of land that her grandfather had given her when she went away to college. Our monthly payments were low, and since I was supremely unhandy, I was relieved by the fact that, if something went wrong, all I had to do was put in a work order and the co-op would take care of it.

Part of me knew that Dad's cousin was right. We might be short of money from time to time, but we would never be poor. In both our families there was wealth to cushion our mistakes and correct our errant aims. We could risk everything we personally had while knowing there would be more, money as deus ex machina, coming in from some family member or another at the last minute to save the day. We did not have to fear bankruptcy or homelessness. We did not have to worry about insurance or medical bills or where our next meal would come from because if things got bad, we knew our families had the resources to back us up.

"For poor or poorer," my uncle Richard said, slapping me on the back and laughing. He and my aunt Susan had made the arrangements for the rehearsal dinner, insisting that everyone wear "bummy old clothes," as I had once declared I would do if I ever got married. As we grow, I realized, we want to shed our previous selves. Family are those people who force us to remember our own pasts, even as they distort them with their own.

Uncle Bully walked up.

"I hope that was serviceable," he said.

"It was great," I said.

"Not as good as the judge would have been," he said.

Judge Dobbs, who was originally going to perform the ceremony, had gotten cancer and been unable to make it. It would have been sad for him anyway, because my grandfather Summey had died a couple of months earlier, in April. He'd been in bad shape when I visited him for the final time, in a nursing home, where he was hooked to a ventilator. I'd stayed all night and sat beside him in a pink floral print chair while he coughed and choked and the machine sucked away phlegm.

Before I left, I'd stood up and taken his cold, splotched hand and started singing to him softly, the Kris Kristofferson song "Sunday Mornin' Comin' Down." We both loved Kristofferson, one of the insurgent country stars of the late sixties who had brought the genre more in line with rock and roll and the rest of popular culture. Along the way he'd become a movie star, acting in films like *A Star Is Born* with Mom's favorite, Barbra Streisand. But in order to do that, he'd had to break away from his whole family, who had much different expectations for their son, a former Rhodes scholar and air force pilot. They disowned him when he moved to Nashville, and the song captured that feeling of abandonment and alienation.

"'And there's nothing short of dying that's half as lonesome as the sound,'" I whispered, and Summey squeezed my hand with an almost imperceptible bit of pressure. "'Of the sleeping city sidewalk'"—he squeezed again and I kept singing—"'and Sunday mornin' comin' down.'"

That was our final communication. At his funeral, Mom played Kristofferson's "Why Me" and Frank Sinatra's "My Way," in accordance with his last wishes.

My links to the world before me were fading. Family consists of those people whom we must remember after they are no longer able to. They are the ones whose lies we must sort out, whose damages we must assess.

I looked over and saw Nanny sitting with my aunt Gaile and walked over and hugged them both.

"Where are you going to be living now?" Nanny asked, although I'd already told her.

"Greenbelt," I said. "It was a New Deal project. Everyone there still loves Roosevelt and has pictures of Franklin and Eleanor hanging on the walls."

"A lot of people sure did love him," Nanny said. "Things were terrible here in the thirties."

"Our town center is Roosevelt Center, and there is a New Deal Café," I said. "We're in the historical center of the city, not the newer part."

One of the things we loved about Greenbelt was just how into its own past it was—a version of the country's past that most places had forgotten. And this environment had helped me to form a new, post-9/11, Bush-era political vision that moved away from my earlier antiglobalization radicalism toward a New Deal kind of liberalism.

"What we need is a New Deal, Willie Nelson Democrat," I said to my cousin Michael a little later that night.

"Yeah," he said, lighting a cigarette.

"Somebody who will promote big social programs but also support drug legalization and will get the votes of the cowboys and the hippies," I said.

"Exactly," he said. "We need someone who can appeal to the white working class more than a rich, Ivy-educated faux cowboy like George Bush."

Talking about electoral politics, when it was OK to discuss demographic trends and group behavior, was one of the only circumstances in which most white people I knew ever explicitly mentioned whiteness at all—but looking back, it feels as if we were all obsessed with whiteness, at least the people around my age, during that first decade of the new century.

White people in their twenties, dubbed hipsters, were wearing trucker hats, drinking PBR, and hanging out at trailer park–themed bars—doing things that we somehow associated with authentic whiteness—in the same way I had reembraced country music and NASCAR in an effort to look for my roots. We were the first generation of southern white people to be born after the Civil Rights Movement, the first generation of southern white people to be told from birth not to notice race, not to talk about it, even though it was obvious there was a lot to talk about, a lot that made us nervous and angry and upset, whenever it came up. And the gulf between these things, the fakeness of our families, made us feel we didn't have a culture at all except for shopping mall, Hallmark bullshit.

"On the one hand, southern white people—rednecks, white trash, hillbillies—are the only people it's OK to make fun of in America any-more," I said, drunkenly, as I lit a cigarette. "But they are also the ones who are swinging elections. We've got to find a way for Democrats to talk to that."

I knew the appeal of having a group of whites to see as worse than yourself. We could look down on them for being racist at the same time they kept us from seeing our own racism.

I had not invited my old friend Chuck to the wedding, partly because he had gone to rehab and was struggling with his various addictions and there would be a lot of drinking. But I had also sent him a story I'd written where Plato's Academy was discovered in West Virginia and the dialogue was rendered in an exaggerated hillbilly dialect, marveling at the absurdity of finding philosophy in *them thar hills*. I told Chuck that I was honoring his neighbors in West Virginia. I could tell he was pissed and felt the condescension dripping from my pages. And rather than deal with that, I just didn't invite him—and did the same with a lot of other old friends I hoped I'd outgrown.

When we returned to make our lives in Greenbelt, I brought back a banjo that my cousin Eric had rescued from Summey's basement, and I set about trying to learn to play and write country music. We spent weekends dancing at honky-tonks and bluegrass festivals at fire stations and empty fields and hanging out at backyard jam sessions, where I met other white people and we romanticized our whiteness. In this music we could peel back the veneer of modern times and bask in an older, pure, and authentic whiteness. But it was all romanticized, whitewashed in our minds.

One weekend not long after the wedding, I went with some friends to a bluegrass festival in rural Maryland where Ben Jones, a Georgia Democrat, was signing autographs. Jones had played the role of Cooter, the car mechanic on the TV show *The Dukes of Hazzard*, and he was standing in front of the car from that show that they'd called the *General Lee*, a bright-orange Dodge Charger with a Confederate flag on its roof that had become the centerpiece of the popular series, which itself had become the centerpiece of white culture. A friend snapped a picture of Ben Jones and me in front of the *General Lee*.

I'm standing in the photo, thirty years old, a married man and a PhD, after decades of trying to rebel against all of what my identity as a white man was supposed to look like. But in that photo, I saw someone who'd found peace, pillaging what I liked in my culture and ignoring the rest without examining the connection between the two. Whiteness is the search for the authenticity of our lies.

Chapter 18

I NEVER REALLY FELT *WHITE* white until I found myself standing up in front of a tenth-grade world history class in Washington, D.C., with twenty Black students and four students from El Salvador, talking about the transatlantic slave trade.

"So why did they think they could enslave the Africans, then, Dayvon?" I asked one of my students, a hefty kid with large, kind eyes, an easy smile, and a script that was nearly impossible to decipher.

"Because they were white," he said. Then his eyes fell, his face flushed. "Oh, I mean, I'm sorry, Mr. Dr. Woods. I didn't mean that."

I wasn't sure what he was apologizing for.

"Because they were Caucasian," he said, correcting himself.

It was a small charter school in a rickety old brick factory building with irregular plumbing and uneven floors in southeast Washington, D.C., a few blocks off Pennsylvania Avenue, in the shadow of the Capitol. It was a rapidly changing neighborhood in a gentrifying city, but the delineations were still rough. The housing projects across from the school sat in an uneasy truce with million-dollar mansions.

We had roughly four hundred students at the school, and around three hundred of them were Black. The other hundred were Salvadoran. There were two white kids, twins, which reinforced the kids' joke that all white people look alike. Most of the teachers were white, and students regularly mistook me for other white teachers maybe because we were all just instruments of authority or maybe because, to them, we really did all look alike.

I'd ended up there in the whitest way imaginable. Paul, the washtub bass player in the band I'd put together, taught English at the school and had booked us to play at their faculty talent show. Wearing cowboy hats and playing archaic instruments, we were kind of like a honky-tonk minstrel show, performing an exaggerated whiteness to a nonwhite audience.

But the kids were going kind of crazy for it, clapping along to the beat, mock square-dancing, jumping, cheering. The applause seemed genuine, but part of me felt the appreciation must have either been ironic or coerced. I would never have cheered for any of my teachers in high school. But when I saw the way they approached Paul afterward, it was clear there was some real affection. "Yo, Mr. B!" they exclaimed. It felt important, like in those feel-good TV shows with the inspirational teacher who changes lives with a white savior complex.

By the time we were packing up our gear that night, I was asking Paul about working there. I had just finished writing my dissertation— about how people unwittingly become bad—and didn't want to pursue an academic career. At least not at the moment. I'd gotten no job offers my first year on the market, and Nicole was working on her dissertation, and she was a much more serious academic than I. I loved teaching, but I really wanted to write fiction, and I was done with scholarship on ancient philosophy. So I applied at the school and started the next fall, teaching history to tenth graders and philosophy to juniors and seniors.

"It's OK, *white* is not a bad word," I said to Dayvon, and laughed. "It's better than *Caucasian*."

I wasn't really sure why *white* was better than *Caucasian* to me, but *Caucasian* felt old, outdated, and not the way I'd ever thought of myself. But *white*, I realized, had been the word on the signs at segregated schools. How could we still use the word *white* at all, with that apartheid history attached to it?

"Do white people really eat bugs?" Dayvon asked.

The class exploded in laughter, slapping their palms against their desks, and filled the room with the enthusiastic hooting high school kids use to prolong a lawless moment, the wild freedom of being off topic.

"No, for real," Dayvon said, looking concerned. "I don't mean no disrespect, and I'm not trying to be funny. But I saw this news report about how white people eat bugs."

"Yeah, I saw that too," another student exclaimed.

"Eww, gross!" a chorus of kids followed.

I had seen it too. The previous year, the area had been swarmed by billions of cicadas, which had come up out of the ground in a seventeen-year cycle, and several different news outlets had run stories about cooking the singing crustaceans.

"Not normally," I said. "But they are a good source of protein."

"Eww," the kids cried out again.

"But back to you, Dayvon," I said. "Why would being white make the Europeans think they could enslave the Africans?"

He looked down, embarrassed. I looked around the room for another student to call on, and they were all suddenly deeply engrossed in their notebooks. Teaching these students about the slave trade was the first time I had ever seriously thought about slavery myself. In philosophy there was Hegel's "master-slave dialectic" and Nietzsche's "slave morality," but it was all metaphorical and abstract—as if the slave trade hadn't been an actual fact during their lives. But now, preparing to teach, I read about the horrors of the Middle Passage and the plantation work camps, and I realized that my family had played a role in this horror that was morally no less repugnant than the Holocaust. But the response of the descendants of those perpetrators was so different. I recalled how Grandmother Woods had truly believed that her forebears had been kind and that the people they had enslaved had loved them. We pass down illusions to our children, the things we want to believe, and they never grow out of them but carry these distorted images into adulthood and on to the future.

I started seriously reading Black literature for the first time that year.

When I read Ralph Ellison's *Invisible Man*, as I rode the Metro for an hour each day from my Greenbelt home into the city, I realized that, in the prologue, it is not just that white people can't see the Black narrator—as white people, we are also invisible to ourselves. Whiteness was everywhere. But because it was presented as the norm, as the standard, as the universal, it was nowhere. This dialectic of whiteness made it almost impossible for white people to really see ourselves in the way everyone else saw us.

The Black students could see us clearly—but they were scared of telling the truth, at least to us. They were as uncomfortable talking about whiteness as their white teachers were. We all talked about Blackness all the time, about civil rights and the achievement gap. We weren't uncomfortable talking about race. We were uncomfortable talking about whiteness. Race, we thought, was a Black thing.

It was 2005, at the height of No Child Left Behind and the school reform movement. The achievement gap between Black and white children was, thousands of us all around the country told ourselves, the civil rights fight of our time. That sense of urgency, along with the logistical reach of Teach for America, brought the "best and brightest" young white kids from the Ivy League colleges to places like the school where I taught, where nearly 70 percent of the kids received free or reduced-price lunches and about the same number read significantly below their grade level, according to the standardized tests with which our success would be measured.

At thirty-three, I was a good decade older than many of the other new teachers and had never been to an Ivy League school, but as we started our classes on the first day, we were all faced with the same choice, one that was new to most of us: we had to decide how we would play our whiteness.

What kind of white person will you be?

We didn't talk about it that way, of course. We talked about "classroom management" and teaching style and authority—but we had to figure out how to deploy the power we represented.

There were a few basic options. There was the White Best Friend. Many of the new teachers, and especially the ones who were only a few years older than the students, tried to make their whiteness as invisible to the kids as it was to them, acting like the differences in both age and race were minor or even nonexistent. "Yo, did you hear that new Lil Wayne song? It's dope," a blond math teacher said one day at the beginning of a class I happened to be observing. The students erupted in laughter.

Closely related to that was the White Parent, the role whereby white teachers wanted to be surrogate parents for their students. Most afternoons you could find them with a crying student sitting in their classrooms, complaining about a boyfriend or another teacher.

To me it seemed like both these approaches were more about the feelings of the white teacher than the success of the Black students. So I took a third approach—the White Drill Sergeant. I had been an antiauthoritarian anarchist for most of my adult life, but when I took the job at the school, I decided that I was going to be a stern disciplinarian. It was part of the rhetoric of reform and charter schools—we owed it to these kids to eliminate the achievement gap and make sure they were performing as well as white kids on standardized tests designed for white kids.

But even though I wanted my students to be treated the same as white kids, I did not consider that, as a white kid, I had slept my way all through school with no stern disciplinarians setting me straight.

I didn't see how the system had been set up to cushion my mistakes. But I thought of my own experience and knew that I would not be the kind of teacher who would look the other way when a kid was screwing up because it was easier. I was going to care enough to be tough.

Instead of trying to be *down*, I adopted the goofiest white persona I could, wearing suspenders and a tool belt with detention slips in it. And rather than ripping off the kids' slang, as so many of the teachers did, I used archaic words—*skulduggery, rapscallion, spiffy*—and was thrilled when I heard them creep into the students' speech. I loved the job and felt electrified every time I walked into my classroom. I was popular with the students precisely because I did not pander to them.

The academic teachers were mostly white, but there was a disciplinary staff made up of four Black men, two of whom had been students at the school two years before. Mr. Marlowe, the vice principal in charge of this staff, was a bulky Black man with his short hair cropped high above his ears and a mustache so thin that it almost seemed drawn on. He was a towering moral presence within the school. He did not argue with students or pander to them either. He enforced the rules and he enforced them strictly, but without emotion or anger. Cause and effect, he said, was what they needed to learn. When the teachers were inconsistent, when they acted out of emotion, the kids never learned anything. "You might not think it's fair to send them out of the class or for us to suspend them," he said. "But it's not fair to the other students to let them disrupt the learning time."

Again and again, the Black "discipline staff" rescued the white teachers from seemingly insoluble conflict with Black students.

I admired the authority with which Mr. Marlowe carried himself among both the kids and the teachers, and I began to model my own disciplinary style after him—with my own flourishes. I loved goofy tactics, pranks, and puns to break up the series of expectations a school day brings. When the school began calling detention "reflection," I started carrying a mirror in my tool belt and would whip it out like a cowboy and flash the kids with their own reflections in order to signal a detention, hoping the absurdity of the gesture would offset the initial negative reaction—but, whatever we called it, it was still detention.

I might have had good intentions, but I also had an extraordinary amount of power over these students—as all teachers do—and that power amplified any mistakes I made.

About a week into my first year there, the academic dean approached my door with a student. Because of spotty school attendance in Baltimore, from where he'd recently moved, the school hadn't known in what grade to put the kid, whose name was Aaron. So even though there was no record he had completed the ninth grade, or even the eighth, it had decided, based on his age, that he would be a tenth grader and put him in my class.

He had light skin and a kind of smashed pug nose and hazel eyes that were almost green. He was new to the school and spent the first class looking sadly off into the distance, pretending to do the work I asked for, hoping not to be noticed.

The next day, I wanted to make a point of engaging him and making him feel welcome, and so I called on him early in class.

"So, Aaron, why is it called the triangle trade?" I asked, pointing at a world map hanging on the wall.

He just looked at his desk.

"Aaron," I said.

My booming voice was an asset in the classroom. It was one of the things I liked about teaching—it turned something that had always seemed like a flaw, something I could not control, into an advantage. Sometimes my volume and cadence kept students captivated. I tried to be entertaining. But it could also really annoy teenage students when they were tired. And it annoyed Aaron then.

"Man, why you keep bothering me?" he asked.

"Because that's what education is," I said. "Did you do the reading?"

He was silent.

"Aaron," I said.

"God!" he said, and sprang up from behind his desk and stormed out of the class.

A few minutes later, my door opened, and Marlowe stuck his head in and motioned me to come out.

"OK, read the next section," I said, and stepped out into the hallway, which was lined with orange lockers reflecting the fluorescent light.

"What happened with Aaron?" Marlowe asked.

"I don't know. I just called on him and he yelled back and then jumped out of his chair and lunged at me and then ran out of the door," I said.

I wasn't scared when Aaron had leaped up, but my account emphasized a sense of danger, adding the word *lunged*, for instance, and highlighted the racial threat presented by the student, perhaps in order to cover any of my failures that may have contributed to his desire to escape.

Describing events in a way that favored me had long been one of my worst flaws, but it was so natural to me, so essential to the white culture in which I had been raised, that I hardly realized I was doing it. I experienced the world in terms of what was good for me and what was bad for me. My reality was dominated by the desire to seem right rather than the desire to be right.

When I was in school, I'd argued endlessly with my teachers, I'd exaggerated and escalated, making every slight against me into a major affront while minimizing each of my errors. Such behavior from a student is annoying but mainly harmless because the student lacks the authority to enshrine this version as truth. But in the reverse situation, where there was a complete imbalance of power, where I was the authority, such an instinctual exaggeration could be detrimental and even deadly.

Marlowe, who was not one to make exceptions, graciously ignored my overstatement to make the case for an unaccustomed leniency for the kid.

"He's a tough case," Marlowe said. "He moved here from Baltimore because his dad was murdered. He's torn up. In a lot of pain and he's confused. He only reads at a third-grade level. But he's a Golden Gloves boxer. Supertalented. He's a good kid."

After that, Aaron and I started to get along. I couldn't imagine how someone could make it to the tenth grade reading at what standardized tests told me was a third-grade level. How many teachers had simply passed him on, overlooked him, made him someone else's problem? I was not going to do that. I pushed him academically, and it seemed he responded, and he started attending school more regularly.

One day, at the end of class, I mentioned something about South Carolina. "Oh, you know, South Cackalacky," he said, using a slang phrase that later became popular but at that point I'd never heard outside the state, as the bell rang and the room exploded into motion. We both laughed.

"My family comes from Beaufort," he said, standing beside my desk as the class filed out into the hall.

"You know, public education began in Beaufort," I said. "With Robert Smalls, a Black congressman, during Reconstruction."

"The guy who stole the boat, right?" he said.

"Exactly," I said, delighted that we both knew the story of Smalls, who had captured the Confederate ship he worked on and brought it over to the Union and later served five terms in Congress. "So if he can do it—"

"See you tomorrow, Dr. Woods," he said with a little smirk, cutting me off as he turned and walked out past the group of students filing in.

"Stay spiffy," I said, and followed him out.

Between classes there was the chaotic energy of four hundred bodies passing in different directions through the narrow hallways of the school building, which had uneven wooden floors and unreliable toilets and had not been built for this kind of traffic.

Many teachers remained in their classrooms, waiting for the students to come to them, but I prided myself on prowling the halls, feeling that energy, and engaging with the students.

This proactive approach was rewarded. During my second year at the school, I had three leadership positions. I was a department chair, a mentor teacher, and the teacher representative of the four-person management team that made the major decisions for the school. But I didn't represent the teachers so much as manage them.

Armed with this new sense of responsibility, not only did I patrol the halls looking for student misconduct, I also looked into classrooms to make sure teachers were following the ever-more-prescriptive lesson plans we were working with consultants to develop.

There was very little money at the school, but during my second year there, through a grant I got sixty copies of *Maus*, Art Spiegelman's graphic novel depicting the Holocaust through the experiences of Spiegelman's father, who was reluctant to talk about it with his son.

The students at our school struggled greatly with reading, and I hoped that the illustrations could help provide the context that would lead to understanding.

"So why are the Jews depicted as mice?" I asked the class, standing in front of them, my voice booming.

"Dang, Mr. Dr. Woods, why you got to be so loud?" Bree said, off to the side. Other students laughed.

"Because it's important," I said. "So why?"

"Because the Germans are cats and they kill mice," Bree answered.

"Good," I said. "And Aaron, what are the Americans represented as?"

"Dogs," he said.

"And why?" I asked.

"Well, hold up. What I don't get. They were Jewish but German too, right? And he, Artie or whatever, is an American but also a Jew. But they are mice. But how are Black people and Caucasians both dogs?"

"White people," I reminded him. "It's OK to say 'white people.'"

"How are Black people and white people both dogs, then?"

A wave of nervous laughter rippled through the class.

"Because we are all Americans," I said.

"But wasn't this when y'all was using dogs on us?"

"It was," I said, feeling uneasy about the pronoun *y'all*, which included me in the group of oppressors. "And you're right that there are very real parallels between the way that segregation worked here and what Art's father is telling him."

In preparing for that class, I'd read that the Nazis had modeled the racist Nuremberg Laws on American laws—but that the Jim Crow system, which had benefited my family at the expense of Aaron's, had been deemed too extreme even by the Nazis. There was a direct connection between the schools my parents had gone to and Aaron's academic limitations. Aaron's struggles and my successes were both part of the world my parents had been born and raised into, the world that my grandparents had perpetuated, and that my parents had never seemed to question.

Inspired by Art Spiegelman's conversations with his father in *Maus* about his experience in the Holocaust, the next time I was talking with Dad on the phone, I brought up school segregation. But where Spiegelman's father had been a victim, I knew that mine had been, at best, a bystander.

"What was it like going to a segregated school?" I asked him on my cell phone as I walked through D.C. one bright afternoon, making my way from school to the Metro.

"I don't know," he said. "I mean, I didn't know then because I didn't know anything different. Did you know that the case that started the whole integration push was in Clarendon County, *Briggs v. Elliott*?"

"No," I said.

"I think it was in 1947, shortly after I was born, and some Black families sued because they couldn't get school buses, so they said that separate but equal didn't hold," he said. "It became part of the famous *Brown v. Board of Education* case and was decided in the midfifties. But South Carolina schools didn't actually integrate until shortly before you were born, and so I never knew anything different."

"When *Brown* happened, were people worried about integration?" I asked, standing now outside the Eastern Market Metro station waiting to go underground so I wouldn't lose my signal. "White people?"

"Oh yeah," he said. "And there were riots in Darlington once it finally happened. I think they tipped over a school bus."

"And Grandmother was a teacher," I said. "Was she at all-white schools?"

"Definitely," he said. "But later she had some Black students too."

"I've been teaching about the Nazis and the Holocaust, and the German writers of your generation are so mad at their parents," I said. "Weren't you furious when it turned out you'd been raised in this system that was so wildly unfair?"

"It wasn't so bad," he said. "Like I said, I didn't know anything different. But I didn't benefit from it anyway. And a lot of people *were* pissed off about that. By the time I was really on the job market, after the Coast Guard, women and Blacks could have pretty much any job that I could and were often favored over someone like me, without a college degree, so when people say I was advantaged it's really not true. Even growing up, we were the only white family on our street, and we were as poor as most of them."

"I mean, sure," I said. "But whether or not your family made good use of it, the system was set up to be really unfair—in your favor. And when you realized that, it didn't piss you off?"

"I'm walking into the grocery store now," he said. "I've got to go."

"All right," I said and stepped on the escalator and began descending underground.

I was mad at him for refusing to see what seemed so evident to me, for refusing to admit it, because, whatever the legal situation, my experience teaching made it feel obvious that we still had segregated schools, and I wanted to know how his refusal to look at what his life had really been like, at his school, in his town of Manning, had made my Washington, D.C., school the way it was.

I knew that when the government forced integration, white people had created segregation academies for white kids, private schools where they had the "best" educations—and as a result had attempted to destroy public education. And I knew that the challenges my students faced somehow resulted from that move. And it made me angry.

As I felt the whoosh of the approaching subway echoing against the tiles of the arched underground ceiling, I felt as if the entire Republican idea that Dad espoused so fervently was just an attempt to go back to that segregated world in which he was infinitely privileged while considering himself as disadvantaged as his Black neighbors who'd had to fight for thirty-four years just for the right to school buses. The doors opened and I got on the train, furious and disgusted at what I saw as a willful lack of courage, an abrogation of reality.

As I rode the train out into the county, I noticed one of my students, a short Black girl with dyed red hair, on the same car. It had become more common to see the kids commuting into the city for school as they got priced out of D.C. Washington is divided into eight wards, and I'd hear them jokingly call the surrounding county, where it was much cheaper, Ward Nine. I pulled out my book—Toni Morrison's *Beloved*—and tried not to notice that the student likely did not live in the city anymore.

Even though I had cast myself as a stern disciplinarian, I was not going to snitch on a student who still wanted to come to our school even though gentrification had forced her family to the county, which was pretty much the same thing Mom had done when she lied about our address when we moved to Greenville. Running such a small school meant every day presented a new crisis, and I had no time to police where the kids lived.

Weekends in those days had that brief sense of relief you get when you are driving in a furious rainstorm and pass under a bridge and it is quiet for just a minute before you rush again into the roar. And that was just for the teachers. Some of the students were dealing with lives that were far more complicated than ours, and sometimes they would just quit showing up for a while.

That's what happened with Aaron. I'd call the roll each day, looking out and hoping to see his hazel eyes challenging me from his seat. But each day I was disappointed. Eventually I asked Roberto, one of Aaron's friends, if he had any idea where he was.

"I think he's, uh, working," Roberto said.

"Where?" I said.

"Come on," he said.

"What?" I said.

"Come on, Mr. Dr. Woods," he said.

"He's dealing drugs?" I asked.

Roberto said nothing. But he looked me in the eyes and gave a little nod before walking away.

I went to ask Mr. Marlowe if he'd heard anything about Aaron, and he said they had been calling but hadn't been able to get in touch.

"I'll try again today and let you know if I hear anything," he said, towering above me in the door of his office.

I was starting to consider leaving the school. I loved it from the minute my feet hit the floors in the morning until I went to bed. I was obsessed. But I also wanted to have a life outside the school. I woke up at four every morning to try to write fiction, but it wasn't going well, and I was starting to feel the strain. Nicole told me I needed to decide between being a high school teacher and being a writer, and we had started saving up money so I could take time off and try to write a book. She had just gotten a job in Baltimore County, and if I wasn't working in D.C. anymore, then we thought we might be able to move to Baltimore and live in a real city, and as I walked away from Marlowe's office wondering what kind of good I was doing, the idea of leaving the school seemed more appealing than ever.

That spring, I walked out into the small lobby on my way to the deli around the corner to buy a sandwich for lunch, and I saw Aaron sitting there on a bench by the metal detectors.

"Aaron, where have you been?" I asked, feigning severity, tilting my brows and narrowing my eyes, but I was happy to see him.

"I'm leaving," he said without really looking at me.

"What do you mean?"

"Leaving school," he said. "My mom's in there with Marlowe and them now."

"Why?" I asked.

"Come on."

"You know, you can do this," I said. "I can help you and you can do it."

"And then what?" he said, looking up at me. "College? You've seen how I read. Seriously, Dr. Woods, what am I going to do? What kind of job is waiting for me? I am making more money now than I could ever make in any job I get no matter how hard I work. And we are fucking broke—"

I raised my eyebrow.

"Sorry. We are gosh-darned broke," he said, causing us both to laugh, despite ourselves.

"Yeah, but," I said, looking at him as seriously as I could, "you know where that leads."

His hazel eyes glimmered with curiosity—I don't think he was curious about what I would say but about whether I would really say it.

He raised his eyebrows, urging me on.

"A bullet in the head," I said.

He shook his head. It was fucked up to say—we both knew I was playing what had happened to his dad against him.

"OK, tell me how you're going to help me," he said. "What is your plan for me? If I follow your route, where will I be in ten years?"

I could not answer. It was racist to believe that in ten years Aaron couldn't be on the same path I was on, to believe he could not do anything I could do. That was the path we offered to our students, the same path I had rejected at his age: work hard, go to college, get a good job, be happy. But it was equally racist to use that path as a cheap answer for someone like Aaron who lacked almost all the support I had and who was, at that moment, in an existential crisis.

"Yeah," he said, and smirked a little. "That's what I thought."

Standing there, by the metal detector in front of the open door, I saw that he had known that I had been lying to him this entire time. He'd known it and I hadn't. I'd thought I had the answers, and it turned out that I didn't have any. I didn't even know the right questions.

He left school that day and I never saw him again.

My cohort of teachers and I thought we needed to learn about the historical and socioeconomic limitations of our Black students so that we could educate them, fix them. But it was not they who were broken. We failed them because we could not see the historical and socioeconomic limitations of our whiteness. Aaron's family in Beaufort hadn't just lacked resources—their resources had been stolen by the likes of my family. When we, the white teachers, wondered why our students lacked skills and resources, we needed look no further than the mirror I carried in my tool belt.

Chapter 19

NICOLE WAS PISSED OFF. WE were standing in the small room that we used as an office, notes for her dissertation spread out on the desk.

"It's bullshit and it's sexist and it's racist," she said. "Just because I'm a woman they think I can't go anywhere alone."

"They" was referring to her family.

Her dissertation dealt with the politics of aesthetics in South Carolina's tourism industry. In addition to South of the Border, the roadside attraction that used racist tropes on its garish billboards, she was doing a study of Atlantic Beach, a historically Black-owned section of the Myrtle Beach Grand Strand, which was now the location of a controversial motorcycle gathering.

Every year Myrtle Beach had two bike weeks. The first was colloquially called Bike Week and, since it attracted largely white Harley-Davidson riders, it was seen as an economic boon, even if it made traffic a nightmare. The second bike week, dubbed Black Bike Week, attracted Black riders of Japanese speed bikes and sparked the moral panic of white residents, cops, and politicians.

And Nicole wanted to go.

It was Memorial Day weekend, toward the end of my last year at the high school, and there was no way I could go with her, and I sort of sided with her family. Even if for different reasons, I wasn't sure she should go.

"The world is sexist. Men are awful," I said. "And it is dangerous to go to a big festival where a lot of people are in from out of town and will be drinking and stuff, and men terrorize women because of patriarchy."

"And because they'll be Black?" she asked.

"No," I said. "My students are Black. I don't think it's dangerous because the people are Black. But I saw the white bikers in Sturgis back when I was on the road with Blake, and that was scary. People are dangerous at motorcycle festivals."

But the idea of her as the only white girl at an almost exclusively Black motorcycle rally did bother me. I would have probably been more worried if she went to the white bike week alone, but it would likely have been a different kind of worry, one I didn't care to parse because Nicole had already decided not to go, succumbing to the pressure put on her by me and her family. But as the days wore on, I started to think that my fears were racist, and I wanted to correct them.

Atlantic Beach was called the Black Pearl. After school one day, I went to a fancy jewelry store at Gallery Place and found a pair of black pearl earrings that I bought for her.

She liked the earrings when I gave them to her, but they didn't change the fact that I had played a role in keeping her from her research for what could really only be seen as racist and sexist reasons.

"We are going next year," she said. "Since you won't be teaching anymore."

And we did.

It was the first year of the Obama presidency, and going to Black Bike Week seemed like a particularly poignant sign of the new, possibly postracial times—even if white people in South Carolina were showing us how racial, and racist, they actually were.

Dad hated Obama. Every time he went on some anti-Obama rant, I would recall when he had tried to tell me that Jesse Jackson was the most racist man in America. During the two decades between 1988 and 2008, the propaganda of white grievance had exploded from paper pamphlets and AM radio to a twenty-four-hour news channel and countless websites, and it seemed as if Dad was always parroting some right-wing talking head or radical, ultraconservative politician.

The cast of political characters leading the charge—Joe "You Lie" Wilson, Jim DeMint, and Lindsey Graham—made it hard to miss the deep foundation of racism baked into the white part of our state. They made it obvious that they hated Obama because he was Black and that they would hate him no matter what he said or did. I had started writing a political column for the *Columbia City Paper*, covering South Carolina's congressional delegation, in which I attacked these heirs of the Dixiecratic governor and arch-segregationist Senator Strom Thurmond, who had spoken against the Civil Rights Act of 1957 for more than twenty-four hours, breaking the record for the Senate's longest filibuster.

We had an Obama sticker on our car on our drive to South Carolina for the biker event, and when we got into South Carolina, white people in trucks would zoom past us on the road and then aggressively cut us off, as if they were avenging the defeat of Sarah Palin, the big white mama bear who had somehow failed to chase the Black intruder away, with their massive, gas-guzzling vehicles sporting stickers of the cartoon Calvin pissing on Obama's logo.

At one gas station near Nicole's family house, where I was filling up, a white guy in a baseball cap walked by sneering.

"Hopey changey bullshit," he snarled.

It felt like high school again, with me lost and alienated in my home state due to my opposing politics. I'd done my best to ignore the bad and accept the good about my whiteness. But now, after Obama's election, the white people in my home state were forcing me to see that I couldn't just ignore the bad.

"What they do with Obama is the same thing they're doing with the bike weeks," Nicole said. "Because this gathering is Black, whatever they do there is going to be seen as criminal. And the other one, because they're white, they can get away with pretty much whatever they do and it's seen as just a few bad apples."

"And if they act like this to us just over a sticker, imagine how they are to actual Black people on motorcycles," I said.

As we got close to Atlantic Beach, we started to notice the beautiful, tricked-out speed of the Japanese bikes zipping between lanes and cars. The bass on the stereos blared from the bikes along with the roar of their engines. The fashion of the riders was as loud as the bass. Like the bikes, which could go upward of two hundred miles per hour, everything was over the top, and it was beautiful.

When we checked into our hotel room in North Myrtle Beach, just beside Atlantic, we were the only white people in the hotel's lobby. After the last year, it was a relief not to be around any white southerners. But we didn't even think about how it might feel for the Black motorcycle enthusiasts to be around us—white southerners, after all.

We saw ourselves as different. I'd been scared for Nicole to come to the bike week by herself the year before, but so much had changed since then. The election of Obama was a stark line for white southerners, who had embraced a full-on culture war. If you supported Obama, you might as well be Black in their eyes. A lot of us white Obama supporters thought that Black people should see us that way as well. *Hey, he's on our team!*

I smoked some weed on the balcony of our room overlooking the beach, and we went to walk around the festival. Atlantic Beach was separated from the town of North Myrtle Beach by a barricade blocking it off from traffic. It was like a different world, with small houses instead of Myrtle Beach's lavish high-rise hotels and dilapidated storefronts in place of garish T-shirt stands. But we both felt more at home here, surrounded by Black bikers with good music blaring and people dancing and neon-green plumes rising from neon helmets, than we did with the dangerously drunken frat boys in baseball caps populating the rest of the beach.

A few people smiled at us as we walked by, and one or two stopped to talk. But for the most part, nobody paid any attention to us at all as Nicole used a DSLR camera we had just bought for the trip to document the festivities.

"A few years ago, we were comfortable at a NASCAR race," I said as we walked through the streets, motorcycles slowly rolling up and down the avenue and a DMX song blasting out through a speaker near the center of the drag. "Now I definitely couldn't deal with that."

"For real," she said. "With the way white southerners are acting after the election, I feel like if we were walking around at a NASCAR race taking pictures right now, they'd attack us as the lamestream media or communist intellectuals."

We stepped out of the way of a procession of sparkling bikes easing by, their engines sending up the faint smell of combustion above the smell of all the sizzling meat coming off grills at stands, at stalls, and in yards on either side of the road.

"And even just last year, you were scared of me coming alone," she said. "And look how cool this is."

"I wasn't exactly *scared* of you coming alone," I said.

I looked over, and she was wearing her black pearl earrings. On her hand the diamond engagement ring gleamed. I thought with horror now of those seven generations who had owned that ring and how roughly half of them would have thought they owned these people. The thought that the ring had been on the finger of my slaveholding ancestors hit me with a kind of muted horror, casting the relic as a physical inheritance from hell.

As I took Nicole's hand, both of these pieces of jewelry had become complicated symbols that went well beyond their intended signification, ornamenting our whiteness and its relationship to Blackness.

"We should definitely move to Baltimore," Nicole said. "This has the same kind of vibe as Lexington Market."

We had fallen in love with Baltimore one Saturday when we drove up to the market, where we stood at a bar and ate oysters and drank beer, surrounded largely by Black people talking and laughing. We'd begun to notice how white our town, Old Greenbelt, was, and we were no longer happy with that.

We had for years now prided ourselves on living in "historic Greenbelt" and "not the new part." But the newer part of the city had a largely Black population, like the county it was in, while Old Greenbelt was almost exclusively white. And Nicole's research—she volunteered as a docent at the local history museum—showed the extent to which that had been by design. As a New Deal government program, Greenbelt was open only to white families in the 1930s, and that demographic decision had gone unchecked, despite the changing makeup of the county, and resulted in what amounted to a segregated city. And though our all-white part of town was staunchly liberal, opposing the Iraq War and voting overwhelmingly for Obama, we felt some deeper undercurrent of white dread when we read the nascent community message boards filled with fearmongering reports of Black youths afoot.

"I'm one hundred percent for moving," I said. "We need to get out of Greenbelt."

We'd already been vaguely looking for houses in Baltimore and preparing to put ours on the market—but we kept convincing ourselves to do it, to make all the pain-in-the-ass work worth it.

While working at the school, I had started to think of myself as a white person who is cool with Black people. Not like someone who was artificially *down*, like the Eminem wannabes, but someone who was at ease and natural around Black people, even though I had very few Black friends and none with whom I was close. Nor was I that white liberal who claims to be equally comfortable with everyone. I felt as if I could recognize and appreciate Blackness and Black people without trying to appropriate or imitate them. But this was still just another way of defining my whiteness in terms of Blackness—it was a way to deflect from actually thinking about whiteness, or a way of grasping to understand a whiteness that remained invisible to me.

When I saw whiteness unveiled, as an organized political force, early the following year, I was struck by how the low-grade horror of the obvious was transforming into the potential for real political terror. Of course this was what whiteness looked like.

It was the first Tea Party rally, on Tax Day 2010. I met my friend Liam at Freedom Plaza early that bright spring afternoon. Liam was a big, tough, blue-collar dude I played country music with. He was a D.C. cop until he got shot. Then he worked on the railroad until two cars coupling crushed half his right hand. Then he became a union organizer, and he was a perfect fit for the job—the loud-talking, confrontational type of organizer who might just slam you up against a wall to make a point. He was the perfect guy to go to the Tea Party with.

When we got there, we found thousands of people wearing tricorne hats and other colonial-era garb along with signs reading "Don't Tread on Me" or "Obama is a traitor" or "My freedom is a big fucking deal." Pretty much everyone was white and over forty-five. I thought of Dad. He wasn't the type to attend rallies—his political actions were largely confined to cursing at the television or the radio—but he shared the sentiments of these Tea Partiers. How much of their anger was the anger he'd expressed when I talked to him about school desegregation? This generation of white men had entered a world where they had to compete with Black people for jobs that had previously been reserved for them. And now, for the first time, there was a postboomer president, and he was Black. And to them that was unbearable.

I started talking with a white guy named John, who had long wavy hair coming out of a white baseball cap. He had on shorts and a loosely buttoned shirt showing off his gold chains.

"I'm ready for the next revolution," he said. "I firmly believe that the guy in the White House is a Muslim. He hates America, I think he hates whitey. He's a self-loathing piece of shit."

"What do you think the postrevolution world would look like?" I asked.

"It would look like me," he said.

After a while, I needed to escape the constant barrage of aggressive whiteness that was almost bowling me over, so Liam and I went to a bar. Then we went to another one, where we ate oysters for a couple of hours. As it got dark, he left and I went down to the main event, where thousands of people crowded the mall. "Hi, I'm with the *Columbia City Paper*," I said to one woman.

"What kind of paper is that?" she asked.

"A newspaper," I said.

"And what's your name?"

"My name is Baynard Woods," I said.

"What?"

I was officially John Baynard Woods Jr., and I had always gone by Bay. But "Bay Woods" was useless in a Google search, which brought up dozens of retirement communities, golf courses, and subdivisions called Bay Woods before anything I'd ever written. So I'd started using Baynard as a byline. But it didn't matter, verbally, whether I used Bay or Baynard because most people didn't know what the hell I was saying on the first try and I usually had to spell it. Nicole's grandmother had thought my name was Gay for a whole year.

"Baynard Woods," I said. "Of the *Columbia City Paper.*"

"Your paper isn't good for anything but wiping your journalist asses," she said.

She turned away, and I shrugged and wandered off through the apocalyptically Caucasian crowd into the heart of what looked to me like white doom.

I spotted one odd sign. "Defend Obama: Outlaw White Supremacy," it said. Then I noticed that people were standing around it, holding other signs with arrows and the word "Infiltrator!" written across them.

I decided I needed to go see what was happening and snaked through the crowd until I reached the sign, which was being held aloft by two young people, a white woman and a Black man. Around them, a crowd of angry old white people were yelling and jeering.

"Hey, what's going on?" I asked, walking up with my tape recorder out.

The couple with the sign said nothing. They just looked straight ahead and did not react.

"We're blocking them off," a Tea Partier told me.

"Is there a reason for that?" I asked.

"Because that's offensive and no one should see it."

"What is offensive about it?" I asked.

"'Outlaw white supremacy'?" the woman sneered. "These Kool-Aid drinkers think all the Tea Partiers are racist."

"If the Tea Party movement isn't white supremacist, why block the sign off?" I asked, doing my best to appear as a neutral journalist. "Wouldn't the Tea Party also want to outlaw white supremacy?"

"They don't belong here," the woman said.

She would not give her name.

A blond woman stepped toward me, aggressively.

"I can't find a white supremacist, can you? Let's go find one," she said, and grabbed my arm, digging her fingers in.

"Hold on, hold on. Let go of me, please," I said, my voice rising to an embarrassingly high pitch.

"Come on, let's go," she said, gripping my arm harder and pulling as people jostled around us. I jerked my arm away from her grasp.

"Let's go find a white supremacist," she said again, reaching for me once more as the crowd that had been focused on the sign now turned all its attention to me.

"Hold on," I said.

"Let's go find one. Do you know one? Do you know one?" she asked, grasping again at my arm.

"Do you have to know a crack smoker to outlaw crack?" I asked.

"Do you smoke it?" she asked.

Then she paused and sniffed, pointing at my face.

"Have you been drinking?"

I stepped back, trying to get away from her grabbing hands.

"You've been drinking," she announced, delighted, her swelling southern accent almost a slur, moving across the word *drinking* like a truck over an oil slick. "You've been drinking. How much did you have before you came down here?"

People chanted, "USA, USA" in the background.

"You been drinking, haven't you buddy?" she said.

The crowd around us loved that. It confirmed all their stereotypes about the liberal media. More people started yelling at me.

"Did you beat your wife before you came here today?" one guy bellowed.

Others started waving their "Infiltrator!" signs at me like tomahawks. I held up my arm to keep one from hitting me in the head.

I had swiftly lost control of this situation.

"Let me show you a picture of my grandchild," the blond woman said as she dug into her purse. "Let me show you a picture of my grandchild."

I knew what was coming. I hated every second of this confrontation.

"Look!" She pulled out a picture.

"He is cute," I said.

"He's Black!" she cried. "Isn't he cute? He's Black. Isn't that great? My grandson is Black!"

"And that means what?" I asked.

"That means I'm not a white supremacist," she said.

"He's been drinking," someone else yelled.

"I didn't say you were one—but if you aren't, why worry about this sign?" I asked.

"We're not white supremacists," the blond woman said. "Obama is a Black supremacist. That's what we're against. To be against Black supremacy isn't white supremacy."

"He's been drinking," a man yelled again.

More white people in tricornes and American flag T-shirts had gathered around. I didn't even know what the couple's sign really meant. It was hard to imagine what outlawing white supremacy would look like in a country where, with the exception of the first Black president, the political and law enforcement establishment was overwhelmingly white. But I applauded their sign and the courage it took to hold it.

"Well, thanks a lot for your time," I said, easing back, hoping no one would push me down from behind. I felt as if I was in danger and I needed to get out.

"Going to smoke some crack?" the blond woman asked.

"He needs another drink," a man said.

I did need another drink after I managed to extract myself from the rally. But more than that, I needed to get my ass home.

On the Metro ride back to Greenbelt that night, I stared at my reflection in the darkened window, exhausted, my buzz already a hangover. And as I thought about the Tea Party and its white anger, it was as if I saw Dad's face superimposed over mine. All of this rage came from insecurity. Whiteness is the fear both of being seen and of not being seen. Whiteness demands to dictate its own terms—and everyone else's terms too. It sees any Black gain as white loss. This anger wasn't confined to the Tea Party event, it felt intimately familiar. It was the same anger and sense of aggrieved loss that had suffused Columbia when I was growing up and the shared feeling in my community that the Wo-ah and the world had turned out wrong.

Chapter 20

THE SKY GLOWED ELECTRIC ON a brilliant, bright Friday after-noon in September. I was standing at the park and ride at the train station near the university where Nicole worked.

We'd just moved to Baltimore two weeks earlier, but I was teaching Greek and Latin at a nearby university and commuted by train. Adjunct work was a good way to make sure I had some income while trying to figure out how to survive as a writer.

"Hey, hon," Nicole said as I got in our silver Corolla.

"How was your day?" I asked.

"OK," she said as I slammed the door and she pulled out. "But I'm still really stressed about the house. I don't want to go back to Greenbelt."

Our house in Greenbelt had sold before we found our new home in Baltimore, so we'd decided to rent an apartment on Cathedral Street in Mount Vernon, a neighborhood in the center of the city that we couldn't afford to buy in, and we loved it. But then, two days earlier, the buyer had backed out of the Greenbelt deal, leaving us with the prospect of rent and a mortgage.

"We won't," I said. "She gave us that five thousand dollars for breaking the deal, and that will cover the mortgage and co-op fee for a while."

The traffic was all going the other way, streaming southward out of the city as the skyline rose up over the highway in front of us, the BRESCO tower spitting a light cloud of smoke into the sky. Nicole took the exit for 395 into the city.

As we drove up Park Avenue, Lexington Market loomed up at the top of a small hill to our left. The streets were teeming with people standing around and waiting for buses or smoking and talking and drinking from brown paper bags. The street life around the market was one of my favorite things about the city. It was alive with laughter and language. I felt at home in these chaotic streets, and I couldn't wait for the weekend to start.

Nicole made a sound, but it was not a word—more like something guttural involuntarily escaping from her lips. Then I saw the black SUV floating straight across Saratoga Street, its wide black hood aimed at my side of the car. The next seconds passed frame by frame like a film until the moment of impact. The velocity of our Corolla combined with that of the SUV suddenly and sent us crashing, spinning, weightless, through the intersection.

When the car had stopped, in shock, I immediately climbed out. Looking over the roof, I saw Nicole doing the same, but standing there on either side of our steaming, crumpled wreck of metal, we didn't know what to do. Faces were all around us, peering in as if through a fishbowl.

"Are y'all OK?" an older Black man asked.

We looked at each other across the silver roof. She nodded and so did I.

"The rich lady hit you," someone said.

"Aw, my back hurts too," someone else yelled.

I looked over and noticed that the woman who had been driving the SUV had not gotten out of her car. As I approached, I saw her through the window, talking on her cell phone as she employed a gesture to shoo me away.

"She's afraid to get out of her car," I said to Nicole.

A crowd of Black people had surrounded us, still asking if we were OK. I nodded and looked over at the "rich lady" in the car and felt a certain sense of pride that they identified with Nicole and me more than with the "rich lady." It bolstered the image I had developed of myself since we had moved to the city, the image of myself as a white person who was at home in a Black city, who could move about the world, comfortable in any situation. It was, in the end, another way of erasing my whiteness, seeing myself as not white at all, ignoring my history again, seeing myself as different from other white people.

At this time in my life, I wanted to shed all the imperfect, fucked-up, stupid, and ridiculous things about my past; to lose my history, and my identity, and just become one facet of this crazy diamond of a metropolis. If I could have, I would have liked to dissolve my whiteness, to be truly postracial. But I was smart enough, even looking around at the crowd around me, to realize that was impossible. So I recognized I was white, but I wanted to minimize it in whatever way I could, to put being white behind being a Baltimorean.

We decided not to get another car, and being carless increased this sense of dissolving into the city. Nicole took the 35 bus for an hour each way to her job at the university in the county, about a fifteen-minute drive. And since I already took the train to work, the biggest difference for me was that getting around the city necessarily happened at a human pace, in connection with everyone else, either on the bus or on the street, face-to-face with people.

The buses were mostly full of Black people, while whites regularly told us it was impossible to get by in Baltimore without a car. Cars were, it seemed, a good model for whiteness. Everything in our cities is designed for the benefit of cars, and yet behind the wheel everyone is furious all the time, trying to get to the next light just a little faster, feeling slighted by the least progress made by someone else.

However much I wished, in my peregrinations around the city, to erase my whiteness, I couldn't escape it. At the same time I was trying to lose myself in the city, my job forced me to see my race in a way I never had before.

"Can I see you in my office a minute?" my department chair asked when I got to work early one morning, his voice soft but uneasy.

"Sure," I said, and followed him into a dim, book-lined room.

I had an idea what this was about. A student had come to complain to him about me and had not been happy with the response.

"That student filed a formal, federal civil rights complaint against you," he said when we walked into his office with soft lighting coming from a desk lamp and the book-lined walls. "She's claiming you discriminated against her."

I felt my stomach lurch up not only because of the fact of the complaint but also because I knew I would be judged, right now and through the entire process, by how I responded to this allegation. The ways we respond to being called a racist seem to say as much as anything else about whether we really are racist. Previously I'd believed that racism was an active stance one took to be bigoted. Now it seemed a whole set of subconscious assumptions could be imbibed from the culture so that we could be racist without intending to be, without considering ourselves bigots. I was starting to recognize that racism could be structural.

I tried to steady myself and look into the chair's eyes.

There was only one Black student in my Latin 102 class. She was supposed to graduate from another local university that semester and needed a Latin credit to complete her language requirement. Since her school didn't offer it, she was taking the course with me. But she had taken Latin 101 many years earlier, and on the first day, as we started working through sentences, I worried she didn't have the prerequisite knowledge to be in the class. I asked her to stay after, and we stood there talking about her previous Latin class.

"I just don't know if you have the background knowledge to succeed in the second-semester class," I said. "You should think about taking my 120 class over the summer, where you get a whole year of Latin in six weeks."

She said she needed the class to graduate and that she would review.

I offered to help however I could, but mentioned the 120 course in the summer one more time. That was when she first went to the chair, who was a person of color but not Black, to complain about me. She told him that she had been recording my class and wanted to play snippets of me acting unfavorably toward her.

The knowledge that I was being surreptitiously recorded so that my words could be used to prove I was a racist made my teaching feel artificial and stilted, every word analyzed carefully before I uttered it.

Shortly after that, I got a call from her father in my office.

"I know you are from the Carolinas and how racist people are down there, and if you weren't racist she would pass," he said.

"I know how racist it is there too. But you don't know anything about me, and assuming you know what I am like because of where I'm from is the only prejudiced thing I've heard today," I said.

I was angry. Pissed off about the whole thing. I had used my PhD to teach underserved kids of color in the inner city. I had even written an article about using Latin to teach literacy to the students who struggled with reading the most. I had written the introduction to a book about literacy as a civil right, and now I was being accused of violating a Black student's civil right to an equal education? I wrote articles attacking South Carolina's racist politicians, and now I was being judged as a racist because I came from the same place as they? I couldn't believe it.

As long as it was just the tape recorders and the phone calls, I could blow it off. But this was a formal complaint to the Department of Education—whether or not I was racist would be examined by the United States government.

"I know this is difficult," the chair said.

"It's OK," I said. "I taught at a mostly Black school and understand how bad discrimination in education can be and the seriousness of this. I've thought a lot about it and even written about it. I've never discriminated against anyone based on race, but I applaud the process of reviewing alleged civil rights violations."

"OK," he said. "That's a good attitude. We'll have to respond. Can you work up a statement with some supporting materials that we can send to the lawyers?"

Because we'd talked about it before, I got the sense that the chair was on my side, and his use of the plural pronoun reassured me here. But I was only an adjunct, and I knew that the department would throw me over if it had to—or if it turned out I actually had discriminated against the student.

"Sure," I said.

I could tell that the whole thing made him as deeply uncomfortable as I was, and I just wanted to get out of his office, as much for his sake as for mine, as quickly as possible. I was a source of embarrassment.

I would write up my version of what had happened and supply any supporting documents, which he would then send to the university's lawyers, who would review them and then be in touch with me, he explained.

I staggered from the colonial brick building out onto the lawn of the leafy campus. I pulled my cell phone from my bag and noticed the pack of cigarettes. I spied a student smoking over by the steps and asked for a light and then walked behind the building, hiding behind a dumpster to call Nicole.

"It's impossible not to look like an asshole when you defend yourself against racism," I said into the phone after I explained what was going on. "Every racist says they're not racist. So how do I say I'm really not racist and not just some racist saying that I'm not racist?"

Writing up a defense, I knew that I'd sound like the Tea Partier who'd shown me the picture of her grandson to prove that she wasn't a white supremacist. I was not racist, or so I believed—but so did that woman who had harassed the kids at the rally with an "outlaw white supremacy" sign. How were we different? I wondered.

Late that night, I could not sleep. I walked into our local bar. My friend Rocky, a short, round Black guy with big baby cheeks and a bigger laugh, sat with a few other friends at one end of the bar in a peach-colored polo shirt. I approached them and did the ritual handclasp, chest-bump greeting and sat down beside them.

"A beer and a shot," I said to John, standing behind the bar.

"What's up?" Rocky asked.

"Our damn house in Greenbelt still hasn't sold," I said. "Thought there was going to be an offer today, but it fell through."

I felt wrong about hiding what had really happened today to get me down, but I couldn't tell these Black men that the United States government was investigating me as a racist.

"Shit," Rocky said.

"Another round," I said.

A little while later, I was taking a piss at the stained urinal in the bathroom when Rocky walked in. He took a bump of coke off of a key with a snort loud enough that I heard it clearly over my piss stream. He shook his head and smiled.

"Want one?" he asked, extending the key to me after I'd zipped up.

I took the bump. He took another. So did I.

We ended up later back at a friend's apartment, snorting blow till 5:00 a.m. Every time I put my face down to the mirror, I thought of the charge hanging over me, the charge that I was racist. What would Rocky and my other friends say if I told them about the complaint?

With a coke-fueled tongue, I almost mentioned it a couple of times, then chickened out and said something else instead.

Over the coming weeks, as I compiled the documents for my defense, the shame kept returning. I worried that any defense I might make would just prove that I was guilty.

The complaint that the student had made—that I'd told her she did not have the background for the class—alleged that I thought whiteness was a prerequisite for Latin. And though I did not think that, centuries of Latin teachers had.

The discipline of classics—based primarily on the study of Greek and Roman languages and cultures—was essential in the creation and propagation of the idea of whiteness. "The glory that was Greece, / and the grandeur that was Rome" served as the foundation of the concept of "Western civilization," which ultimately justified colonization, genocide, and slavery.

In the South of my ancestors, the slavers had studied ancient Greek while the people they tortured built colonial-style plantation houses with Greek columns. These white slavers often gave the names of famous Romans like Cato or Cicero to the Africans they prohibited from learning to read—on pain of death.

In the Ivy League schools up North, Greek and Latin were used as an elitist barrier. W. E. B. DuBois was the first Black person to get a PhD at Harvard in 1895, which was only possible because he had studied and taught classics, which forced white people to take him seriously as an intellectual.

Reading about this history as I prepared my defense, I understood the wider context of the student's complaint. I had not meant that Blackness was not an appropriate background for the study of classics—but that assumption had been an essential part of the discipline since its inception. Teaching classics, I felt, was kind of like hanging out with a skinhead—when a Black person assumed you were racist because of it, it was not without cause, even if it was, I hoped, without merit.

I was conflicted and confused. It was the first time that an outside force had made me think seriously about my whiteness. Before that, this awareness had been like a seed growing within me as I hung out in Baltimore, where I was now the minority as a white man and could actually see my whiteness, when I hadn't really needed to notice it before.

When my parents were kids, race had been inscribed in every public space, above every door or facility, "White" and "Colored" starkly stating the centrality of the category. I'd known this but hadn't lived it. By the time I was born, only eight years after the Civil Rights Act, white people mostly acted as if they didn't see race, and they taught me not to see it either. The Civil Rights Movement was ancient history overcome—even as the Civil War was remembered as an ever present tragedy.

Now I understood that whites like me hadn't forgotten race, we had repressed it, repressed the shame. The monstrous looks on the faces of the white southern racists screaming at Black children integrating schools must have embarrassed my parents, made them bury the experience of growing up in Jim Crow. Sacrificing that reality had been the only way to retain positive memories of their childhoods.

So every time we are reminded that we are white, we feel that shame afresh. It makes us angry, and we want to blame whatever and whoever reminds us of who we are and makes us suffer this shame. When white people get upset about Black History Month, it's not because white history is excluded from the picture. They are upset because it reminds us of the reality of our history.

But maybe, I thought, the repression was a conscious decision, a strategy for oppression. Whiteness had been a source of power for white people for hundreds of years before the Civil Rights Act made discrimination illegal. In order to undo those centuries of privilege, we would have to discuss race and the imbalances it created. So we white people quit "seeing race" and refused to talk about whiteness—and kept the spoils of our plunder.

If you spend four hundred years creating a world that favors a particular concept—whiteness—pretending that concept no longer exists is a good way to keep from examining its residual benefits.

In the end, I did not argue that I was not racist. I documented what had happened as accurately as I could and compiled a number of documents to show that I had thought about the role of race in education in the hopes that it would show I do not believe that a Black person is less qualified than a white one to study Latin or any other subject.

But I still had to grapple with the difference between what I'd intended my words to mean and what they may have actually meant. The reality lay somewhere between the student and me, my experiences causing me to think of the words one way and hers causing her to hear them in another.

After I submitted the materials for my defense, I just had to wait. Meanwhile the student remained in the class. I was aware of my whiteness at every moment, aware that, with the complaint filed, anything I said or did subsequently could be used against me in that case or even seem like retaliation.

I couldn't tell how much the white students knew about this whole business. I didn't know if the Black student had told anyone about it. If they did know, I didn't want to know what they thought, and so I tried to just focus on the work and keep an even head, making sure my sense of shame didn't manifest in any negative way against any of the students.

The student started coming to office hours more often to retake quizzes and ask clarifying questions. She said she was using YouTube videos to catch up. I told her I was happy to help as much as I could. But though she asked a question when she had to, she had no desire to work intensively with me.

Still, by the end of the semester, she had gotten her grade up to passing. Because of her university's graduation date, I agreed to grade her final exam first. When she passed the exam and the class, I was flooded with relief because I had told myself I wasn't going to pass her if her grade was not legitimately passing, because I thought that would be racist. Such a belief had been the basis of my entire identity as a teacher at the high school, and I still held on to that as an adjunct at the university. But for me to make such a decision would have put us both in a terrible position and escalated the whole problem.

Shortly after graduation, I received an official letter noting that the Department of Education Office for Civil Rights was closing the complaint. Reading the letter, I felt as if a flu had lifted, as if for the last several months my limbs had been suffused by a dull awful ache that was suddenly gone. That weight was a consciousness of whiteness. When the letter allowed me to feel vindicated, I didn't have to feel my whiteness anymore. I could be unconscious again.

I would learn that I couldn't ever be entirely unconscious again. I had seen enough of my whiteness, detected the ways it intersected with a larger history and distorted my own actions, casting them into a context I didn't understand, that I knew enough now to at least be wary of it.

"Let's go out and celebrate," I said to Nicole. We would tell no one what we were celebrating.

Later we were walking up Chase Street and we noticed a bar called Singers and decided to stop in for a drink.

"That's Lafayette Gilchrist," Nicole said after we sat down, pointing to a spiffy-looking Black man about my age with a porkpie hat at the next table, watching the drummer on the stage. Gilchrist was one of the best-known jazz musicians in town, and after a few minutes, we introduced ourselves to him.

By the end of the night, we made plans for him to come over to our place the following Sunday so I could start interviewing him for a profile I was going to pitch to a magazine.

We put a pot of red beans and rice on the stove that Sunday as we got ready for Lafayette to come over. I stirred the pot and turned to grab a beer. I noticed the magnets on our refrigerator for the first time since we'd moved from Greenbelt. Someone had given us a set that depicted Jimmy Carter, Ronald Reagan, George H. W. Bush, and Bill Clinton dressed as pimps. I'd never really thought much about the magnets. Now I was wondering if they were racist. I decided to take them off the fridge and figured I should scan the house for anything else that a Black man might deem racist.

Immediately I noticed the photograph of me and Ben "Cooter" Jones standing in front of the *General Lee* from *The Dukes of Hazzard* in a red frame on the wire bookshelf in the kitchen. I walked up and looked at it closely. The Confederate flag was clear.

I dug through a drawer with some photos and found one of me and Nicole and slid it into the frame covering the photo of me, Cooter, and the *General Lee*. It seemed obvious that an image of two white men and a rebel flag on a muscle car would appear racist to a Black man. And I'd never even considered that before.

I had been defending myself against charges of racism and had grown so angry at the student's father for assuming things about me because of my home state, and I hadn't even recognized that there was really no way to interpret the rebel flag that was not racist.

Because of my upbringing, because of where I was from, I not only had the image on the shelf, I had kept it there because a part of me had loved it. It represented my childhood in a way that actually hit me, emotionally. In order to deflect the reality of that emotion, I, and many others of my generation, had developed an ironic read of the "colorful" parts of white culture. I had never thought of racialized irony, but that's what the whole hipster thing felt like at that moment. Only a white person could look at a picture of the Confederate flag with this specific kind of irony.

But it was the emotion under the irony that was the dangerous thing. Irony fades like fashion. But a visceral feeling born in childhood is hard to shake. It can inform our choices in ways we aren't aware of, in the same way that the history of classics shaped the way my words to the Black student were received. Whiteness is the intersection of the hapless individual honky with the power relations embedded in our country's racist institutions.

Whiteness is institutionalized skulduggery performed by actors largely unaware of our roles. We don't even know we're wearing masks. But we are, I realized then for the first time, still responsible for the crimes committed beneath their cover.

Chapter 21

DAD RAISED A GLASS OF iced tea for a toast, his stark white beard catching the dim, flickering light of the candle on the table of the bar in Beaufort, South Carolina, where we were celebrating the publication of my first book. The front of the bar looked out onto Bay Street downtown and down to the water. Through the window, over Dad's shoulder, I could just see the red light on the bridge spanning the bay separating the town of Beaufort from the Sea Islands to the south.

Mom sipped her Diet Coke next to Dad, and on his other side were my uncle Richard and aunt Susan, who raised their glasses of red wine. Larry, Dad's old Coast Guard buddy, occupied the other end of the table.

"To the White Prince," Dad said.

Everyone laughed.

"The Witchdoctor Sheriff," Richard added.

These were names given to Sheriff Ed McTeer, the county's highest elected official from 1926 to 1963 and the subject of my book. The greatest challenge to his power had rested in Black root doctors like the famous Dr. Buzzard. After years of being bested by the root doctor, the sheriff started a rumor that he was a powerful witch doctor who could counteract Dr. Buzzard's spells. I wrote about the battle between these two men— but the fight between the tradition of Anglo-Saxon law enforcement and Gullah-Geechee spiritual practices lay at the heart of the book.

We had just come from the county council chambers, where there had been a packed room for my presentation about the book. Looking out over the crowd, I saw so many familiar faces who had helped in my reporting, which included my family.

When I'd first come across the sheriff's story, Richard had started introducing me around and let me stay at his house anytime I needed to research. He mailed me copies of the sheriff's books. And when I was on reporting trips, Dad would come down and share my motel room, driving around or visiting with family and friends as I pored over old issues of the *Beaufort Gazette* in the library before feasting on seafood each night.

"I am so proud of you," Dad said. I took a gulp of beer. He'd told me he was proud of me before, it was just that I'd never believed him. His previous professions of pride had never really been credible. This time I could tell he meant it.

"It was standing room only," Mom said. "People were crowding in the back. I couldn't believe it."

I had escaped my repressive home state, ignored all familial advice, and now I was welcomed back here, honored as some sort of hero in the family, because I had brought their world, the world of South Carolina, back to them in a way they'd never seen it before. They felt proud of me, but I also felt proud of myself. I was, in some small sense at least, victorious.

Though I was flush with a feeling of success, something kept bothering me. I'd interviewed quite a few Black people in the area for the book, but only one or two had been at the talk, which was sponsored by the public library. Gullah-Geechee culture was essential to the story that the book told, and I had tried to do it justice, and I was struck with a momentary fear that maybe I had not.

"Your grandmother would be so proud too," Dad said as the server brought the check.

"Yes, she would," Richard said.

"We'd better be getting back home," Dad said. "Long drive."

"Same here," Larry said.

"Yeah," I said. "I am on the radio early tomorrow morning."

We stood out on Bay Street in front of the bar and said goodbye in the cold December wind, and I felt that for the first time I had finally reconciled all the jangling, contradictory pieces of my identity. I had told everyone I was going to be a writer and now I was, even if it was a very minor publication. And though I had rejected my family's advice and the scholarship to USC, I had over recent years become a journalist, or at least a nonfiction writer.

As I watched their taillights disappear, I pulled out a cigarette and lit it. Then I walked back to my motel room.

The next morning I was up early. After a continental breakfast at the motel, I pulled up the address for the small radio station I was going to. It was a Black religious station located in a small house out on the outskirts of town. When I walked in, there were crosses and lambs and other religious iconography scattered about on nearly every surface, in both two and three dimensions. It was dusty, and light eased in through the blinds, strips of black glowing in gold lines. Gospel music was playing softly. The room smelled of incense or perfume. A red sign above a door at the back of that front room read, "ON AIR."

At a commercial break, I entered the studio, which felt extremely hot. I was sweating.

"Ready?" asked the host, a middle-aged Black woman with a silk scarf around her neck.

Sitting in the small radio booth, with a microphone to my mouth, I was vain enough to feel proud to be the one revealing these aspects of Black history, to be telling the story of Dr. Buzzard and all the others. But I also felt a certain sense of uneasiness creeping up under my skin. I figured it was just the typical hesitation or uneasiness that white people have when talking about race. It was as if I was violating some strict taboo.

I proceeded to discuss all the ways that the sheriff had been a friend of the Gullah people until the end, after he'd been voted out of office, and how he'd found meaning in his own life through his practice of hoodoo.

The host seemed fascinated, smiling and nodding and going a bit beyond the questions she'd asked me to send.

When it was over, I walked back out again into the bright, cool morning. The sun glanced off the grass, flaxen with winter, glowing gold. The gravel driveway sparkled. I got into my rental and drove back to my motel, which I had not checked out of yet. I stood in the parking lot smoking a cigarette and looking at the giant oak across the street bent down over the bay.

I walked down the familiar block toward the commercial strip of town until I reached Prince Street and turned. Behind a gate was the former home of Robert Smalls, the great figure of Reconstruction in Beaufort. He had been a five-term congressman, owned multiple newspapers, and wielded a wide-ranging power in the postwar South Carolina Lowcountry, where there was suddenly a large Black voting majority after the passage of the Thirteenth, Fourteenth, and Fifteenth Amendments.

As I looked at the white mansion and its black shutters and wrought-iron gate, I realized what had been nagging at me about the book. I hadn't really taken into account the end of Reconstruction there. I didn't know how it had come about. But when I made the case that Dr. Buzzard, the root doctor, had been the major political power for the local Black community, I was missing something else, something that felt too big to ignore, even if it wasn't directly in the time frame I was covering. This was, after all, where Sherman's field order had freed the enslaved people in 1863. There was a long history of Black politics that had nothing to do with conjure. How could the book fail to take the legacy of Smalls and the Reconstruction era into account altogether?

I recalled the vague story about my great-grandfather helping to redeem the state. By now I knew that "redemption" just meant the overthrow of Reconstruction. I turned and looked down the street, leaflessly stark against the taut skin of the winter sky. No one was out on foot, though the occasional car tooled by, belching small clouds of gray smoke against the cold.

I turned to see Smalls's house again. The great magnolia tree had not yet dropped its leaves, and the ferns crawling up the sandy brick wall around the property were still green. Maybe I would write something about Smalls, I thought, and fill in the pieces that I'd missed. That vague plan helped me minimize the questions I had about my work.

As I strolled Beaufort's wide streets back to the motel, I thought about my student Aaron, who had left high school to deal drugs. He had come from here—or at least his family had, and they had migrated to Baltimore. From teaching the Great Migration, I knew that it was not just economic conditions that had inspired Black southerners to leave and move up North. It was also the terror that white people in the South had inflicted through both Jim Crow laws and vigilante enforcement of extralegal social codes.

I understood then that one man's redemption is another's damnation. But I did not dwell on it.

Back in Baltimore, a website I wrote for helped throw me a big book release party at the Midtown Yacht Club. Lafayette, who was still coming over almost every Sunday for long interviews, played music. People dressed up as witch doctors and in various other wild costumes. A beatboxer performed. I played the banjo and read, attempting to cast a kind of spell.

And all of that led to more work.

I'd published enough stories with the *Baltimore City Paper* that I was invited to the meeting where the editorial staff and some freelancers determined the "Best of Baltimore" and assigned blurbs to various writers. It was the biggest issue of the year, and people took it seriously. All around the city, I saw the yellow-and-black awards hanging proudly on establishment walls.

I was thrilled to be invited. I'd done a couple of cover stories, and the paper liked my work, and I wanted to get a job there more than anything else.

The paper was housed in an old mansion not far from my apartment, but I was disappointed to learn that the meeting was in a nearby art gallery. I wanted to see what it was like at the office. But the firewall between editorial content and the advertising salespeople required that a meeting of this import be held away from the office so the salespeople wouldn't try to influence or snoop on the picks. I loved that seriousness even more than I would have loved going to the office. I rode the creaky, graffitied old elevator up to the gallery. There was a big table in the center of the room and a cooler of beer and bottled water.

"OK, Best Shoes, any ideas?" the white middle-aged editor asked, rushing through the boring categories.

"We did Downtown Locker Room last year, I think," said the white middle-aged art director with a gray ponytail.

"How about Ted's, by the Lexington Market?" I asked, cracking open a beer.

"I've never heard of that," said the dude to my left, the tall white middle-aged staff writer. "What street is it on? Eutaw?"

"No," I said. "Paca."

"Sold," the editor said. "What else do we need for goods and services? Or can we move on to nightlife?"

In addition to the staff writer, the art director, and the editor, the paper's editorial staff boasted a few more Gen X white people. There were, I knew from reading the paper, several Black freelancers, but none of them were in the art gallery that day as we went through the countless categories of superlatives the paper would dish out in September, including those that were backhanded at best, such as "Best Politician in Need of a Slap Upside the Head."

I left the meeting that day with somewhere around a dozen blurbs to write at fifty dollars a pop.

Each of the blurbs was about a hundred words. The week before that issue came out, the *Washington Post* used about the same number of words—ninety-nine, to be exact—to report that my former student Aaron had been murdered.

"A man's body was discovered in the street in the 8100 block of Manson Street at about 9 p.m. Monday. Police said that when officers arrived on the scene, they found the man had suffered trauma to the body."

The story went on to say that Aaron, whose death I'd blithely predicted, had been pronounced dead at the hospital and that police believed he had been shot. There were no leads.

I eventually got a job at the *Baltimore City Paper*. I'd been an editor there for three years when the Baltimore police killed a young Black man named Freddie Gray. He was twenty-five years old—the same age Aaron would have been in 2015, had he lived that long. I had been reporting at the center of the protests for a week, on the front lines, covering skirmishes between cops and residents, and I had never felt so alive.

My eyes were still burning from the flames engulfing police cars and the pepper spray and tear gas filling the air only a few blocks away from where Joe, the paper's photographer, and I stood at his car waiting for our phones to charge at a media staging area where news stations had satellite vans on that explosive spring day.

We'd been in the middle of the mayhem when I got a call from an MSNBC producer asking if I would go on air to talk about what was happening with the riot following Freddie Gray's funeral. Over the past two weeks of covering the growing protests, I'd seen so many waves of parachute reporters coming in from the networks and mischaracterizing things that it felt nice to finally get a chance to share the perspective of someone who had been living here.

Two nights earlier the big protest downtown had gotten intense as a fight started between Boston baseball fans and Black Lives Matter protesters and windows got smashed. The protest finally dispersed, but Joe and I had driven over to the Western District, where we'd found hundreds of cops in riot formation staring down a couple of dozen residents at the edge of Gilmore Homes.

"The empire strikes back," said Joe as we walked up. Like me and most of the paper's staff, he was a middle-aged white guy. He'd grown up in Dundalk, the working-class, conservative white suburb just outside the city, which had been devastated by the closing of the steel mills. Joe was a bulky blue-collar guy, an army veteran who wore a green flak jacket and a black-and-orange Orioles hat.

We were there for about an hour before the cops charged the crowd and, in the process, started stomping Joe as I filmed, screaming, "He's a photographer! He's press!"

Even though I was trying to distinguish Joe from the average resident—who is also protected by the First Amendment—as if it is OK to stomp them, the Black residents rushed to our aid. The video of the attack went viral. We were providing vital information to the city that no one else was getting, I thought. And we were willing to put ourselves in harm's way for it.

After that, we knew it would get worse. The cops were being questioned, and they wanted revenge.

The storm had come a few hours earlier that Monday, after the funeral, when the city closed schools and shut off all public transportation. When kids arrived at the transit hub of Mondawmin Mall, they were met by hundreds of riot cops who began using pepper spray and rubber bullets almost immediately. The kids fought back with rocks and water bottles. That fracas migrated down to the corner of Penn and North, which was now on fire. And Joe and I had been there for all of it. We had witnessed it.

My phone rang. It was the MSNBC producer.

"We're ready to go live," she said.

"Let me bring in Baynard Woods. He's a reporter with the *Baltimore City Paper*," the familiar voice said. I hadn't thought to ask who would be interviewing me, and I knew the voice but couldn't place it.

"Baynard, you were right in the middle of the clashes today, what's the scene now?" the voice asked, and I realized that it was Al Sharpton, the reverend and civil rights activist, interviewing me. I almost laughed at the absurdity of the situation, but instead I hit him with a barrage of language, pouring out the adrenaline that had been building all week.

"We ran over from the office to the mall today. It was a war. It was tactical, with the riot police shooting gas, shooting rubber bullets at the protesters, and the protesters throwing rocks and bricks at them and everyone trying to maneuver, and when we got to the corner right about where Freddie Gray was initially picked up, or spotted by the police when he ran, people were really, really angry and serious. They were flaming police transit vehicles and vans," I said in the middle of a long monologue.

I told Sharpton how the protests had been building for the past week as Baltimore's Black residents decided to rise up against the way police treated them.

"We got a sense, two white guys, what it's like for them in this area every day," I said. "I walked around the neighborhood asking people— everyone said, 'I can't go to the store without being hassled or searched or having to sit on the curb and sit there for an hour while people come by and you're humiliated.' So we saw that. So I wasn't really surprised."

I'd been focusing my attention on West Baltimore for barely two weeks, since police had arrested Freddie Gray and thrown him into the back of a van, severing his spine, on April 12, and already, in my passion, I was an expert, not surprised at the plight of poor Black people living in and around Gilmore Homes.

But I was also starting to think of myself specifically as a white guy now, and recognizing the limitations of that reality. I understood that the facts of my gender and my race would change the way I saw certain issues. But I could go only so far in seeing exactly what was affected or how it was changed. I knew that my whiteness and my masculinity were my own blind spots, and I couldn't know what I couldn't see. That was the problem.

That perspective was at odds, though, with my deeply held view that I needed to be out here covering this. That it was my duty to tell these stories, regardless of my race or my sex. My white skin and press pass afforded me some extra protection against these cops, and I wanted to use it to document what they were doing to poor Black people when they thought no one was watching.

When I finished the interview, I told Joe I needed to get back to the office. It was a Monday night, the night we put the paper to bed so it could be printed on Tuesday and in the bright-yellow boxes on the street on Wednesday morning. I was managing editor by this point, and normally I would have been there all day on a Monday, especially since we had scrapped the entire issue in order to devote it to Freddie Gray coverage, and I felt lucky to have spent so much time out in the field.

When the protests broke out, I was already training my colleague Brandon to take over my role when I left the paper two months later. I'd been working with a production company to develop the story about the sheriff and Dr. Buzzard for TV, and when Will Smith's production company signed on as a partner, I figured it was a good time to get out of the paper before it failed. It had been bought by the *Baltimore Sun*, and I couldn't imagine it even existing two years in the future. Besides, I was burned out.

As I found myself standing there in the middle of the biggest story in the country, a story about the white policing of Black communities, I felt again as if I'd really missed something in my presentation of the sheriff in that book. I'd relied so much on the accounts of the *Beaufort Gazette*, and yet the coverage of Baltimore was showing me how racist and pro-cop the mainstream press was, even today, and I knew that the early-twentieth-century *Gazette* would not have told the truth about race and policing.

But I countered this thought with the idea that the Black Lives Matter movement would make the show we were planning both more relevant and more useful, and I figured that there I could correct my error. And if Will Smith didn't think it was racist, well, who was I to say?

Dad texted me as Joe and I drove back to the newsroom through smoky streets.

Good job, Dad wrote. When you talk so much that Sharpton can't get a word in, that's really something.

Windows all around the paper, in my neighborhood, had been smashed. Downtown was now empty, locked down; the city had an eerie feel. The front door of the *Sun* building was locked, and the security guard came to let us in. When we made it up to the third floor, our small office was full of people. The writers D. Watkins and Lawrence Burney, Black native Baltimoreans, were using the office as a space to work, and to be with other writers, in the craziness of the night. There were some reporters from the *Guardian* using our Wi-Fi in another room, and our staff was all hands on deck trying to pull a new issue together.

My phone rang, and it was a friend who worked as an editor at the *New York Times*. He asked if I knew anyone who could write a story about what was happening. As much as I wanted to be in the *Times* again—I'd had a piece a year earlier when the *Sun* bought the *City Paper*—and as much as seeming like an authority on the city, a frontliner at the protests, mattered to me, I knew it wasn't a job for me, and I said, "Hold on" and handed the phone to D, who actually had a firsthand understanding of the way Baltimore police treated Black men in the city.

I'd been living in the city for five years, and I had never been stopped and frisked. I had never been searched. I had not been pulled over, and I had not been threatened by police. But all of that was an everyday occurrence in East and West Baltimore, where the city's Black majority lives.

I was starting to think of the segregation in the city as apartheid. And I finally understood that my teenage drug arrests did not mean I understood the nature of oppression in America. I knew that I had gotten off easy because I was white. At one point I'd thought that those laws benefited me as a white person because I got off easier than a Black guy. But the racist drug war hurts white people too, whether they get arrested themselves, as I did, or simply share in the loss of resources—social services, transportation, sanitation, and education—sucked up by ballooning police budgets when they could be used for bettering their cities and our nation. White people had it better than Black people when it came to criminalization in the drug war, but we also lost more than we know. Without Baltimore's apartheid system, our city would be so much richer and we all would benefit. One of the great things about the uprising was that it got many white people to take lives of Black people in the city seriously for the first time and that got us out in the streets advocating in solidarity with Black people.

Other than D and Lawrence, everyone in the room was white—our whole staff, including interns, the *Guardian* reporters, everyone. And for the first time, as I handed the phone to D, I realized how much of a problem that was, even as I continued to be praised on social media, essentially for being a white guy who would go into the Black neighborhoods where things were happening.

There would have been no protests if a Black man named Kevin Moore had not filmed and published the video of the police dragging Gray into the back of the van screaming, but still, white people wanted a white filter to reflect and interpret what was happening in Black Baltimore. And I was happy to play that role, if that was what was necessary, but I also knew when to step away. As small as it was, the awareness that I was not at the center of the story, that it was not about me, felt to me like an advance in character.

We worked on the issue of the paper until sunup, when we finally sent it to the printer. Our third-floor office overlooked I-83 as it came into downtown. I walked over to watch the sky turn pink, a celebratory beer in my exhausted hand, as I waited for the final word from the editor that we were good to go.

I saw a caravan of military vehicles rolling into town on I-83, the sky glowing pink behind their khaki desert camo. "Holy fuck, look at this," I said.

The skeleton crew still in the office stood there gawking at what looked like an invasion.

"National Guard coming to enforce the curfew," Brandon said.

"I guess we won't get any sleep tonight," I said.

We were issued official papers that allowed us to be out after the new curfew, but that night, when we were told the media had to remain in a pen, taped off, behind the cops, Joe and I balked. Fuck that. We got heavy doses of tear gas as we stood with the protesters defying the curfew. But there were so many cameras that we left and drove around the neighborhood, where we saw armies of police from other jurisdictions rounding up Black citizens on the street.

We were standing on a dark sidewalk as a unit of armed police from New Jersey ran toward their requisitioned transit bus with a hog-tied Black man. It was horrifying. We photographed and tweeted it.

Wherever shit was popping off, Joe and I were there. But Nicole noticed what was happening. I had already lost the self-awareness I had gained in the office that night when I passed the phone.

"It is not about you," she said on one of the rare occasions we ate together that week.

"I know it's not," I protested, glancing at Twitter on my phone.

"I don't know if you do, sometimes," she said. "I know what you're doing is important, but you can't let it go to your head."

During one of the early protests, I'd ordered her to go home, and she'd gotten pissed off, and she was angry that I had a pass that allowed me to ignore the curfew, which she had to abide by. I thought it was natural: because I was a reporter and because I was covering the city, I should be able to be there and witness what was happening in the streets.

But I knew what she meant. I loved this story, even if it was a story that, at its heart, was about Black suffering. The fact that I saw it as "a story" to love was the problem, and I knew that Nicole was right and that I needed to make sure I didn't enjoy myself too much. But I also knew I needed to report on this important movement that felt like the start of a revolution.

That feeling came to a head the day that the state's attorney announced charges against six officers who had been involved in Gray's death.

There was a march that afternoon, heading uptown. Thousands of people crowded the streets. Joe and I had both gotten good at maneuvering through crowds, but we knew we would not be able to make it to Penn North before the march arrived. We wanted to be there to capture that moment. Joe disappeared into a crowd. I started talking to a guy with a sign reading, "No Justice, No Peace."

An old pickup truck pulled up to the corner on a side street; Joe was standing in its bed, his hat on backward, snapping photos.

"Hop on," he said.

"I'll get y'all there," said the driver, who I suddenly realized was an artist I'd once written about.

I hopped on. We cut through some side streets and at North Avenue met back up with the march and got in the middle of it so that the bed of the truck, where Joe snapped pictures and I tweeted words about the scene, felt like a parade float. Or, even more, like a triumphant military procession.

"All night, all day, we will fight for Freddie Gray," people chanted as the truck eased along North Avenue, in the Arts District where we both caroused and which we covered. A few white people standing along the side of the road cheered us.

We passed a bar where I hung out. I saw Nicole amid the crowd, just as she was walking in the door.

"Be right back," I said. I hopped off the back of the truck and dashed through the thick crowd. I opened the door. The bar was cool, dark, and chaotic with an overflow of people from the march looking for a bathroom or a quick beer. I saw Nicole with a group of our friends at the bar. I walked up to her, grabbed her shoulder, turned her, and kissed her. Then I took a gulp of her beer, ran back out the door—to a few more cheers, this time for the kiss—and ran behind the truck, hopping up into the bed as it lurched forward.

It was one of the most glorious moments in my life, the closest thing I'd ever experience to something like the liberation of Paris, but even as I felt it, the spring sun against my cheeks, the wind in my beard, I knew I would never tell anyone that. As Nicole kept reminding me, none of this was about me. I was just bearing witness to what was really important. A man had been murdered by the police. This was not about my career or my Twitter followers. It was about telling the truth, sacrificing my ego and my comfort for something greater.

That's what I would tell people, at least. And it was true, for the better part of me. But it was also true that my ego gloried in the front-row view of history and the feeling of importance it bestowed upon me.

All my life I'd seen myself as the hero, with everyone else playing supporting roles, and that was what I did in that moment, even though I knew a real hero would not see the world that way, so I resolved not to see myself as a hero in order to be more heroic.

I knew I'd made the right decision when I read D's story in the *Times*.

It was so much more insightful, more powerful, than anything I could have done.

As I covered the horrible conditions in Baltimore, I was freed from the responsibility of truly implicating myself in the apartheid system I saw around me because I cast the cops as the bad guys and I was against the cops. I was not like them. I was innocent, I thought, even as I recognized my guilt.

I couldn't square what I'd written about the "Witchdoctor Sheriff" with what I saw as the reality of the white policing of Black communities. I wasn't certain if my book was racist, but I was sure that I had been naive.

I had painted the sheriff in the same way I saw myself, with a mixture of heroism and innocence. In this, after a Black uprising against racist policing, I could see the contours of my whiteness clearly—but the focus would not last. Still, I realized, however briefly, that whiteness was a compilation of the stories we tell about ourselves and to ourselves. Whiteness brought together all the stories that cast us as innocent heroes. This made me think that maybe we could tell different stories, changing the meaning of our whiteness for the future. And we can start by sometimes passing the phone.

Chapter 22

MY SLOW JOURNEY TOWARD UNDERSTANDING how my whiteness worked underwent a radical change in pace and focus on June 17, 2015, as Nicole and I were packing our bags for a flight to South Carolina the following morning.

We'd been going to stay with her family at a house near Myrtle Beach for the past decade, and my parents, who were close with her family now, had started coming to spend a few days as well. But over the last several years, when I was busy at the paper, I'd come late, left early, or worked while we were there. This would be my first real vacation in years. And I needed it.

It was only a month after the Baltimore Uprising had tamped itself down into the long wait for the trials of the six officers charged in the death of Freddie Gray, and I was exhausted from the intensity of the coverage.

We wore little but bathing suits at the beach, so the bulk of our thoughts about packing revolved around which books to bring. My mind was locked in a debate between *Don Quixote* and Tom Wolfe's *The Electric Kool-Aid Acid Test* when I heard a report on the NPR station playing in the background that there had been a mass shooting at Charleston's most historic Black church, the Emanuel African Methodist Episcopal Church.

I forgot about my books and logged on to Twitter. Details were scarce. When police released an image of the shooter entering the church, I was chilled. The guy in the picture could have been a slightly less well-adapted version of my younger self. It was as if part of the little bowl-cut boy I'd been, the boy who was raised on stories of the Civil War and rebel pride, had broken off from me and grown up raging about our repressed history. Dylann Roof, as police identified the shooter, seemed to me to be a monster made up of everything that I had repressed about what it means to be white.

This initial impression was heightened as more information dripped out. Roof had grown up in Lexington, South Carolina, only ten miles from the house we'd left when Dad lost his job. When reporters discovered Roof's website, the Last Rhodesian, there were pictures of him at historic sites connected with slavery in South Carolina, waving the same kind of souvenir rebel flags I'd carried as a kid. All of the history that had been whitewashed—the country's hundreds of years of enslavement, a terrorist campaign to overthrow Reconstruction, and the Jim Crow apartheid regime that had followed—was not only acknowledged but celebrated by Roof. To him, the plantation concentration camps we had dehistoricized and turned into tourist sites and wedding venues were sacred representations of the racist vision South Carolina was founded on. Roof had harvested the history we'd discarded and made its inherent horror apparent.

In that first flush of information, I felt personally responsible for Roof's actions in a way I had never felt responsible for the actions of a stranger before. A little later, I read his manifesto with horror.

"I have no choice. I am not in the position to, alone, go into the ghetto and fight. I chose Charleston because it is most historic city in my state, and at one time had the highest ratio of blacks to Whites in the country," he wrote. "We have no skinheads, no real KKK, no one doing anything but talking on the internet. Well someone has to have the bravery to take it to the real world, and I guess that has to be me."

I thought of Grandmother Woods telling me about the large Black majority in the Lowcountry and the fear it had engendered in the white minority. I thought of my slaveholding ancestors in Charleston and my skinhead friend in high school.

How had this kid who'd grown up ten miles from me arrived at this place? I wondered, even as the outlines of his trajectory became clear. In the manifesto, he wrote that he had not been raised in a racist home environment, but that the internet had radicalized him, that the Trayvon Martin case "prompted me to type in the words 'black on White crime' into Google, and I have never been the same since that day."

One wrong Google search is all it takes, when the soil for hate has been fertilized by a lifetime of propaganda for a bowdlerized whiteness. When I was young, I'd had the impression that it wasn't easy for my friend Glenn to get his racist literature from David Duke. But in 2012, when Roof typed in "black on White crime," he'd come to the Council of Conservative Citizens, an organization that attempted to legitimize racism in a way very similar to Duke's NAAWP. It was part of a self-validating circle of hateful sites. Discovering it, by Roof's own account, was the defining event in his trajectory toward mass murder.

Roof was the return of everything we "good" white people had repressed, everything we felt we could just wish away. By pretending to be color blind, by hoping to be postracial, we had ceded the floor to the white supremacists anytime a troubled kid did a Google search about whiteness.

I stayed up all night that first night writing an essay in which I addressed my whiteness and its history for the first time in any real way. I acknowledged, for the first time, that my ancestors were the kinds of people who'd put heads on pikes. And I knew that my failure to previously acknowledge the hundreds of years of these atrocities had helped produce people like Dylann Roof.

The *Washington Post* was interested in my essay. The editor, who was also white, asked me to be specific about a time when I'd allowed a racist remark to slide, when I had not stepped up, when I had been racist. A lifetime's worth of whiteness flooded my mind, but I fumbled around for something and settled on a weak admission of professional obligation, admitting to ignoring subtly racist remarks made by people I wanted to get information out of as a reporter.

I finished the edits in the morning, and we went to the airport and caught our flight to Myrtle Beach, where Nicole's family would pick us up.

The story was out when we landed.

I read it rapidly, anxiously, standing there in the airport with tourists in Hawaiian shirts and baseball caps streaming past me as if in a dream. When I opened my email, I saw dozens of new messages, most of them attacking my story. The first one I clicked on even questioned my whiteness, noting that I looked Jewish in my photo on the website.

The comments section was even worse. Women I worked with got vile comments all the time, but this was the first time that I, a white man, had been told to go kill myself—because I was questioning whiteness.

Nicole's mom picked us up. We would go to the beach house the next morning, and Mom and Dad would join us in a few days. Dad sent an email to family members linking to my story and telling them to "judge for yourselves." It was obvious he hated my conclusions but couldn't help but feel pride at my accomplishment.

I wanted to go to Charleston. I felt a need to go, partly for professional reasons—I wanted to compare the way Charleston responded to the murder of Clementa C. Pinckney, Cynthia Hurd, Susie Jackson, Ethel Lee Lance, Depayne Middleton-Doctor, Tywanza Sanders, Daniel Simmons, Sharonda Coleman-Singleton, and Myra Thompson—all Black people— with the way Baltimore had responded to the murder of Freddie Gray. But there was something a lot deeper and more basic than that. I hurt and needed to be there to grieve.

Nicole's mom let me borrow her car, and I drove two hours to Charleston for the mayor's vigil for the slain churchgoers. As the tires spun over the Ashley River on the new sparkling white suspension bridge, the sweeping cords rising to white points in the sky, they looked to me like the outline of an invisible Klan hood, and I wondered if that is what my whiteness is: a Klan hood that the wearer can't see.

I knew that Roof had also driven this same route into town with weapons in his car, whiteness in his mind, and murder in his heart. I wasn't sure why I needed to retrace this course, to track the steps of this killer, to go to Charleston tonight, but I knew I needed to be there.

The North American slave regime was centered in Charleston. Edisto, where my grandmother's family lived, was one of the richest plantation areas supporting the nearby city's economy of crops and human bondage, and as I tooled through the traffic clogging the sorrowful streets down-town, near the church, I realized that this was where my ancestors would have come to buy and sell the humans they enslaved. Every street name, every statue represented a slaver.

Passing through this now-gruesome landscape, I contemplated the logic of the massacre. Roof had said he had gone to Charleston because it had once had the largest Black majority in the country. But it had had the largest Black majority because people like my family imported and then "bred," often through rape, a vast Black population over whom they felt entitled to exert absolute control in order to extract absolute wealth.

Roof also chose to massacre members of Emanuel AME church, known as Mother Emanuel in Charleston's Black community, because it was founded by Denmark Vesey, who had led a revolt against the slavocracy in 1822. Someone snitched and the revolt was crushed, Vesey was executed, the church burned, all much to the relief, I am sure, of my slaveholding ancestors who profited off Black pain. They rightly assumed that Vesey had wanted to overthrow their totalitarian system. And though Vesey's revolt was brought down by a snitch, the totalitarian system was ultimately overthrown around forty years later—and white people like Roof, like my ancestors, have been clawing and fighting and scheming and lying and killing to bring it back ever since.

I parked in a downtown parking garage and walked out of its neon lights onto the crowded street. I was struck by the way the city's mood seemed split. There was a sorrowful air to individual people and groups passing by on their way to the arena at College of Charleston, where the memorial would be held, and yet the crowd as a whole had a collective carnivalesque feel due to the influx of news crews and television cameras, everything bubbling with energy.

In front of the gleaming white facade of Mother Emanuel, where the news crews all had their trucks set up, I saw DeRay Mckesson, the Black Lives Matter activist who had become famous for his tweets from Ferguson, Missouri, during the uprising there. We'd met in Baltimore, out in front of the barricade at the Western District police station, and recognized each other on the street here in Charleston.

"Hey, what are you doing here?" he asked, surprised to see me.

"My family is from here," I said. "I feel an obligation."

I asked him some questions for a story I planned to write, but as he talked, I noticed a white guy behind me butting into the conversation. The more I ignored him, the louder the white guy got.

"There are things like the Confederate flag that serve as symbols of hate that are deeply embedded into the fabric of this place," DeRay said.

"You're a liar," the white guy yelled. He had white hair covered in part by the American flag bandanna wrapped around his head. He had a sign that read "MSLSD" and "Communist News Network."

"The flag wasn't a problem until people made a big deal out of it," he said. "Just because other groups misuse it doesn't mean it's hateful at all."

The white man seemed desperate to engage DeRay, but just as he finished this spiel, he noticed Chris Hayes beginning to broadcast for MSNBC behind us and turned to wave his flags and heckle, hoping to get on camera.

As I drove back up the coast that night, the white guy's words stuck with me. I realized that for every white person like me who felt that Roof's massacre indicted their whiteness, there were dozens who believed it justified theirs. I could imagine all the casually racist white people now saying, "See, I'm not racist. I don't go shooting up Black churches or anything."

As the headlights cut through the dark night on Highway 17, I started to think about what Dad had told me about how his grandfather Dr. I. M. Woods had murdered a Black man because he couldn't accept that the

Wo-ah was over and was trying to "redeem" the state. Rather than seeing the story as some picaresque adventure, as I had twenty years earlier, I now saw it as a precursor to Roof's attack. In Roof, I could see my great-grandfather's face for the first time.

When Dad got to the beach three days later, I asked him about it as we sat on the screened porch.

"You told me about your grandfather killing a Black man," I said. "Do you remember anything else about it?"

The leaves of a palm tree scraped against the screen in the wind. The chains holding up the hammock that Nicole lay in, reading, creaked. The surf crashed against the sand below us as a cloud passed over the sun.

"Daddy didn't tell me much," Dad said, his beard a stark white in the bright light, his cheeks flushed a rosy pink. "He just told me that granddaddy had killed a Black man after the Wo-ah and had to escape the state and cool down for a couple years in Texas and that's why he named Daddy Hernando."

"I thought about that when I was driving back from Charleston," I said. Dad looked off at the horizon.

"That what he did was not that much different than what Dylann Roof did," I said.

"What about all of the white people who are killed by Blacks every year?"

"What?"

"It doesn't mean that every Black person in the country is responsible when a Black man kills white people," he said. "So why should we be responsible for what Roof did? It was terrible, horrible, reprehensible— just like a crime if a Black person kills a white family or something."

I was flooded with frustration and anger. I took a gulp from my beer.

"Because he said he did it in our name. Because my great-grandfather did something similar and then became a hero for doing it and ended up in the legislature, and the fact that whatever it was that he actually did was erased and covered over might have something to do with what Roof did," I said. "Because I was taught, like him probably, that the South was noble, and the Yankees were evil and they were the ones that turned the enslaved people against their kindly masters—those are the kinds of stories that y'all passed on to me."

"What about someone like Al Sharpton?" he said. "You were on his show and he openly hates white people. How is that different?"

"I can't believe this," I said. "We're talking about a massacre that happened a couple hours from here, in the place where your family comes from, the place you taught me to be proud to be from, and the kid who did it grew up in basically the same place I did, and he went in and killed nine people, and you're asking me about Al Sharpton and how that is different."

"Well, isn't hate hate?" he asked.

"No," I said. "It's not. White supremacy is hate with an army and a navy. The police who killed Freddie Gray in Baltimore were part of the same system as Dylann Roof here. They are all coming out of the slave system that we've never recognized or acknowledged."

"That's crazy," he said with a theatrical laugh that infuriated me.

"He went to slave sites and took pictures of himself there," I said. "Literally."

"And he is terrible," Dad said.

Nicole got up and walked away, leaving the hammock swinging in her wake. I could tell she was annoyed. She wasn't afraid to argue, but she didn't want to waste her vacation with this.

"But he was connecting it to the larger culture," I said. "I mean, you went to segregated schools and—"

"But we were the minority on our street. The only white family, and we were about as poor as anyone else," he said.

"But legally, there was a great chasm between you and your Black neighbors. Every door said 'White' or 'Colored' above it, and the *Brown* case, which started in your town, ruled that separate was not equal because of the Black schools' deplorable conditions. It's still called the freakin' corridor of shame," I said, my voice rising far above the surf, like a big wave ready to crash.

"But white kids also go to those schools now," he said.

"The few who don't go to segregation academies," I said.

"The Obama girls go to private schools," he said. "Is that a segregation academy? Or what about Chelsea Clinton?"

"Goddamn it, Dad," I said, shaking. "Why do you always do this? We can't talk about anything without you just saying what about something else."

"Well, how is it different?" he asked.

"I'm trying to talk about Dylann Roof," I said.

"Well, he went to the same public school as the Blacks in Lexington, didn't he?" he asked.

"Oh my God."

"And you did too."

"That's my point," I said. "Everything I was taught in South Carolina is on a continuum with Roof."

"That is crazy," he said. "Most white people aren't going into places and shooting them up. A lot more Black people—"

"Just stop," I said, getting up from the rocking chair so that it tilted back, almost tipping, and then rocked forward with an aggressive lurch on its curved timber legs.

"I need another beer," I said.

Even in the face of death, it was the same thing he always did, a constant dance of deflection that pushed meaning away for the sake of argument itself. As I walked from the humid porch into the air-conditioned kitchen where the beer cooler was, I realized this was the logic of whiteness. Always deflect and defer and change the subject when your innocence is questioned, your power noted. Whiteness is like a chameleon, camouflaging its own power in order to maintain its simultaneous sense of innocence.

"Good God," Nicole said, walking out of the bathroom. "I couldn't take it anymore."

"I know," I said.

"Want to go to the beach?" she asked.

When we walked outside, my chair, empty now beside Dad, was still rocking.

"We're going to the beach," I said.

"I think I'll make a sandwich," he said. "And then maybe take a nap."

I scooped up my copy of *The Electric Kool-Aid Acid Test*, whose cover had been wilted soft by the salt air.

I felt a little better as we walked down the hot, weathered gray boards extending out over the dunes, speckled with the green and gold of sea oats shimmering in the wind.

The tide was coming in, and the waves demolished the day's sandcastles spread out across the strand.

I settled down into my canvas chair in the umbrella's shade a few yards from the waterline and just sat watching the white foam lap a little closer to my feet each time. The other white people splayed out on towels or splashing in the surf now all seemed suspect. There were no Black people on this section of the beach, and I thought of Atlantic Beach only a few miles north, and I figured it must be by design.

"You've already worked a lot," Nicole said. "You really need to try to relax. You don't have to argue with your dad while you're on vacation."

"If he's saying racist shit, I do," I said.

"I'm not saying you shouldn't do that," she said. "But you were the one that brought it up in the first place."

"I know," I said. "It is obsessing me. I feel like this entire state is haunted with the totalitarian hatred that has defined it for so long, and it almost physically hurts to be here right now."

"I know," she said, and took my hand across the small chasm of sand between our chairs. After a minute she bent over and reached into the cooler at the base of the umbrella and handed me a beer.

"Thanks," I said. "I'm going to read a minute and then I'm going to go try to catch some waves."

I had been wanting to reread *Electric Kool-Aid*, Tom Wolfe's book about the Merry Pranksters that I had loved in high school, in order to study the literary technique, but I had decided on it, over the *Quixote*, after news of the shooting broke, partly because I recalled thinking of it as an antidote to Glenn's white supremacism back in high school. When he told me about David Duke, I'd thought, since he also liked acid, I could turn him on to the Pranksters and he might see a different light.

I opened it up to the page I had folded to mark my place, a good ways into the book already, where the Merry Pranksters are holding the Acid Tests—the multimedia acid-fueled happenings where the Grateful Dead had first played. I read on as Wolfe detailed a conversation between Jerry Garcia, singer and guitar player for the Dead, and the Black guy who let them use the hall where the Acid Tests occurred, and I stopped cold when I saw that Wolfe called the landlord "Big Nig."

What the fuck? How had I missed that?

"Big Nig stares at Garcia with the deepest look of hip soul authority you can imagine," Wolfe writes with acid disdain for the Black man, going on to explain how the landlord tells the stoned Garcia that he hadn't charged them to use the venue but that people needed to kick in so he can pay the rent.

"A freaking odd thought, that one. A big funky spade looking pathetic and square. For twenty years in hip life, Negroes never even looked square. They were the archetypical soul figures. But what is Soul, or Funky, or Cool, or Baby—on the new world of ecstasy, the All-one," Wolfe wrote.

"What's wrong?" Nicole asked from her low-slung beach chair beside me, my face reflected in the lenses of her sunglasses. "You are scowling."

"I can't believe I never even noticed how racist this is," I said. "It's like the whole hippie movement was an attempt to create a specifically white counterculture."

I'd been noticing hints of this throughout my rereading of the book, but with this passage it became glaringly obvious. During the previous generations, the way a white person became "hip" was to mimic Black dress and behavior; from the Beats to Elvis, hipness was a matter of appropriating Black culture as what Norman Mailer called "the White Negro."

But here the Merry Pranksters, as protohippies, rejected that appropriation and attempted to create a new form of hipness with a broader appropriation of American Indian and Asian spiritual traditions and fashion. And because they felt they no longer needed the approval of "cool" Black people, they blithely dismissed the Civil Rights struggle as somehow square.

"The thing that gets me is how I just didn't even see it," I said. "I loved this book, and I thought all of these people in it were supercool. And I didn't even notice the blatant racism. And no one else seems to have noticed it either. When people talk about Wolfe, they don't mention it. It makes me wonder what I am missing now."

"My dad and I used to talk about that," she said. "He used to say, 'Most white people who lived in the slave system didn't realize it was wrong. What is that issue that the future will see as so obviously bad but that we are missing?'"

I looked at her beside me in her red one-piece bathing suit, gray tortoise-shell sunglasses, and floppy straw hat, and I thought how grateful I was to be with her, to have someone to try to work out all of these complexities with. Our awarenesses were growing together as we each worked in our own fields toward greater understanding of the world, even when it meant we indicted ourselves. Our younger selves seemed almost silly now in our search for authenticity and roots in our southern whiteness, but that only meant that we had grown, and that made me love her more.

"But I think they did know it was monstrous," I said. "I think they had to know. But they distorted their view of the world so badly in order to justify it that we still haven't recovered from their contortions. Once you see it, white supremacy is obviously everywhere."

We sat there a minute in silence, sipping on our drinks.

"Put on some more sunscreen," Nicole said, handing me the plastic tube.

Everyone over forty in our families had had some kind of cancerous growth cut or burned or frozen from their skin, many of them with great regularity, and she had some precancerous growths already and was careful in the sun.

"Our white skin will even kill us," she added as a joke.

"Skin cancer is like a cost of very pale people coming to colonize these very hot climates," I said.

I stared at the swelling waves. They were choppy, and I needed to feel as if I were beating something or being beaten by it. I remembered when I was little, playing in the surf with Dad and punching the waves.

"I'm going to go fight the waves," I said, getting up from my chair. The lowering sun stretched my shadow across the sand as I stood.

"I'll be here," Nicole said, and picked up the book she was reading about the soul singer Tammy Tyrell.

I jogged off toward the rumbling ocean, looking at its shores for the first time as those to which my ancestors had shipped thousands of Africans. I stepped in the cold water as the foam remnants of a wave rushed over my feet. As I walked farther out, the surf rushed around me and then started breaking, swells coming at me with their white crests. I've loved the ocean my entire life, especially in Edisto where my grandmother lived and which I saw as a foundation for who I am, but this time I saw the reality of that foundation and I swung at it. I punched it with all my might, fully aware that I really wanted to punch myself, my dad, my grandfather, and that which is tied and buried within the roots of who I am.

When we returned to the house an hour later, Dad had gone to the store, and I was relieved not to feel the responsibility to fight with him as I cracked open another cold drink.

I learned that week that sometimes whiteness is murder. The rest of the time, it is a cover-up, which is much quieter but still violent in its silencing of everything but bluster, its silencing of all the moral self that makes the murder possible and even inevitable.

Chapter 23

I PUSHED MY PLATE AWAY, a few potatoes scattered around the remnants of a burrito. Mom was sitting beside me, and across from us were Dad and my brother Chris. We were at a chain restaurant in a suburb outside of Charlotte, where Mom and Dad had moved to be near Chris's kids.

"You know me," my brother said. "I've never even voted before—but I think he might be what we need to shake things up."

"That's crazy," I said. "Shaking things up means deporting immigrants, threatening reporters. It's just crude racism."

"No, now hold on, now," Dad said. "There's nothing racist about him. He might be crude and crass, but that doesn't mean he's racist."

"What the hell?" I said. "He started his campaign by calling Mexicans rapists and murderers."

The server walked up to the table, her glasses reflecting the neon light on the window behind us.

"Another beer, please," I said.

"Me too," my brother said.

This was our third or fourth pint. We didn't see each other much, but at least we had alcohol in common. I could feel myself getting buzzed, and I knew how things would go. Dad would keep pushing and everything would escalate until we were all yelling, or everybody but Chris, who never yelled.

At first Dad had resisted the call of Donald Trump, rejecting his bombastic and brutish demeanor in favor of the less blatant fascism of Ted Cruz. But he loved white masculinity—and hated Hillary Clinton—enough to overcome his distaste and embrace the failed New York City developer-cum-wannabe-fascist-dictator after he became the Republican Party's candidate.

"He has a lot of faults, but they all do. And at least we know what we're getting with him," Dad said.

"But what we're getting, what he's telling us we are getting, is racism and violence and an attack on the free press," I said.

"That's just campaigning," Dad said, taking a sip of tea from a red plastic cup.

"You just said he meant what he said and now you're saying the opposite," I said. "That's just like him."

The candidacy of Donald Trump forced a divide among white people because it was so clearly based on a chauvinistic and racist vision for America. It was as if the meaning of whiteness was on the ballot. Supporting him was supporting a certain version of ourselves as white people, and so to those of us who didn't support him, it hit like a slap to realize that loved ones had fallen under his sway.

This kind of divide was happening in white families around the country, I was sure. It was an important conversation to have, but I didn't give a shit right now. I couldn't wait to get home.

I'd flown into Charlotte three days earlier, but Greenville was the real destination. Nanny was starting to sink into serious dementia, and Mom and I had driven the hour and a half to Greenville, where Nanny lived in a small townhouse in a gated community for the elderly. She would not be able to live there alone much longer.

Mom and Aunt Gaile went to the store, and I sat with Nanny that afternoon in her rococo room, her case of Hummel figurines between us, these little idealized emblems of whiteness frolicking upon her dustless shelves with bright-blue eyes, blond hair, and ruddy ceramic cheeks.

"I picked the wrong man," she said, somewhat suddenly beginning a story that I had not expected. She told me that she had been in love with another boy when she met Summey. The other boy was better. He came from a better family, had more prospects. People made fun of Summey for being poor, and she felt sorry for him, and that pity mixed with a primal attraction—she said she liked his butt. On top of that, we all knew he could be awfully persuasive when he wanted to be, and she left the other boy for him. But the other man never quit loving her. Even after she married Summey, the man would send her a letter every year, on her birthday.

"'I'm still waiting,' that's what it said. Every year," she said. "The same note. Even after he married the town slut. He married her because he knew he would not love anyone who he married. It might as well be her. And even after he married her, he would find a way to get the letter to me."

She was looking directly at me, with an intensity I'd never seen in her before.

"The same note every year," she said. "Until he got Alzheimer's. He got it early. When he was forty-five, then I never heard from him again."

I couldn't believe she was telling me this.

"I tried to leave him," she told me. "He hit me and I wasn't going to take that and I had everything arranged, but then he found out and he said he had a dozen men in town he could pay to say they slept with me and I would never see the children again."

"I'm so sorry," I told her.

The image of her sitting there like that, her romanticized German peasant Hummel figurines beside her, still haunted me as I argued with my parents at the restaurant in their suburb two days later.

"I can't believe you're falling for all that shit," I said, my voice rising above the din of the plates and cutlery. "The whole 'Make America great again' thing is, at best, wanting to return to the good ol' boy system Summey enjoyed, but more likely either the Jim Crow you grew up under or even slavery."

"I like that he says he is going to stop these protests," Mom said. "They can peacefully protest, but what happened here was just shameful."

"What, that the police murdered a Black man?" I said.

"No, even if they did. You have to follow the law. You can't be throwing rocks and blocking traffic and destroying property," Mom said. "They should throw the book at those people."

"And not the cops who shot Keith Lamont Scott," I said. "They shouldn't have to follow the law."

"He had a gun," Dad said.

"He did not," I said. "They had a warrant for someone else. Something totally unrelated."

"People should protest peacefully, but they have to obey the laws," Mom said.

"So should the police," I said.

"Another beer," Chris said as the server came by.

"I'll have one too," I said, taking a big gulp.

I was furious that they had no idea what actually happened at Black Lives Matter protests but acted as if they were the authorities.

"I wasn't here for those protests—but I was in Baltimore, and I can tell you it was the cops who made it worse," I said, anger spilling through the spaces between my words. "They escalate the situations."

"People didn't have to go out and smash stuff," Chris said.

"No, and the cops didn't have to shoot a guy either," I said.

"We need respect for law and order," Mom said. "And why does it have to be Black Lives Matter? Don't all lives matter?"

"Mom!" I exclaimed. "You're not serious?"

"I hate Trump," Dad said. "But Hillary is so much worse that I have to go for him."

"I agree that the mainstream Democrats suck," I said. "I don't like Clinton at all. But she is infinitely better than the buffoonish Mussolini that Trump wants to be."

"She is the most corrupt person who has ever lived," Dad said. "Although Obama and Susan Rice and a few others come close."

"Now that's probably not true," Chris said. "Obama has not really had any corruption scandals that I know of."

"So what past do you want to go back to?" I asked. "To slavery or segregation or what?"

"I'd be fine with Reagan," Dad said.

"What, when big mergers happened and you lost your job?" I said.

"What would you like—Black rule Reconstruction?" he said.

"Yeah," I said.

"Reconstruction was a terrible period," he said. "Our family lost everything."

"If everything is the people they thought they owned," I said.

"But also the land," he said. "Some of it. And the silver. They had to bury it and hide it to keep any."

I told them about a story I'd written just before the South Carolina primary about the legacy of Reconstruction. Robert Smalls, who had escaped from slavery to serve in the Union Navy throughout the war, bought the house in which his family had been enslaved. The man who had enslaved Smalls's family was dead, but his wife showed up at the door one day with dementia, and Smalls let her stay.

"That was very kind," Mom said. "They must have been kind to him."

"No," I said. "You can't think someone is property and be kind to them."

"You can't judge the past by our standards," Dad said.

"But hold on, let me finish," I said. "Smalls let the woman stay—her name was Mary McKee, and I think, way back, she might even be related to us. But every day, she forgot about the reality, that she didn't own the house. That she didn't own him. And to me, that's what race relations seem like for the last hundred and fifty years. White people forgetting the history when it's convenient for us."

"That's ridiculous," my brother said, draining his pint glass.

"I have to agree," Mom said.

"And you don't think Reconstruction was corrupt?" Dad said.

"You mean when they were trying to create a democracy in the South for the first time after hundreds of years of totalitarian rule," I said.

"That's ridiculous," Dad said. "It was not totalitarian."

"Making it illegal for the majority of the population to read, to play drums, to congregate, to move around without passes, to remain with their families—if Communists did something a tenth as bad, you'd never shut up about it," I said.

"That's the way the Yankees saw it," Dad said.

"We should just go home," Mom said.

"That's a good idea," Dad said.

"The check, please," my brother said.

He covered the check and we got up to go, all of us on edge.

"I think I'm somewhere between Bay and Dad," Chris said when we were waiting for the server to come back with his card.

"Me too," Mom said.

To me, Dad's statements implied an embrace of fascist right-wing white supremacy, but like Trump, he always kept a rhetorical distance from his own remarks, reserving the right to scold anyone who was too dim to see he was joking.

After a quick stop at Chris's house, we were heading back toward my parents' place, frustrated and tired. Dad was driving, and I was in the seat beside him, while Mom sat in the back.

"Trump is against abortion," she said. "Don't you think Jesus would be willing to tolerate some bad behavior for that?"

"Mom," I said. "You can't do that. First, I support abortion rights. And I don't believe in Jesus. You know that. But you always act like I do and then— you're already doing it. You can't just cry when I tell you what I think."

"This conversation stops now," Dad said, attempting to exercise his outdated authority as the head of the household.

"No, it doesn't," I said. "That's not something you get to determine."

"I can't believe that you don't believe in Jesus," Mom said, tears running down her face. "I thought you just didn't like churches."

"That's because you always bombard me with your religious beliefs, but you won't listen if I ever try to tell you mine," I yelled. "Or you cry. And that's fine, but you just can't talk to me about it anymore."

262

"I said this conversation stops here," Dad said, pulling into the driveway.

"And I said this is a conversation between me and Mom that she started, and I just want to make sure this doesn't happen again," I said.

We got out of the car and Mom hugged me, in tears.

"OK," she sobbed. "I won't talk to you about Jesus anymore."

When we got inside, Dad turned on Fox News. I went upstairs, exasperated by how hard it was to have a simple conversation about anything that mattered—and especially about race—with my family. Whether they found theirs in the Bible or on Fox News, we lived in different realities that, at best, overlapped. I had come from them. They had given me my earliest definitions and values. And yet I saw the world so differently from them now. It was almost funny. I had tried for most of my life to be different, and now that I could so clearly see the difference, I was shocked, sometimes wondering who the hell these people were.

But I knew it was nothing new. I remembered a time back in the eighties when Mom would repeat Summey's claim that "they ought to just put drug dealers against the wall and shoot them." Whiteness shares a frontier with fascism. Or rather, fascism is the obvious form of whiteness. Capitalism is its more subtle, less escapable cousin. Trump had given permission to all the white people who had kept statements like Summey's to themselves to let whatever racist thoughts they had rip.

I was furious and wanted to yell out to them that I was scheduled to have a vasectomy in a couple of weeks, just before the election. I hadn't yet told them. Neither Nicole nor I had any desire to have kids, and she'd been carrying the burden of our birth control for over a decade, and I felt that it was my turn.

I decided to tell them in the morning, calmly, before I left. But I was going to be clear. I was not asking for advice. The decision was made.

The alt-right was obsessed with "white genocide" or the "replacement theory"—arguing that white people would die out without aggressive nationalist action. The more I learned about my family's history, the less I wanted to have any part of passing it on. I was content to do my part to let whiteness wither away.

I knew Mom and Dad would be disappointed, but I was forty-four years old and they already had two grandkids, so they must have seen it coming. Just before they drove me to the airport the next day, I brought it up.

"Hey, so I wanted to let y'all know that I'm scheduled to get a vasectomy in a couple of weeks," I said.

Dad nodded. Mom looked down.

"Neither one of us wants to have kids. I just don't think the world is in any condition to bring a kid into at this point," I said.

"Well, it's your choice," Mom said. "But that's not a good reason."

"There are a lot of reasons," I said.

"You would be a good father," Dad said.

"A great one," Mom said.

"But I understand," he said. Two of his brothers had long, happily childless marriages, and I felt he really did understand the decision to avoid reproduction.

"How could I bring a kid into a world where Trump might win?" I said.

I was joking, but there was something serious behind the joke. If Trump could bring out such hatred in relatively stable and prosperous times, I could only imagine how grim a future where climate change limited resources would be. Trump showed me how susceptible most of us were to racist propaganda because of the emotional level on which it operates.

What I didn't tell them was that I could see myself in Trump, or Trump in myself. It was the part of me I hated on display on every station all the time, the worst parts of my whiteness and masculinity personified. But those parts, I realized, were what my parents, and especially my dad, liked about him. Conversations white people were having about Trump were so emotionally charged because we were talking about ourselves.

Watching Trump debate Clinton, I could see my whiteness play out in human form. The way I sometimes talked over women, he talked over her. In Trump, I could see the way my own use of rhetoric, like Dad's, lost all reason when I argued, overwhelmed by the desire to win.

I thought more and more about how Trump was a referendum on whiteness, a way in which white America was going to decide which version of itself it was going to be. My negative identification with Trump may have been a little extreme, but he increasingly seemed like the naked projection of the collective sum of white desire and ambition onto a single person rendering all our awful appetites plain to see.

The majority of white people saw it and loved it, bringing this racist strongman to the White House. In doing so, they were endorsing a view of the world that I knew. It was the unreconstructed southern white view of history, a view where to be white meant to be both indignantly privileged and also angry and aggrieved, always demanding more. I was pissed off and disgusted with Mom and Dad and with all of the generations of our family who had never addressed slavery or Jim Crow. We'd invented the goddamn "alternative facts" with our myths about plantations, slavery, and the Civil War. It was an awful time to be white, but it was an even worse time to be Black or Mexican or Muslim or anyone else who suffered because of our whiteness.

Similarly, it was also a terrible time to be a man—but not as bad a time as it was to be a woman. With the flood of #MeToo stories on top of the Trump victory, Nicole felt the same disgust for me that I felt for my parents. Or something close. She'd get drunk at the bar around the corner from our apartment and start accosting me. Finally, she would call me Trump.

"I can't believe those fucking fascists," I said, scrolling through Twitter one night.

"It's not about you," Nicole shot back, tipsy after two stiffly poured shots at the bar.

"I know it's not about me," I said. "But that doesn't mean you have to be hostile to me. Can you just be nice?"

That was the worst thing I could have said. She was done with *nice*.

"No, I will not be *nice*," she said with a slight slur. "I am done being nice. Men are always asking women to be nice. It means be weak. It means don't question me. Just go put on your hair, why don't you, Donald Trump."

"Come on," I said. And then I fell silent. I was crushed that the person I loved the most regularly compared me to the person I hated the most.

But at least I didn't feel innocent. In addition to stoking white rage on the right, Trump gave white liberals a chance to indulge in their own sense of innocence. As an antifascist leftist, I tried to avoid that, looking down not only on the Trumpists but also on the liberals desperate to paint themselves as the "resistance" for carrying out the same old pro-corporate, mass-incarcerationist, warmongering policies that had brought us to this position in the first place.

Even as I made such distinctions in an attempt to separate myself, Nicole, and my friends from the "white people" who were propelling the country toward doom, I worried whether, if my parents were so susceptible to racist rants, I might also be harboring an inner fascist.

⌒

Nanny died in July 2017. Nicole and I flew in for the funeral. After the somber ceremony, we all sat around, going through papers and documents. Dad found the original deed to the house that Summey had built on the top of Piney Mountain Road, overlooking Greenville.

The house had been sold years ago, after Summey died, but I still had a sentimental attachment to the idea of it, to the storage room in the basement with all its old clocks and bottles, as a repository of lost time.

"Look at this," Dad said, pointing to the deed. "It's one of those restrictive covenants."

I read it:

> No person or persons of African or Asiatic descent shall use or occupy any building or any lot, except that this restriction shall not prevent occupancy by domestic servants of a different race domiciled with an owner or a tenant.

"That's horrible," I said.

"It's fascinating that it was just written in the deed," Dad said.

Dad viewed this document with historical curiosity, rather than as a covenant with conventions that affected the lives of "African or Asiatic" people in Greenville, preventing them from acquiring wealth from property. It was an extension, a written expression, of the larger, more general covenant that had rescued me from trouble as a teen. It was the good ol' boy system; it was white supremacy. A conspiracy to advance the interests of white people.

"Redlining caused so many of the problems we're still dealing with today," Nicole said.

Nicole and Dad were still outwardly warm to one another, but we were far from the days of attending NASCAR races together. Since the election she could hardly deal with him anymore, the bluster and "just saying" offensiveness. In him were all the parts of me she didn't like, but worse.

"What year does it say?" I asked.

"Nineteen forty-seven, I think," he said, peering over the faded document.

We flew back to town that evening, and as I lay in bed that night, I wondered what else had been going on in Greenville in 1947. A quick search revealed that 1947 was the year of the last lynching committed in South Carolina, which had happened in Greenville when a bunch of white cabdrivers captured and killed a Black man named Willie Earle. I stayed up all night, following the trail of the story, trying to figure out the world my mom had been born into.

On February 14, 1947, the night after Summey's thirty-third birthday, a white cabdriver lay on the road beside his car in a puddle of blood. Police said they followed the blood to the door of a twenty-year-old Black man named Willie Earle, who was arrested and held in the Pickens County Jail.

A bunch of white cabbies in Greenville heard that Earle had murdered their buddy. They gathered at a café directly across from the sheriff's office and planned to go bust Earle out of jail and lynch him. A caravan of more than thirty white men menaced up the road from Greenville to the Pickens County Jail. The jailer let them take Earle out of his custody, reportedly asking only that they not curse and disturb his wife as they did so.

The white cabbies drove Earle into Greenville County in the back of one of the cars. They dragged him from the car. They beat him, repeatedly. They cut and stabbed him. Finally one man, Roosevelt Carlos Hurd, shot Earle twice in the head with a shotgun.

The state solicitor ultimately charged thirty-one men, prosecuting the lynching as a conspiracy. As a reporter, I'd covered enough trials to find this legal maneuver fascinating—and it gave me a model to use to understand how whiteness worked. Whiteness was a conspiracy, in the legal sense, in which "the hand of one is the hand of all."

The defense attorneys proved the conspiracy even as they appealed to its power, the white solidarity of the all-white, all-male jury, even though the judge prohibited open discussion of race.

"Willie Earle is dead and I wish more like him were dead," one of the defense attorneys said, to the delight of many of the white spectators who filled the court each day.

Another defense attorney told the jurors that if they convicted the lynchers, not only would they "rankle the hearts" of men all across the state but "the ghost of Hampton's men"—who had overthrown Reconstruction— "would rise to haunt you."

I stopped cold at the supernatural threat that ghosts of the "Redeemers" who had overthrown Reconstruction would haunt anyone who betrayed the conspiracy. My great-grandfather I. M. Woods had been one of those men. And the attorney was, in some way, right. They haunted me.

I knew what would happen in the trial, of course. The jury came back with not-guilty verdicts on all counts. The prosecutor had gambled on the conspiracy charge, but it seemed to me he did not understand the extent of the conspiracy. Greenville was an entirely segregated, Jim Crow city. Its very existence was a conspiracy to favor its white residents at the expense of its Black ones.

Hundreds of white supporters packed the court on the day the jury came back with a verdict. Rebecca West, who had recently covered the Nuremberg war-crime trials of Nazis, described the scene in the courthouse as one of "orgiastic joy."

The defendants "were kissing and clasping their wives, their wives were laying their heads on their husbands' chests and nuzzling in an ecstasy of animal affection, while the laughing men stretched out their hands to their friends, who sawed them up and down. They shouted, they whistled, they laughed, they cried; above all, they shone with self-satisfaction," she wrote in the *New Yorker*.

Self-satisfaction is the essence of whiteness. When I look at the photographs of the jubilant defendants and their white supporters in court on the day of the acquittal, I see the pale features of a people I have known and loved all my life, and I would see them again in subsequent years in the faces surrounding acquitted cops and vigilantes.

I thought of my family members, like Summey, who might have been there among the glad-handing friends and supporters of the lynching party in Greenville. This was all part of the same conspiracy that had been kept alive in my bloodline, in the culture that had created me.

I studied the photographs of the courtroom celebration, looking for Summey. I did not find his face, but in the white faces of the freed lynchers I could easily discern the warp and weft of the fabric that has protected me. The actions of the cabdrivers worked in tandem with the covenant on the deed preventing "African or Asiatic" ownership. It was a conspiracy to concentrate wealth and power in the hands of whites. Even though the original acts of violence had been covered over and forgotten, their repercussions reverberated throughout my own life, insulating me from trouble as the same good ol' boy system that had protected the lynchers protected me forty years later.

The next day I called Mom to ask her if she had ever heard of Willie Earle.

"No," she said. "I don't ever remember any racial problems in Greenville at all."

Whiteness is a conspiracy that hides its actions from coconspirators, pacifying them with the benefits, which come to seem natural over time. Mom didn't see the gruesome murder or the grotesque miscarriage of justice at the trial. Instead, she saw the benefits that had accrued from the violence as natural. She never questioned them, and neither did I.

Ultimately I inherited $80,000 from Nanny's estate. I thought about where the money had come from and how it had been maintained. I thought about its relationship to the white power structure in Greenville, to the racial covenants designed to keep it out of the hands of Black and brown people. I knew that it was dirty blood money, but I fell into the same trap as all the white liberals I criticized. I thought the best thing I could do with it was use it to supplement the paltry income I was making covering Trump and the alt-right for alternative weekly papers.

Chapter 24

THE FURIES OF WHITENESS HIT me with full force when racists rallied in Charlottesville, Virginia, to defend the statues of the same slaver generals my parents had taught me to revere as a child.

I arrived in town early that morning with my friend and colleague Brandon. We'd been covering the far right for a couple of years at that point, and we were expecting a sad but still potentially dangerous little rally of cosplay Confederates, neo-Nazi numbskulls, Facebook fascists, and a smattering of seriously scary militia dudes. But when we saw the torchlit march, where dozens of khaki-klad office bros chanted, "Jews will not replace us" the night before, we had begun to expect that this march would be different.

The moment we arrived at the perimeter around Emancipation Park, where thousands of racists were rallying, we saw a phalanx of white guys in white shirts with black shields and black helmets charge a group of antifascist counterprotesters. One of the white guys swung a club that smashed into the face of one of the antifascist women a few feet from me, landing with a horrible crack, which I could hear amid the grunts and cries and the sounds of the wooden shields knocking together.

For the next several hours, we were swept up in this sea of violence. A moment of calm would be disrupted by another Nazi group marching in formation toward the statues, attacking counterprotesters on the way. A white man fired a gun toward a Black man in the park. Others beat people down with flagpoles and baseball bats.

Brandon and I split up, but we checked on each other via text every five minutes or so because the situation seemed so dangerous. It felt as if it could erupt into a mass shooting at any moment. Finally, late that afternoon, after hours of skirmishes, the various factions of racists fled. There was a celebration in a nearby park, where antifascists burned Confederate flags.

A rumor swept through the group that some cadre of racists were planning an attack on a mostly Black apartment complex nearby. After a quick discussion, this group, mostly white antifascists clad in black, mobilized and began marching in that direction, probably one hundred strong. Brandon and I were running along opposite sides of the group, tweeting and taking notes as we moved through the city.

I was thinking that this is the way to be white: the Black people in the apartment complexes didn't need the white antifascists to come and "save" them from the white Nazis—but they also shouldn't have to deal with shit that is our problem, as white people, shit that is a problem *in* white people. If there's one thing white people are good at, it is being defensive. If we change the angle of that defense, to be white offers the possibility of putting yourself in the way of white violence, of positioning yourself to shield others from white harm.

There were no Nazis at the apartment complex, and the crowd of antifascists marched triumphantly toward Fourth Street, where it met up with another large group of mostly white counterprotesters in black, chanting an antifascist song and waving antifascist banners in black and red.

The two marches converged with a jubilant cheer. Then a thunderous sound ripped through the marching crowd. I thought it was a bomb and I started running away, down a small path beside the road, toward a bridge where I thought I could take cover. I couldn't tell if the sound in my ears was my heart pounding against my rib cage or my feet slapping the pavement until I finally stopped and turned around to look. It was my heart.

From my new vantage point twenty yards away, I couldn't tell what had happened, and I started walking back toward the mass of people. Everyone was standing around stunned, like extras on a movie set waiting for directions. As I got closer, I noticed more concerted activity in small clusters.

I realized that street medics—people at protests trained to give emergency aid—were racing to tend to severely wounded people. What the hell had hit us?

One medic, a white guy with brown hair, bent frantically over a woman. I saw blood. Two other people ran up with a flag and held it in front of the injury.

"What happened?" I asked.

"A car came driving down that street and just slammed into us," a woman said.

"I thought it was a bomb or something," I said.

"Me too," said another guy. "I couldn't see anything because of the crowd. But I could feel the concussion go through the air."

More than a dozen people were injured. It felt like an eternity before sirens finally announced the arrival of an ambulance. By the time Brandon and I left the scene, it seemed certain that at least one person would die, but I knew that had it not been for the street medics, there would have been more deaths.

We wandered around in a daze for a while before finding the rental car where we'd parked it eight hours earlier. It had been the longest eight hours of my life, and I was not the same person I had been when we arrived that morning. We drove mostly in silence, pulling off at the same Dunkin' Donuts we'd stopped at that morning, for coffee. But everything seemed sinister, tainted now.

Waiting for my coffee, the crash still swirling in my mind on replay, I looked at Twitter to see that my old friend Chuck, the kid I used to skateboard with, the guy who'd lived with me and Blake and then on the farm in West Virginia, was tweeting about how Antifa was responsible for the death of Heather Heyer that afternoon in Charlottesville.

I tweeted at him that he was wrong, that I had been there, that he was defending Nazis who were intent on causing harm to my Black neighbors and friends. A fascist had killed Heather Heyer and could have just as well killed me or anyone else in the march that day.

We'd been arguing on Twitter ever since Trump announced his run. Chuck tweeted obsessively about Pizzagate, the conspiracy theory that alleged a massive child trafficking ring in the basement of a Ping-Pong and pizza joint I'd often eaten at in D.C. He endlessly shared stories about antifascists instigating violence.

One day, shortly before Charlottesville, he'd tweeted, "conservatism is the new counter culture," parroting an InfoWars acolyte, and it struck me how most of the countercultures I'd experienced now seemed conservative. All of my rebellion—as skater, punk, Deadhead—amounted to a demand for more freedom for a white dude, namely me, to be an irresponsible dick.

When Chuck and I used to skateboard and we got chased by security guards, we'd turn back and yell, "Fuck you, man, I'm having fun," as we rode away, and his online shitposting for Trump partook of that same aesthetic. "Fuck you, man, I'm having fun" is the ultimate form of the white man's protest. It isn't just "Don't tread on me," but "I can tread on you if I want to."

I'd thought of myself as a rebel all my life, and I saw suddenly, in an online encounter with my old friend, that none of my rebellion acted against the system at all—it was a part of it. The rebellion of young white men was built into the system of white supremacy. During slavery, rebellious white men had expanded the range of their own sexual freedom by raping enslaved girls. Though they were violating the stated social norms, they were aiding, rather than damaging, the white, patriarchal slavocracy. If the enslaved women became pregnant, the offspring would become the property of the white slavers. The rebellion of young white men was built into the system.

After the Wo-ah, a group of young white men got drunk on whiskey in Tennessee and started dressing like the ghosts of dead Confederate soldiers to terrorize Black people, under the banner of the Ku Klux Klan. Though white newspapers occasionally condemned violence, they almost all supported the aim of white supremacy, ensuring the safety of the terrorists. And even the white hippies were simply carving out more space for whiteness, forgoing the Civil Rights struggle for their own chemical enlightenment. All rebellion can be forgiven as long as it is intended to expand the freedom of the white man.

Chuck had not changed—it was I. When we had become blood brothers two decades earlier, we were camping at Stone Mountain, a giant monument to the Lost Cause, and drinking Rebel Yell whiskey. That now seemed preposterous to me. I wanted to blow those monuments up, and Chuck wanted to save them.

Now I had begun to see that the only rebellion that whiteness cannot forgive is working to end the oppression of Black people, rebellion that seeks to limit the power of whiteness. That was the only rebellion worth its name. And by that token, the antifascists in Charlottesville were among the only white rebels I'd ever seen.

"You have called me a Nazi for the last time," Chuck DMed me. "Goodbye."

"You ready?" Brandon asked, walking up to me and shaking me from my screen.

"Yeah, let's go," I said as I took my coffee from the counter.

I cranked up Neil Young's *Tonight's the Night*, and we drove for a long time back toward Baltimore without saying much.

I thought about Chuck and our different trajectories and how we'd each gotten to where we were from our little suburb outside of Columbia. The differences between the communities we lived in now as adults seemed to play a big role in our divide. He had spent the last decades in a poor, rural, almost-all-white county, while I lived in a poor, majority-Black city. We also consumed different news sources, followed different people on Twitter, and really saw the world through different eyes even though we were both white.

I'd also finished college while Chuck had not. I thought about Dad and how he was the only one among his brothers who hadn't finished college and the only one who had voted for Trump. That was part of Trump's appeal. Both Dad and Chuck were smart but felt their intelligence belittled because they didn't have academic degrees, and Trump spoke to that chip on their shoulders. Resentment against the so-called elites was the other side of his racism. It was parallel to southerners like my family blaming the Yankees for turning the once-loyal Black people against their "masters."

I recalled a message Chuck had sent me on Twitter. "I'm dead serious about this Civil War thing," he wrote. "A lot of people are. I've been prepping Bay. If things do break down in this country you're going to want to be with your tribe man. Get out of the city and come here bro. I'm not trying to preach doom, but, well I've seen things, I can feel them happening, and it's been this way for many years now."

That message was from back in February. And now I had seen the civil war he'd predicted breaking out that day in Charlottesville. Chuck and I had ended up on opposite sides. Brother against brother, as they said of the Wo-ah, eliminating the role of the enslaved altogether, making the conflict into a family spat among whites.

Two years earlier, Dylann Roof had seemed to embody everything I had repressed about my own whiteness. Since then, the monster had multiplied into a swarm of furies, come out of hiding. The white subconscious had been pried open and the horrors in our hearts were emerging in a fearsome storm of terror.

When I got home, I fell into Nicole's arms and wept. The army of racists in Charlottesville had told us all what the statues of Confederate generals meant to them. We could look around the country and see what they wanted to do to vulnerable communities, to people who were not white. But what was it to a suburban white mom if hate crimes against people of color were skyrocketing along with all the white nationalist rhetoric, as long as her life was good?

The next day, Nicole and I met a friend for brunch at an Irish bar near the house. I was still feeling shaky, but I thought I would be fine. But as we sat at one of the tall marbleized tables across from the long wooden bar, I gripped Nicole's leg harder and harder under the table as our friend talked.

"I've got to go," I said, and jumped up and ran out the door.

I didn't know why I was affected so deeply, why this was making me feel crazy, but I felt as if I was falling apart. I staggered down the sidewalk, past the Catholic church and then the Unitarian one, people streaming from each as the services ended, white people mostly wearing their dresses and their suits and on each and every one of them I looked with a suspicion that amounted to hatred.

I hated the way so many white people would express a vague sense of moral outrage, or share thoughts and prayers on Facebook, while simultaneously condemning the tactics of the antifascists who had saved lives. Charlottesville made it obvious: it's not enough to be an ally standing on the sidelines, a good white person praying at church. White people need to learn to play defense, the way the antifascists in Charlottesville courageously did. We need to be abolitionists. But I knew, for myself at least, that I had to abolish the racist systems of violence that had infiltrated the barely conscious mind of childhood at the same time that I tried to challenge the racist systems outside me.

The buildings looming over me seemed to lean in, blocking my sight in the bright sky. I needed to get home, where I did not have to see anyone, where I could breathe. It felt as if everything were closing in a static that filled the space behind my eyes, and I gasped and hurried through the littered, sweaty streets.

My phone rang. I looked at the screen, standing, holding on to a lamppost at a red light.

DAD WOODS, the caller ID read. No fucking way. I had texted Mom and Dad to tell them I was safe, but I dreaded talking to them. I did not want to hear what they might say—what they might reveal about themselves. I didn't answer. When I got into the house, I fell down on the couch and buried my head.

That night, just as I was falling to sleep, I got a text from a source telling me that a truck was about to carry away the monument to Confederate sailors on Mt. Royal Avenue. It was 1:00 a.m. I jumped out of bed and ran ten blocks to the intersection where the monument sat and got there just in time to see the truck driving away with metal mermaids on its bed.

All the Confederate monuments in the city were coming down "under the cover of night," a phrase usually reserved, in Baltimore, for discussions of the Colts' move to Indianapolis. Just before dawn, about a dozen of us stood out on a leafy street by the art museum as the equestrian statues of Robert E. Lee and Stonewall Jackson swung from ropes, casting wild, galloping shadows across the ground in the industrial spotlights used by the removal crew.

I remembered standing in front of the state capitol in Columbia when I was little and looking at the statue of George Washington gripping a broken cane, and how Mom had told me that the Yankees hated democracy so much that they stoned the father of the country and broke his cane when they were burning Columbia. It was one of my earliest memories, but it was a myth, a complete falsehood, and standing there in the morning dew as municipal trucks drove old Dixie down decades later, I realized that was why the people in Charlottesville felt so passionate about the images of these Confederate generals. When we said Lee or Jackson was bad, they heard us calling their mamas liars, and that is always a fighting offense in the South. Whiteness, as Chuck put it in his DM, was about "your tribe," extending the myths your mama spun when you were in your crib into an identity.

The sun was high in the sky before I got to bed. I had a busy day and barely slept. I recorded a podcast in a hot, closed-in closet at the *City Paper* office, and I felt woozy as I walked out the door and up Centre Street toward my apartment. I was sweating the whole way back to the house. When I walked in, I fell on the floor, clutching at my chest. I thought I was having a heart attack. I thought I was having a stroke.

Nicole bent over me. I could see her face, so beautiful, but so panicked, a mask of urgency, hovering above me. It looked as if she was talking, but I could not hear. I wanted to say something but I could not respond. I was shaking. I crawled to the bathroom and puked and shit for an hour, alternating from end to end. I could hear her on the phone with a nurse friend. When I made it to bed, I slept for nearly twenty-four hours.

When I woke up, I went to the doctor, who diagnosed me with

PTSD. I felt silly, aware of all the things other people go through, whether reporters covering real war zones or Black people attacked by police in West Baltimore or women terrorized by the sexual violence of men. I knew my trauma was nothing in comparison, and I didn't want to think of myself as the kind of wussy white guy reporter who sees the violence of racism and gets all weak at the knees. But I was. Something was wrong with me.

The furies of whiteness were haunting me. I had to expiate the sins of my family, I felt, even while recognizing the absurdity of this quest. At the least, I had to know more precisely what atrocities my family had committed so I could make an accounting of what they had bequeathed to me.

In this reflection, I realized that my own name was like a Confederate monument perched above every story I wrote, and I had to, at the very least, know what miasma the names bore.

Online, I started looking through the so-called slave schedules, census and tax documents for slavers and the people they held in bondage. In 1860, I quickly learned, the Baynards had held 781 people in bondage.

The Woodses, at that time, held only about twenty-three people in bondage. Then the absurdity of my own formulation struck me: in comparison to the eight hundred people that Grandmother's family, the Baileys, had enslaved, I found myself using the word *only* to limit the twenty-three people the Woodses felt entitled to control in every respect.

When we think about the horrors of slavery, we almost always neglect the psychological state of the slaver. We act as if the slave system were a natural phenomenon, a storm or something, when instead, it was a series of decisions and business ventures made by people who moved about the world as we do. What kind of moral monstrosity could make them feel entitled to own other people? Such actions could be undertaken only with the help of a powerful ideology. That ideology is race. We have never exorcised it.

We did this. We bought and sold. We raped and tortured. We put heads upon pikes at the mile markers. We gouged and burned and cut flesh. We engaged in every form of indignity. I needed to go back only three generations to find an ancestor who'd fought a war for the right to treat people as property.

When I finally talked to Dad again, he sounded like Trump. It wasn't so much that he mimicked Trump's talking points as that Trump was tapping into a deep well of white aggrievement from which Dad also drank.

"Where is it going to stop?" Dad asked. "Are they going to take down statues of Thomas Jefferson?"

"They should," I said.

"You can't erase history," he said.

"What do you think the statues did? These heroic images of Lee and Jackson—they lost the Wo-ah. The statues were trying to erase that fact. And that they lost in a traitorous war. But the statues tried to hide all of that and cast them as noble American heroes."

"They were acting by the standards of their time," Dad said.

"Sure, but there were a lot of people who lived in the same time that pointed out the monstrosity of the system," I said. "John Brown for instance."

"John Brown was a terrorist," Dad said. "When I was growing up, his name was a curse."

"He may have been a terrorist," I said. "But he wasn't a monster like our ancestors. He killed some people and caused some others to die. But it was in the service of liberation. Ours systematically tortured hundreds of people for hundreds of years and only fought to maintain that absurd sense of privilege."

"I don't think it was as bad as all that," he said. "The Yankees weren't any better. They wanted the labor, they just used us to do the dirty work."

"At least the Union, which is the United States of America, by the way, finally fought to end the practice, while our family fought on the other, wrong side," I said, my voice echoing through my apartment, causing the dog to quiver on the bed where he sat.

Dad was silent a minute.

"What?" I said.

"Clearly we just disagree," he said.

"Disagree about what?" I said. "That the South was wrong in the Civil War?"

"It's just more complicated than that," he said.

"Whatever," I said. "I gotta go then."

Baynard Woods, I thought, shaking my head. He had passed on his name to me in ignorance and pride. I felt as if I could no longer carry that name, but I had no idea what to do with it.

I knew I could no longer look away. Whiteness is a moral pollution that demands expiation. I had to unravel the details of the murder my great-grandfather had committed.

Chapter 25

THE PORTICO FRONTED THE WHITE plantation house like the smile of a sociopath. I got out of the car and stood there, staring at the ancestral Woods home, aware that enslaved people had built this house, hoisted the six columns of the portico, framed the walls, built the roof, cut the windows.

In the nearly two years since Charlottesville, I had begun to sporadically research my family's history, between writing assignments. The ignominy of my family radiated in countless directions—slavers tended to marry slavers—but I kept finding myself returning to the story Dad had told me about his grandfather Dr. I. M. Woods, the most illustrious member of my family, who had murdered a Black man in Clarendon County and fled to hide out in Texas before being welcomed back with a fulsome embrace.

He fascinated me because he'd had a clear choice. No one could say he was just a man of his time—history had placed different options clearly before him. When his father died in the late 1850s, I. M. was too young to inherit slaves directly—though some were put in a trust. When the Wo-ah started, he could have chosen to leave home and join the Union Army. Instead, he was an enthusiastic Confederate, who fought for four years to maintain his right to own and torture people. After losing the war, he could have made another choice. Reconstruction offered the possibility of a multiracial democracy in South Carolina. He killed a man to redeem white rule, which he later encoded as law.

Each of these actions was a choice he made, and by thinking about why he'd made those choices, I figured I might be able to learn something about my own whiteness and the way it functioned both in my mind and in the world around me, the world I help to make with each of my decisions each day. And so I went to the home where I. M. Woods had lived, both as a boy and again when he returned from the Wo-ah, his older brothers dead, to take over the family farm, which would have to function, for the first time, without the labor of enslaved Africans.

I looked out at the yard and the fields beyond, green flora shimmering in the heat of the horizon. Enslaved people had farmed this earth under the threat of whip and lash. The people who'd propagated me tortured this labor out of them. How many enslaved people died in bondage here, were buried in this earth? I wondered.

How could a white person bear to live here? I wondered as I got out of the car. But it's not just that white people can live in old plantation houses—it's that we desire to. Plantation homes were considered the height of respectability not long ago, and elite resorts still proudly call themselves plantations, which should strike us as monstrous as an elite, gated community at Auschwitz.

A lot of antebellum mansions are now museums or wedding venues, but smaller manses such as this one have remained in private hands and are cherished. Whatever details I knew about the house came from an old photocopy of a "tour of homes" listing that detailed its restoration with a loving pride.

I felt exactly the opposite. As I walked through the yard, I was filled with so much shame that I thought, or maybe wished, that the earth itself might swallow me up as it sometimes did to people in mythology.

The sound of a barking dog followed me as I walked up the short brick steps onto the porch. Even though it was summer, Christmas lights were draped in a triangle from the center of the portico roof to a column on either side. A weathered wicker couch and two chairs sat off to one side, wilting in the humidity, as some wildly flowering bush reached toward them with overgrown branches.

The shutters and the door were a stark black against the white paint. A knocker hung from the mouth of a brazen lion mounted just above the peephole. A mane of cobwebs was spidering around it on the door. I avoided the lion and used my knuckles to knock. Rather than stare at the door, I turned around to inspect the yard. A giant dead oak stretched out in the center, its bottom engulfed by a lacy clamor of saplings and weeds.

Dad and I had planned to come and see Henry, who was his cousin Mary Lou's widower, and their son Ricky at the old Woods house in order to look over documents that Henry had. But Dad had fallen off a ladder trying to clean my aunt Gaile's gutter and hurt himself pretty bad, and so I had come alone. Henry was suffering from dementia, but Ricky had said they would put aside some folders of old documents they'd amassed for me.

I didn't even know what I was looking for, but I hoped to find some clue about I. M. Woods that might help me understand our own world, as irrational as that might seem. It was also a chance to connect with real people, my family, whom I didn't know very well.

I knocked again and then took out my cell phone and called Ricky.

"Give me just a minute," he said when he answered, his voice gruff and scratchy like mine. "Come around the side and I'll meet you there."

As I made my way around the house, Ricky emerged from the side door with a cigarette in his mouth. He had a thick dark beard and stepped toward me with a forward-sloping gait.

We shook hands and he invited me in.

"Dad, you remember Bay," he said to Henry, a tall, bony bald man, who was sitting slumped in a chair in the darkened living room. I had not seen either of them in years.

Henry straightened each section of his long, crooked body until he rose out of the recliner. We shook hands, and the three of us stood there sharing news of various family members for a few minutes.

"So you're interested in the family history?" Ricky asked.

"Yeah," I said, although I felt a little silly saying it. I'd been pretty dismissive of the genealogical craze, which struck me as inevitably aggrandizing and romantic. It wasn't surprising that only porn was more popular than genealogy online. For white people, it was so often an onanistic enterprise of ancestral aggrandizement—how did everybody trace their lineage back to some nobility, while nobody seemed to ask what it means to come from monsters?

Of course, plenty of people did ask that—but most of them were not Americans. The Germans had, of grim necessity, made an art of it—and self-examination has helped them resist the lure of hate in the years since the Holocaust. But instead of inheriting an attitude that swore, "Never again," I'd inherited one that promised, "The South will rise again."

I didn't know how to talk about that with Ricky and Henry. If they were strangers, I would be comfortable initiating the conversation in journalistic mode, or if I knew them well, I would feel free to talk and argue as I did with my dad. But I knew Ricky and Henry just well enough to not know how to talk with them. At least that was what I told myself, while wondering why it was so hard to discuss what I really wanted to know about our family's history. Whatever discomfort and reluctance I felt proved to me that there was something powerful lurking there just beneath the surface, something that still held a serious emotional charge today.

Standing on these floors that had been leveled and laid under the threat of the lash, I thought again of the concept of miasma, the inherited curse. I wanted to ask Ricky about that, about how he felt about living here.

"I don't know where a lot of the stuff Daddy had collected, the documents and all, went to," Ricky said. "But we put together some stuff for you."

He showed me a map on the wall that purported to show the 1775 grant from the king giving this bit of land to the Woods clan.

Then he seemed to answer the questions I was too pusillanimous to ask.

"That room is haunted," Ricky said suddenly.

He was pointing from the hallway where we stood across the large living room and into a smaller parlor on the other side of the house.

"Haunted?" I said. "Like a ghost?"

"I've seen her clearly," he said. "A Black girl, about thirteen years old."

I didn't know if I believed in ghosts, but I could hardly imagine how the house would not be haunted. Even if it was not an actual ghost, the horrors of the house itself constituted a haunting.

"My brother said he seen her all the time," Ricky continued. "Always in that room. I came in one evening and there she was as plain as day. Probably a slave. Thirteen or so, little braids, a white dress."

"What did she do?" I asked.

"She didn't seem mad or nothing," he said. "She just sat there looking at me. Surely she was a slave."

Ricky was directly addressing the grave reality of the house's history. He was not hiding from it, in a way that felt refreshing but also flat, affectless.

"Somewhere around here there is a will that deeds a slave in it," he said. "You want to see it?"

"Yes," I said in my reporter's tone. "I'd love to see any documents you have."

I wanted to know more about Ricky's experience of this ghost and what it meant to him, but I didn't know how to get into that conversation with him, and I turned to the documents when I should have plumbed our emotions.

Ricky walked toward the kitchen. I lingered there looking into the haunted parlor, cast in the kind of shadows sunlight never hits and tinged with the mustiness of a hundred years.

This house felt like a symbol for South Carolina, for America itself, in all its genteel horror. This building I was standing in had been built by people who my family thought they owned in the same way that so much of the country was built on that bitterly coerced labor.

I understood how so many northern whites had been able to wear cotton, profit off it, without thinking about the conditions under which it was grown, because I did something similar every day when I used my iPhone with a vague knowledge of the horrible conditions the construction of that device required.

But to live in this house in the nineteenth century in the middle of a concentration camp and to consider that way of living the natural, right, and highest form of human life while witnessing, and inflicting, tremendous suffering every single day—that was almost unimaginable. Who could live among people and believe them to be property?

We white people have still not asked this question of ourselves, failing to interrogate the mindset that made us. There is some deeply fucked-up shit just a few generations back, and it is still destroying us. And we won't ever be able to look at it as long as we want to heroize men like Thomas Jefferson. By any moral standard, a human who believed he had the right to own other humans is a monster. We have to come to terms with this as a culture, or else we shall remain monsters as individuals, granting ourselves all the same ethical excuses and heroic fantasies that we grant the slavers we still memorialize. Their fantasies formed our minds. We must exorcise them.

A perverse part of me wanted to see the ghost, wanted it to mean something. I was, like so many well-meaning white people right now, waiting for a Black savior to come and tell me the answers—only now in spectral form.

Waiting for a word from the parlor, I missed the opportunity the ghost had already opened, the opportunity to talk with Ricky about the family's history, to wonder together how they had managed to live such monstrous lives and to figure out what it means to be the heir of that kind of horror. Instead, I stood there, chicken. I was trying to discover something, and yet I was scared to really talk about it.

The phrase *white guilt* had recently become popular, but most people thought of it solely as a subjective state—the way white liberals feel when confronted by race. But I was thinking that this ghost haunting Ricky and his family was a manifestation of white guilt, whether only in their minds or in this space where they continued to dwell. The ghost demanded we recognize what our ancestors did. White guilt was an objective fact. Not a feeling. We are guilty whether we recognize it or not.

When I walked into the kitchen, Ricky was hoisting a crumbling old valise onto the table. I started going through the case while he talked and smoked cigarettes for the next half hour. Mostly there were pictures of Henry and his wife, Mary Lou, when they were young. He hadn't said much before, but standing tall and bald in the corner, Henry livened up as I flipped through the pictures, recounting the story behind each one. It was moving, but it was not the history I was looking for. I was seeking something further back, something like the ghost, that might help me see what had been hidden. I wanted to know the debt we owed.

"Want to go to the cemetery?" Ricky asked.

"Sure," I said, happy to get out of this house and back into the fresh air, away from the ghost and the smoke and the dust.

When we walked outside, the day had reached a thrumming peak of humidity. I started sweating immediately, in the few steps between their door and the car I'd borrowed. I got in and followed Ricky and Henry out to the Midway Cemetery, a couple of miles from the old house. We parked in the church lot across the street and dashed together across the country highway. As soon as we crossed into the graveyard, Henry bent down and began picking weeds. Ricky and I ambled around the rows of stones planted like a Tartarean crop awaiting harvest at resurrection. We paused our peregrinations over the flat granite grave marker of Ricky's grandfather:

RICHARD RYAN WOODS
Nov. 18, 1893
Sept. 23, 1973

"I was named after him," Ricky said, a buzzard circling the skies over us. "I always heard that Dr. Woods, Irvin McSwain Woods, our

288

great-grandfather, named him Ricky after an Irishman who had saved his life at Gettysburg during the Wo-ah."

"What?" I said. "I was told that my grandfather was named Hernando Jennings Woods because a Mexican woman saved Dr. Irvin McSwain Woods when he was hiding out in Texas, and he named the son after her husband."

"Oh no," Ricky said. "Irvin McSwain had a brother named Hernandez. He died in the Wo-ah. You can find him in the slave schedules and the census. He was named, I think, after a Spanish general."

Family lore is made up of twisted, distorted, half-heard whispers warped in time. The story I had heard about the name was a mashup of other stories, a mess of misunderstandings passed on again, always in whispers, always in whispers.

"Do you know any more about that Texas story?" I asked.

"That he killed someone?" he asked. "I never heard no more than that."

We kept walking. There on a flat stone, the carved name faced the sky.

DR. IRVIN MCSWAIN WOODS
JULY 17, 1841–JAN. 21, 1921

Beside it, on an identical stone of speckled gray granite, age-worn and stained, was his wife's name.

LYDIA MCFADDEN WOODS
JUNE 30, 1857–OCT. 22, 1933

Beside these horizontal stones, one stone stood vertically, made of a more roughly hewn rock, with the figure of a sleeping infant on top.

MART. GARY
SON OF
DR. AND MRS. WOODS
FEB. 8, 1892–AUG. 3, 1892

"That son was named after a Confederate general," Ricky said. "He obviously died as a baby."

Ricky lit a cigarette, and I stared for a moment out at the hazy pines, trying to place the name. I turned and saw Henry still bent down in his plaid shirt pulling weeds.

"I should get going," I said.

While saying this, I knew that I had not spoken to them directly of whiteness or about the shame and guilt of our shared history. I was still constrained by the omertà that made such discussions off-limits in so many situations. It wasn't exactly that I was scared—but I stalled out of something that felt like family politeness. That is the purpose of ideas such as family decorum: to keep us all from having to confront the truth. The South had such an elaborate set of manners because the reality they were intended to hide was so noxious. Perhaps had Ricky and I gotten drunk together, we would have grown comfortable.

As we got into our cars and drove in different directions away from the bones of our ancestors, I cursed myself for failing to be more direct with my family, wondering why I couldn't say that our past troubled me and I saw it as a challenge. I had written it in the *Washington Post* for the goddamn world to read, and I couldn't sit at a table with a cousin and try to have a real talk about whiteness.

But I had still learned a few things. When I got home, I looked online for the 1860 census and for W. H. Woods's 1855 will. As I used my fingers to enlarge the scrawled print on the PDF document I pulled up on my iPad, I saw Ricky was right. When William Hagood Woods died, he willed twenty-three people whom he had enslaved, dividing the "property" between his second wife, Charlotte Woods, who was I. M.'s mother, and his two sons by his first wife, Hernandez and John, who shared a name with my father and with me.

Hernandez was about twenty years old in 1860 when he inherited a twenty-seven-year-old Black woman, a seven-year-old Black girl, a four-year-old Black girl, a sixty-year-old Black woman, a seven-year-old Black boy, a thirty-three-year-old Black man, and a twelve-year-old "mulatto" girl, who was likely either his half sister or his niece. Among a dozen people "passed down" to I. M.'s mother and Hernandez's stepmother Charlotte, there was a one-year-old "mulatto" boy who had also likely been fathered by one of the white Woods men.

Rather than feeling superior to my ancestors, I wondered if I would have been any different, if I would have been any better. I tried to imagine what it would be like to inherit that kind of raw power, the power of life and death over human beings, at the age of twenty. Hernandez inherited that dominion. The Civil War ended the legal sanction of that dominion, but it did not eradicate the belief that it was right. That belief sickened me, but I tried to keep thinking about it, forcing myself to actually encounter it. What traits of mine come directly from the mindset that had allowed my forebears to buy and sell human beings? My entitlement, my belief that I should always be heard, my rebellious streak, my moral forgetfulness, my objectification of others. The conditions in our worlds were different, but how distant are my traits of character from those of Hernandez Woods? I wondered.

Again my mind turned to Hernandez's younger brother, my great-grandfather Irvin McSwain Woods. Like me, he'd had choices—and he chose, it seemed, to overthrow Reconstruction in the name of creating a new apartheid system that would come as close as possible to slavery. In every iteration, whiteness is an imitation of its earlier, more extreme form. Jim Crow tried to approximate slavery, and the current Republican party was dead set on fashioning a form of whiteness as close to Jim Crow as it could manage.

But there is another way. Whiteness had been invented to justify the enslavement of Africans and the genocide of Native Americans, and when the slave system collapsed under the weight of the general strike of the enslaved and the war, there was a chance to try to undo whiteness, to deal with the trauma it had wrought.

But the whites knew how bad the slave system had truly been, and they were terrified that Black people, if they had any power at all, would demand revenge. They were certain of this desire for vengeance, because if anyone treated them the way they had treated their slaves, they would be ready to burn down the world. And so they covered the crimes up and enforced the cover-up with violence while trying to claw back as much power as possible. They passed down the cover-up and the attitudes it protected to their children, where it became history, holy writ, and a replacement of reality.

Expanding on my attempt to trace the lines of whiteness as a white-wash, I started going more places—archives, slave sites, the locations of lynchings—in an effort to make myself really think about what this horrible past means to me, what it means to us, collectively, and especially to all the people who are not white and are harmed by our unexamined whiteness.

At the beginning of 2020, Nicole and I arranged to spend a month in South Carolina at my uncle Richard and aunt Susan's house, while they were away. Nicole was on a sabbatical and would spend her days writing, and I would drive from there to various archives around the state, which, I came to realize, had been one of the longest-standing and most brutal totalitarian regimes in history, where the small white minority had staked its entire identity and culture on the ability to extract absolute value from and exert absolute control over the Black people who made up a vast majority of the state's early population.

Thinking about the brutal mechanics of such control must have utterly destroyed the moral capacity of those who insisted upon such a vile task. The white minority outlawed drums, limited move-ment and congregation, prohibited education, created policing with slave patrols and badges, prohibited Africans from bearing arms but mandated white males always be armed. Almost the only laws im-pinging on the liberty of white males involved punishment for failing to be properly vigilant against the enslaved majority; they required white men to punish any insurrectionary activity with brutality, detail-ing precisely where and how heads were to be placed on pikes along the road.

I found it easy to trace the policies of South Carolina's current politicians back to these deeply totalitarian slave codes. But I was trying to do the harder thing and see where their legacy reverberates in me.

Just as my pale and freckled splotchy skin is the place where I meet the world—part me and part world—my whiteness is where my subjectivity intersects with the power structure of race, capitalism, colonialism, and patriarchy.

Chapter 26

ON A WARM DAY AT the end of February, Dad and I stood knocking on the door of the Clarendon County Archives. I had been in South Carolina for a month, but I had not been to Clarendon County yet—even though, more than any of the other details of my family history, I wanted to know about the lynching Dr. I. M. Woods had participated in.

Dad had driven down from the suburb where they lived, and we'd had lunch at McCabe's, his favorite barbecue place, before coming to the archive. I was worried that he would hamper me—or worse, make racist or insensitive remarks about whatever history we might find.

Dad now looked like a stooped old man. He'd gotten out of his car and walked to the archive's door limping on a cane, his face wan, his beard looking almost yellow in the sunlight. He'd had to hoist himself up the three steps to the archive building. I was worried about whatever was happening with his health, but I didn't want to diminish him by saying something.

The door was locked. I peered in through the glass. I didn't see anyone, and immediately I grew frustrated. I'd told them I was coming. I'd called to verify my appointment. I usually had more patience, but something about me was off that afternoon, everything irritated me.

A month of poring over old racist documents about my family, a month of thinking nonstop about the vast web of crimes my ancestors had engaged in, had started fucking with my head. I didn't know what I'd do with all of this, how I would be able to go back to my regular life and talk about it, how I would be able to face my Black friends when I got home to Baltimore. I had been delving into this racist history as a way to fight it in myself, to learn the roots of so many problems white people were causing right now, but after spending a month thinking through racist thoughts all day and observing them more acutely than I'd ever done before, I wondered if it was actually making me more racist.

Standing there outside the empty office, I felt like a fool. It would have been better for me to not do this, easier for me to pretend that this racist history of my family had no relation to me nor I to it. I should have just kept reporting on police—done something useful.

Dad looked weak and frail standing there with his big belly and his white beard, gripping the handrail. His leg had been giving him a lot of problems, and they thought it was something wrong with his spine. He shifted his weight and winced.

Suddenly the door opened. The archivist, a Black woman named M. L. Witherspoon, emerged from the shadows inside. I'd been corresponding with her about my great-grandfather, but I had not known that she was Black. Standing there at the door, looking at her brown skin and friendly smile, I felt vulnerable. It had been naive and racist for me to even assume that the archivist was white, and I was immediately disappointed in myself. My own unexamined assumptions about race polluted so many of my thoughts, reminding me that I would still always be a human being, acting on a partial view of reality. I would never be perfect, but I could always revise my erroneous impressions. That seemed to be the point.

We walked in, and Dad started cheerfully explaining to Witherspoon that he had grown up down the road and that we were looking for information about his grandfather.

"It's rare for someone of my age to have a grandfather—" Dad said, and then he paused. I knew he'd normally finish the sentence with "who fought in the Wo-ah." But Dad stopped himself short, recalibrating. He finished the sentence with "who was born in 1842."

Even though Dad would never admit it, in that moment he had been aware of the weight of this history and what it might communicate to someone with a set of experiences that were not like his. In that moment, he saw our history through Witherspoon's eyes and, I think, realized that bragging about a Confederate grandfather would necessarily sound racist.

It felt at first like progress, but then I began to second-guess. Instead of facing our reality as white men with a racist past in America, Dad quickly improvised to avoid past truths, covering over the unpleasantness of reality with a more neutral birth date. It was good that he took Witherspoon's perspective into account, but this impulse to hide the truth also spawned the false version of history that formed and deformed his view of the world. It was his inheritance, and he had tried his best to pass it on to me.

I smiled awkwardly, anxious but now feeling a bit relieved that Witherspoon was Black. I thought that she might understand my mission—even if I didn't—and aid me in my hope for redemption. I thought she might see me as a good white guy who desired to tell the truth about America's racist history. I wanted her to validate me as a less bad white person because I was doing this research. I recognized this feeling. Because the harm of whiteness lands primarily on people of color, and especially women of color, white people who are trying to do better expect to be praised by Black women for not hurting them. It is a ridiculous proposition, but it courses through the breast as an emotional need.

On the other pole of my emotional state was the fear that my interest in my family's past might come off as prideful and racist, especially with Dad there. I could imagine how many whites visited there looking for information about their plantation home or the illustrious Confederate ancestor they'd named a child after.

"I've made some copies for you," Witherspoon said to me.

She handed me a manila folder. When I took it, I could tell there were only a couple of sheets of paper inside and I was disappointed, having hoped for a more robust representation of our family's historical record.

"You can use one of these tables to look through it," she said.

296

Dad hobbled up beside me on his cane as I sat down and opened the folder, looking through a stack of census records extending from the 1840s through the 1910s. Then I came to an 1847 newspaper ad put out by William Hagood Woods, I. M.'s father and my great-great-grandfather. The article read:

> Absconded, from my premises, on Friday the 5th inst, my Negro man Joe. Joe is a stout heavy built fellow, about five feet high, with a scar on his forehead just over one of his eyes; he is rather slow in speaking when first spoken to, with a kind of sly-looking smile on his countenance. A reward of Five Dollars will be given for his apprehension and delivery at my residence, or Ten Dollars, if safely lodged in any of the district jails in the state.

In the top left corner of the ad, there was an illustration of a black man with a walking stick and a traveling bag, looking over his shoulder. Sitting there between Dad, an elderly white Republican man, and Witherspoon, a much younger Black woman, reading this description from my ancestor, I was overcome by a vertiginous sense of shame, my mind stretching in two directions, wondering what Witherspoon was thinking about me and hoping Dad would not say anything to make this moment worse.

The meaning of the notice was indisputable—there it was in newsprint. The ad meant that at that time any white person was free to apprehend Joe and they would receive a reward for doing so. If the three of us had been standing there in 1847, Dad and I would have been permitted to take Witherspoon into custody because she was Black and we were white.

I. M. Woods was five when his father placed this ad offering a reward for the capture of a man he thought he owned, and I wondered how such an atmosphere would warp the mind of a child. I contemplated how that warping had been passed down to Dad, and then to me. Our family psychology had been shaped for generations by a mindset that conceived of Black people as mere property. I knew that this domineering mentality or miasma could not have been lost after two or three generations, because I was still seeing evidence of it today.

Only four days earlier, a couple of hundred miles away, in Brunswick, Georgia, two white men had seen a Black man named Ahmaud Arbery jogging through their suburban neighborhood. Gregory McMichael and his son Travis got a pistol and a shotgun and got in their pickup truck with a Confederate flag decal on it and they began to chase Arbery down, the son armed in the back of the truck. When the chase passed the house of another white man named William "Roddie" Bryan, he joined in. His lawyer later said Bryan "[saw] someone he doesn't know followed by a truck that he does. He does, with all due respect, what any patriotic American would have done under the same circumstances."

Bryan used his own truck to try to block Arbery, hitting him with the vehicle at least once. Eventually Arbery stopped, and Travis McMichael got out of the first truck and shot him. And, to make sure there was no confusion, called Arbery a "fucking n*****."

At that point, no charges had been filed. The prosecutor cited a law that stated a "private person may arrest an offender if the offense is committed in his presence or within his immediate knowledge."

Gregory McMichael later told investigators that he "had a gut feeling that Mr. Arbery may have been responsible for thefts that were in the neighborhood previously." His knowledge was his "gut." The trust of the white gut, the belief that the white man apprehends reality correctly, also governed the advertisement placed by my great-great-grandfather W. H. Woods. His ad articulated the power of whites to act upon the Black body as their gut saw fit.

I kept turning through the pages, looking at the culture I'd inherited. When we want to turn away, to close our eyes to the reality that racism belongs acutely to us white people, that's when we need to look closer, pay attention. Only a relentless search for self-knowledge can help us find our way out of this nightmare we help make.

The three of us stood there in an awkward silence until Witherspoon discreetly went back into her office as I continued to thumb through the pages. Dad stood beside me at the table, propping himself up. I turned the page.

I hadn't found the names of the people that the Woodses enslaved, but looking through the census records Witherspoon had collected, I could see that our family lived next to the McFaddens, who owned a mansion and held more than one hundred people in bondage in 1850.

"Lydia McFadden was my grandmother," Dad said, leaning forward on his cane to peer at the page.

"I guess they were neighbors first," I said, thinking how every marriage of slaver families, every branch of the generational tree, only complicated our guilt. I was no less descended from Lydia McFadden than from I. M. Woods, and she had been raised in an environment where one hundred people were deemed to be property. She was my great-grandmother. How many lives had my direct family destroyed?

"We should probably get going soon," Dad said.

"Yeah," I said.

We were both hours from where we were staying, and I had to get up in the morning and drive back to Baltimore.

I was both sad and annoyed that I had not discovered any details of I. M. Woods's crime. I felt like a detective in a backward crime story where I had a culprit and no victim—the traces of the man he'd killed had been wiped away entirely, it seemed.

This crime was small compared with the monstrous history of "owning" hundreds of people, accounting for countless deaths. But that does not mean that this murder does not matter. A person dead is irreplaceable, and somehow, I felt that if I could sweep this lynching away as if it was insignificant in the face of the greater crimes, I would just be giving myself an out, an excuse to go about my life as a sleepwalking white man, exercising all my power blindly.

I knocked on the door to Witherspoon's small office to tell her we were leaving.

"I just wanted to thank you," I said when she gestured for me to open the door. "We're going to head out now. I didn't find exactly what I was looking for, but I'll be back."

I thought I would be able to talk to her more freely without Dad there anyway. I could tell her more about what I was looking for without worrying about him saying something racist or starting an argument with me. Again I imagined the kinds of white people who came into that place looking for the moonlight-and-magnolia version of their forebears.

As she walked us to the door, I noticed on a shelf the book *Black Majority: Negroes in Colonial South Carolina from 1670 through the Stono Rebellion* by Peter H. Wood. It was an astounding book that had opened my eyes to the truly totalitarian origin and nature of South Carolina's history. It had helped me see the extent to which the white minority had set out to fashion an ideology of race in order to dominate the Black majority. I wanted to mention it—but not because I really wanted to talk about it. I wanted to signal that I was coming from some kind of allyship, some racially good place, but when I realized that, I stopped myself, because I thought it would be like mentioning that rapper you love when you meet a Black person or talking about feminism in order to get a date.

The afternoon sun streamed in through the windows and cast a golden glow as we walked toward the door.

"I'll be back again sometime soon," I told her again.

"Definitely stay in touch, and I'll keep an eye out for anything else about Dr. Woods," she said.

As I turned, I looked down and noticed a big binder on the floor labeled "McFadden."

"You know, he married a McFadden," I said, pointing at the red binder. "Dr. Woods did."

"Oh, we have a lot in there," Witherspoon said.

In retrospect, it seems there was weight in her words. I want to think that she'd left it there to catch my eye on purpose and was trying to reveal to me something important, but that is just another fantasy.

She picked up the binder and hoisted it onto the surface of the aged wood table in the middle of the room. All three of us, my father, the archivist, and I, began to flip through the binder.

I reached down and turned the page:

"Dr. Woods + Maiden Slave."

The words, typed in bold font, leaped off the page at me.

In pencil, someone had drawn a line from Dr. Woods and written "I. M. Woods" and above it "W. H. Woods" with a question mark after each.

Another hand-drawn line connected "Maiden Slave" with the name Eliza, followed by another light, hesitant question mark.

Below those names, in printed ink, a genealogical chart extended, documenting several generations, on pages and pages, detailing different unions, generations rising and falling, starting from Dr. Woods, a white man, and Maiden Slave, a Black woman.

I had come looking for evidence of a murder and I'd discovered what seemed to be a rape.

We all three stood there looking down at the paper in silence.

Eliza, it seems, had a child named Liza, who married a man named Major McFadden, a Black man who had likely been enslaved by my great-grandmother's family. They had eight children who had children who had children, sprawling out on page after page of names.

"There's a whole other family," I finally said of the revelation that my great-grandfather I. M. Woods seemed to be great-grandfather to a number of Black people as well as to me. I meant "Black family" instead of "whole other family," but I didn't say it.

I looked at Dad, nervous but also curious about how he might react. He smiled, awkward, and blinked.

This is why it is hard for white people to talk about race. How did Dad and I acknowledge what this chart was saying, what the hand-scrawled names above said about us? What was the appropriate response? There is no appropriate response, and yet a response is demanded.

The lines drawn on the pages, the lines connecting the subsequent generations to an act committed by Dr. Woods against Eliza, held me there, frozen.

"Would you like copies of that?" Witherspoon asked.

"Yes, please," I said. "Do you know where these came from? Like who donated it?"

"Let me look," she said.

I continued to flip through the McFadden files as she walked over to a desk at the side of the room. I noticed the dust motes in the air by the window in the corner and the way her blue blouse shimmered in the light.

"No," she said. "That must have come in here before my time. And I don't see any record of it here."

I had known on a theoretical level that it was likely we would have Black relatives, but such facts are much easier to bear in the abstract. Looking down at the McFadden book, I imagined that a young I. M. Woods—he was eighteen when the war broke out—impregnated a woman enslaved by the parents of his future wife.

Such relations were another part of the system of slavery that white people do not think of. We may acknowledge the horrors of sexual abuse that enslaved women must have suffered, but we don't think about what it means for us, as white people, that our forebears, the people who decided we would be white, practiced a systematic kind of rape, driven as much by the capitalist desire for wealth accumulation—offspring would increase the family's property—as by lust.

The particularities, the details, made it feel real, too real, which was why I had to keep looking. Details work by association, and now this information forced me to confront my whiteness and my family's past as if looking directly into a mirror.

Then I thought of I. M. Woods the legislator—he had passed laws intended to limit the rights and freedom of his own Black descendants in an effort to keep these families apart, to hide and displace his Black offspring from his white and to privilege the white over the Black, legally and financially. All of I. M.'s white children had the chance to go to college. My grandfather Hernando quit the University of Maryland after two weeks to run off with a vaudeville singer, and he ended up with little of the family's wealth, but far more, I was sure, than the Black family ever got.

I thought of a story Dad had told me about I. M.'s youngest son, Steve. When he was a child, the doctors told I. M. that Steve only had a short time to live. I. M. did everything possible to give Steve a good life. Once, at a horse race, Steve was infatuated by the winning horse, and I. M. bought it for him. But Steve didn't die young. He lived a long life and never had a real job. He only applied for a Social Security number when he was sixty-five and could start collecting. That, I thought, is whiteness.

Dad and I walked out the door. He struggled with his cane to make it down the three steps into the parking lot. My own legs felt weak as I struggled with what I had just read about our lineage.

"Want to see that new nature walk you pointed out?" he asked.

"Sure," I said, hoping that the swampy setting would be a good place to contemplate what we had learned and what it meant. We drove in silence to the new boardwalk over the Pocotaligo Swamp and walked out on the trail suspended up over the water, which reflected the trees and the sky, creating an endless loop as I looked out over the soupy scene.

"What do you think?" I asked as we stood there, looking out over the swamp.

"About what?" he asked.

"What we found," I said. "Dr. Woods and Maiden Slave."

He shifted his weight and reapplied that involuntary smile.

Below us, a dragonfly landed on the surface of the black water, sending concentric circles outward in every direction, expanding until they merged into stillness.

"On the one hand," I said to Dad, looking up from the dragonfly, when he still hadn't said anything, "I think it's a great thing. There must have been a hundred names on that chart. They are all our family in some sense."

"I don't know of that many Black Woodses around," he said. "Of any, really."

I was surprised that in a small town like Manning, Dad wouldn't have known about a Black Woods family if they were around. But then I remembered that he had lived in a Jim Crow apartheid system that was designed to keep Black and white separate and unequal.

"I think they may be McFaddens and not Woodses. It was in the McFadden file and not the Woods file," I said. "And we saw on the census that the McFaddens lived beside the Woodses in the previous generation. So I think he must have raped a woman enslaved by the neighbors. But then that means he would have later also married their daughter?"

"I'm not sure if Great-Grandmother was from the same McFaddens as the ones next door. There were a few different branches of McFaddens."

"But it seems like he raped a woman enslaved by whichever McFaddens," I said.

"I don't know that it would be rape," he said.

I thought about the ghost of the thirteen-year-old Black girl that Ricky had seen in the parlor of the old Woods homestead.

"How could 'Maiden Slave' consent?" I asked.

"Well...," he said. His face paled against the shadow-cast swamp.

"Owners and slaves had relationships all the time," he said. "Just look at the Democrat Thomas Jefferson."

He laughed. I tried to offer a small chuckle.

"Whether it's Sally Hemings or Eliza, it is impossible for someone who is enslaved to consent," I said, frustrated that I even had to say this. "Because you have to ask what would have happened if she said no."

"I guess so," he said.

"So there's this whole family that is our family—but they might not want to know us at all because it comes from that!" I said, spitting into the water.

He nodded.

"It would be nice to meet them," he said. "I'd love to know our Black relatives. I wouldn't have anything against them."

"I know, Dad, but what I mean is they might not want to know us. They have a reason to have something against us," I said.

"We didn't have any more to do with what that man did than they did," he said.

"But it seems that he and the other white men like him worked awful hard to make sure we had it better than them," I said. "He made sure that story was hidden from you—although whoever made that chart knew a lot."

"Yeah," he said.

We stood there in silence a few more minutes until it seemed like we had nothing else to say.

Dad limped heavily on his cane as we walked back to the car. The doctors thought it was a cyst on his spine and wanted to operate. He was scheduled for surgery in two weeks and, because his bad heart made anesthesia dangerous for him, I realized it was possible this might be the last time I saw him. Even with this knowledge, I was ready to go. Not just to leave him and to leave Manning, but to escape my home state again. To be back in Baltimore, where I could resume my life in the twenty-first century.

But we were going to make one more stop first.

We drove a mile or so to the courthouse, where there was a plaque dedicated to Dr. I. M. Woods, who was the district's representative in the statehouse when the building was constructed.

In front of the courthouse a stone Confederate monument loomed, a soldier standing at attention atop an obelisk thirty feet above the square, overlooking the tobacco-and-cotton town's main drag.

The soldier is leaning on a rifle and looks, from beneath, as if he's holding a big boner in his hand, a priapic satyr statue uniting rape and enslavement in Italian marble.

"'Erected to the soldiers from Clarendon County who served in the War of Southern Independence. Charleston, 1861–Appomattox, 1865,'" I read aloud.

"'The War of Southern Independence,'" Dad said, the euphemism too much even for him.

I walked around the obelisk and read the next panel, which said the monument was erected in 1914.

"'As we view their patriotism through half a century past; as the last time stage of their deeds recedes, their lustre brightens; generations unborn will proudly claim their ancestry.'"

"This generation unborn is not impressed with their luster," I said.

"You are claiming their ancestry, though, aren't you?" he said.

"Not proudly," I said. "I would reject it if I could."

"You can't change the past," Dad said.

I turned to look at the courthouse.

"No. But we can change the present. This is in front of a courthouse. How could there ever be a fair trial held here?" I said. "A statue like this is clear intimidation. Every Black or even northern defendant should challenge the venue."

We said goodbye that afternoon in the shadow of the monument. Ordinarily, when we hugged, his belly would repel mine, bouncing it back a little, keeping our faces from coming too close. But now in my arms he felt frail, and I felt his beard against my face, and it whisked me back to my childhood.

He had willed this world to me, one where a statue like this could sit for a hundred years, unremarked upon, in front of a courthouse, proclaiming devotion to the idea of white supremacy for which the white men of this region, white men like my great-grandfather and his brothers Hernandez and John, had been ready to die.

This monstrosity was my inheritance. It was all of ours.

Chapter 27

I HAD BEGUN TO DREAD my phone calls with Dad.

"Well, what about Nancy Pelosi wearing a kente cloth?" he asked one day as I tried to talk to him about the history of Edisto.

"What about it?" I said, sighing.

During the year of quarantine, which began only two weeks after Dad and I returned from the archives in Manning, I spent days obsessively organizing the notes I'd found at the archives and tracing my family's infamy back further and further with each day. Every bit of research stripped away another piece of the mythology that surrounded my life as I realized how deeply white supremacy ran in South Carolina and my family. Sure, I'd known South Carolina was racist, but I somehow hadn't understood that racism had been the defining feature in its politics and culture.

Edisto Island, far from being the idyllic place I had romanticized growing up, was in many ways the dark heart of the slavocracy. On the island, in 1830, to take a random year, 318 white people enslaved 4,233 Africans. By 1850, the Baynards alone held 718 people in bondage on the island. Sherman's field order of 1863 gave the land to those who had been enslaved there. Two years later, the US government returned the land to the white slaver rebels. A committee of newly emancipated freedmen submitted a declaration to the US government declaring my people, the whites of Edisto, "all-time enemies."

You ask us to forgive the land owners of our Island. *You* only lost your right arm. In war and might forgive them. The man who tied me to a tree & gave me 39 lashes & who stripped and flogged my mother & my sister & who will not let me stay In His empty Hut except I will do His planting & be Satisfied with His price & who combines with others to keep away land from me well knowing I would not Have any thing to do with Him If I Had land of my own.—that man, I cannot well forgive. Does It look as If He Has forgiven me, seeing How He tries to keep me In a condition of Helplessness

This had been in the archive all that time and my family chose not to see it, or not to believe it. We had all continued to erase the reality of the people our ancestors had enslaved. That infuriated me, the way they willfully overlooked evidence to inculcate pride in themselves and their lineage.

But it wasn't only the ancient past. I thought about the trip I had taken to Edisto right before Grandmother died, when I told my cousin Michael the story I had heard about our grandfather lynching a man. I recalled the way the Black man at the bar had looked at me, and my face burned with shame.

I figured now that that man at the bar had been around sixty that night of our brief encounter in 1995. If my estimate was close, then he would have been twenty-five years old when the lifeless body of a twelve-year-old Black boy named Fred Robinson washed ashore on the beach in 1960 with its eyes gouged out and its skull crushed after he was accused of teaching white girls to dance. The boy's mother would urge the FBI to close the case because of the threats she had received from the island's white folks.

The Black man in the bar would have likely remembered 1963, when the state decided to close every single state park in South Carolina rather than accept a court ruling desegregating the beachfront park a few yards from where we stood. A group of Black activists, the "Edisto 13," were arrested trying to integrate the beach in 1965. It wasn't until 1966 that the first Black man was finally legally allowed into the water, only to see the white family already swimming there scream as they rushed out of the water, as if he had leprosy.

The Black man at the bar would surely have heard that the town of Edisto Beach had been incorporated in 1970 as a result of the integration of the beach, after a group of angry white citizens started to lobby for an entirely white jurisdiction so that they would not be subject to the island's Black majority. And he would have had to know, for his own safety, that the town of Edisto Beach had remained a "sundown town"—one where no African Americans were allowed after dark—well into my own lifetime, when my friends and I would walk on the beach at night.

I knew none of that when I felt all puffed up and offended that he would somehow see a connection between me and my great-grandfather, about whose crime I was loudly talking. I was aggrieved and angry then, lost in my illusion of innocence, operating in my whitest register.

But now I was aware that, despite the blinders of whiteness, Dad must have also known all of that recent history and he must have kept it quiet. He was, as my father, at least partially responsible for my ignorance.

And the more I learned, the less patience I had with his willful and insistent refusal to recognize reality.

"Come on, Dad," I said. "What does Nancy Pelosi have to do with anything?"

"I bet you didn't know that the tribe that used the kente cloth owned slaves," he said.

"I'm trying to talk about our family, which you always taught me to be proud of, but when I bring up the real history, suddenly you care about a group of people whose name I'm sure you don't even know. What tribe is this that interests you so much?"

"I can't recall their name right now," he said.

"But you care more about that than the incontrovertible proof we have that our direct ancestors were involved in a monstrous practice for hundreds of years, causing endless suffering to thousands of people?" I demanded.

"It wasn't endless," Dad said. "The slaves were freed and the playing field was leveled and after that everyone was just responsible for lifting themselves up. If some people fail to do that, it's not my fault."

"Level playing field," I said. "OK, take the Seibels family. I came across that name in the slave schedule the other day. They made at least some of their money as a big slaver family in Columbia—which they then used to start the insurance company that you worked for and loved so dearly. When you taught me how great it was, 'a homegrown company right here in Columbia' and all of that stuff, you didn't mention the vast head start they got from stealing the lives and labor of thousands of people."

"They were in Columbia—think of how much they lost when Sherman burned the city," he said. "And you didn't see them complaining about it."

"How much they lost?" I exclaimed. "All they 'lost' was the claim to human property. I mean, you were standing there with me when we found that genealogical chart. And you know that your grandfather then went into the state legislature to help pass Jim Crow laws that advantaged your dad and his siblings over them and theirs. All of your dad's siblings at least had the chance to go to college and medical school and whatever they wanted. How many of the Black siblings did that patriarch give that opportunity to?"

"My daddy never finished college, and we were—"

"As poor as the Black families you lived around," I said. "I know. But that's because your dad blew his chance. But he and his siblings all inherited opportunity and wealth. The Black descendants of I. M. Woods only inherited Jim Crow oppression."

I had been unable to verify the genealogical chart or to find any living descendants who knew anything about "I. M. Woods + Maiden Slave," but eventually I did learn, as the racist and sexist heading suggested, that the genealogy seems to have been put together by a white rather than a Black family member, and I felt somehow dirty for being fascinated by it—as if it was just another instance of whites attempting to monitor Black people whom they saw as property.

Shortly after the kente cloth argument, I wrote an email to Dad, his brothers, and one of my cousins, asking if they knew of any Black Woodses or McFaddens who had been close to the family back when they were growing up. They did not. But in that exchange, I discovered why Dad had been interested in helping me with my research, at least in part.

"I'm going to tell all of your friends that your ancestors...were slave-holders," Dad wrote to his most ardently Democratic brother, who was on the thread.

On another occasion, he gloated about how the Klansmen of his grandfather's generation were all Democrats.

"From Granddaddy to today, it's the Democrats who are bad for the Blacks," he said.

Dad was trying to use my research to score points against his brothers, whom he still seemed to resent for their college degrees and for the flak they gave him over his support for Trump.

I was so disappointed in him, and my heart broke a little bit. But I was not really surprised. As the election approached and he made it clear that he intended to vote for Trump a second time, I knew he had no interest in the reality of our history. If he did, he would not want to make America great *again*. It was all just ammunition in his endless quest to seem right, regardless of the truth.

When I asked him how he could vote for a racist, he told me that "Joe Biden is the most racist man in America."

I was reluctantly going to vote for Biden, though I despised the corporate Democrats and considered Biden a mass-incarcerating war-monger, but when Dad's hyperbole cast him as the most racist man in America, he reminded me again that he had boiled politics down to its basest foundation—scoring a point against your opponent. The more I challenged him, the more he deflected, and if I kept pushing, he would cite his health—he now had to use a walker to get about and was facing a second surgery—to stop the conversation.

Throughout that summer, the operations of whiteness were on a garish display. Armed antimaskers protested state governments and plotted to kidnap governors who were declaring lockdowns or mask mandates over COVID. Video of the three white men lynching Ahmaud Arbery was released, showing that the prosecutors had mischaracterized what had happened in their initial refusal to charge the perpetrators. A white woman was filmed threatening to call the police on a Black man because he'd asked her to follow the laws and keep her dog on a leash in Central Park. A police officer, Derek Chauvin, was caught on camera kneeling on the neck of George Floyd as he cried out for his mother and died. A seventeen-year-old white kid, Kyle Rittenhouse, drove to Kenosha, Wisconsin, with an assault rifle to protect property and ended up killing two protesters.

Each of these instances, overwhelming and daily, filled in an aspect of whiteness. I kept thinking about a passage by Frank Wilhoit that had been bouncing around online recently.

"There must be in-groups whom the law protects but does not bind, alongside out-groups whom the law binds but does not protect," he wrote.

At first, I mistook the author for Francis M. Wilhoit, who wrote an important book about the "massive resistance" to desegregation, and so I read the quote in that context. It turned out that Frank Wilhoit was another person entirely, a classical composer. Still, his passage gave me the perfect definition of whiteness, which I'd been struggling to define even for myself. Whiteness was the belief that people defined as white should be protected but not bound by the law and that everyone else should be bound but not protected.

It was the logic of the police officers who broke the law beating protesters all around the country each night; it was the logic of the so-called Karens who are always ready to call the cops on Black men, even when they are the ones breaking the law; it was the logic of Trump, the logic of my dad, and it had so often been the logic on which I acted.

Each stage of rebellion in my life had been another way of saying that I should be protected by the law and not bound by it. This logic came directly from my ancestors, the slavers who'd arrived at Edisto Island in the late seventeenth century, and had been passed down all the way through the wretched generations to I. M. Woods and the terror campaign against

Reconstruction. Law in South Carolina had been designed to bind the enslaved population and protect the slavers. That logic has not changed, and that was why I tried to explain to Dad over and over again that it was important for us to understand our history.

The more research I did, the more the necessity of reparations became obvious. It was clear that Congress needed to do some bare minimum to finish the job that Reconstruction had left incomplete—thanks to people like my ancestors. But I also began to see the need for personal microreparations. It seemed obvious to me that I had an obligation to do something directly beneficial if I could. I didn't want to be a savior or to force my beneficence. I didn't want to signal my virtue like all the corporations putting Black Lives Matter statements on their websites or like the cops kneeling with protesters, but I felt the need to do something practical.

I'd spent much of my career writing about criminal justice. Day after day I had seen young men marched into the reception court, where trial dates are set, only to be turned away for another few months because of some scheduling conflict that a lawyer might have, another few months in chains without having been convicted of anything.

When a local legal group I trusted began to post about the juveniles awaiting trial, which meant they had not been convicted of a crime, in COVID-infested jails, when the only barrier to home detention for many of them was an inability to pay the fee of seventeen dollars a day necessary to be assigned an electronic ankle monitor, I knew that this was a small way to begin stumbling toward repair. The home detention practice—known as e-carceration—is itself unjust and cruel, but at least the kids would be home, where they could be free of COVID.

I had always refrained from giving money in any realm I might write about, but to me freeing Black boys from chains was more important than any journalistic moral dilemma I had. The government stimulus check had just been deposited into my account, and what better way to kick-start governmental reparations than by funneling federal money toward freeing the same youth the government was simultaneously trying to lock up?

I immediately donated half my check, which would only keep one kid out of lockup for one month. I spread the rest to people I knew in the service industry or spent it at Black-owned businesses and a little later donated another $600 to help keep one more kid e-carcerated rather than incarcerated. The action was deeply imperfect—I was giving money ultimately to a private e-carceration company that had a government contract—and minuscule, but it was a small attempt that I could make personally, without waiting for the government entity itself, at actually performing reparative action.

My ancestors had been responsible for the enslavement of thousands of people. And as a reporter, I had sat there and watched as Black men accused of crimes walked around in chains as impassively as they must have sat at the auction block. Whether I took pride in those ancestors or felt ashamed of them, whether I was earning hundreds or millions of dollars, I was part of the deeply unjust system they had created.

It was also my responsibility to keep digging for answers about the ignominy of my family because I knew that only when we know the cost can we begin to count the enormity of the reparations that are due. And I didn't feel bad about violating any journalistic moral code because, the more I read old newspaper accounts of Reconstruction, the more I realized how deeply white supremacist so much of American journalism had been. I realized that relying on news accounts was the fatal flaw in my book about the "Witchdoctor Sheriff."

The *Beaufort Gazette*, I discovered, had not even acknowledged the death of Robert Smalls, unquestionably the most important person to have ever lived in Beaufort, only years before Ed McTeer became sheriff. I knew then that my old book was unwittingly racist, as I too had been for much of my life, repeating the fabrications that had been handed down as fact. I needed to renounce the book. But when I looked down at its cover, my larger concern lay in my own name, which I now saw clearly as a problem. It marred every introduction and every greeting. I could not change it, like Malcolm X or Amiri Baraka, because to do so would be to conspire with my ancestors to cover up their crimes. But neither could I let it sit there on the cover of a book like a monument to bondage and torture, to the cutting of ears and the burning of flesh, to rape and to murder. The furies do not forget.

Though there was a long tradition of Black people casting off "slave names," I had never heard of a white person renouncing, or even questioning, a slaver name. But as Confederate monuments began to come down around the country, I wondered again, What is a name if not a monument?

I cannot use my name, and I cannot change it.

The question of what to do with my name—which was also my father's name—became a question of how to deal with my father.

The culmination of my argument with him came after supporters of outgoing white supremacist president Donald Trump stormed the US Capitol on January 6 in an attempt to overthrow the 2020 election. The insurgents were following almost precisely the same playbook used by the so-called Redeemers who'd managed to overthrow South Carolina's state government—and ultimately the entire Reconstruction regime—in 1876.

We were discussing the January 6 insurrection on a Zoom call with Mom, Dad, Nicole's mom, and our nephew the next day, still reeling with shock, trying to make sense of it. Then Dad derailed the conversation.

"You know what nobody is talking about," Dad said. "The crazy Democrat who shot at those Republican congressmen while they were playing softball."

"I can't with you," Nicole said to the screen as she got up from the couch, throwing up her hands in frustration. "That is so wrong."

"Goddamn it," I yelled. "That was five years ago. Do you really think that is relevant now?"

"Yes," he said.

"Of course you do," I screamed. "This is your fault. You supported this, you brushed it off. I kept telling you this would happen because it is the same thing your goddamn grandfather did. I wasn't surprised at all because the plan was easy to see."

I'd tried to tell him all this before: how Reconstruction in South Carolina was overthrown when a group of Red Shirts—members of various local "rifle clubs" who would prevent African Americans from voting—tried to steal the election and then stormed the Capitol and occupied it until their candidate was declared the victor through a racist and pusillanimous compromise.

The entire plan had been concocted by a man named Martin Gary—the Confederate general whom I. M. Woods named a child after in 1892.

Martin Gary had refused to surrender at Appomattox and joined up with Confederate president Jefferson Davis, who'd convened the final cabinet meeting of the Confederacy at Gary's mother's house in South Carolina. Later, Gary became known as the most fervent and violent white supremacist in the state where secession began. He regularly predicted and called for a full-on war between the races. He was terrified of democracy because he was terrified of the "numerical negro supremacy" in the state.

As some white South Carolinians advocated a "qualified" franchise for Black men who held property or had educations, Gary called openly for a "white man's government under the dominion and management of the sons of the Caucasian race."

In 1876 Gary crafted the "Edgefield Plan" to use violence, intimidation, terror, and ballot stuffing to steal the election for Wade Hampton, a Lowcountry "bourbon" and celebrated general running for governor.

After the coup, Wade Hampton's name was ubiquitous. Both Mom and I attended Wade Hampton High School in Greenville, and for many years I drove daily on Wade Hampton Boulevard. Hampton was one of the politicians, like Trump, who could inflame white violence and then claim neutrality. "Good people on both sides."

But Gary stood solely for white supremacy and to name a child after him, that could only mean a deep devotion to the cause.

"I tell you there are certain men you must put out of the way—men you must kill...they must be killed; for they are the leaders of the negroes," Gary said in one campaign speech. "Go in masses, armed and try to force the negroes to vote our ticket...shoot them down and cut off their ears, and I warrant you this will teach them a lesson....Even if we are not elected we will go to Columbia in force, surround the statehouse, and tear it down, and show them we will rule."

Pitchfork Ben Tillman, a Gary acolyte who later became a US senator, explained away the thousands of murders committed to steal the election that year. "Gary's doctrine of voting early and often changed the Republican majority of 2,300 in Edgefield to a Democratic majority of 3,900," Tillman later boasted. "It was Edgefield's majority alone which gave to Hampton a chance to claim to have been elected."

There was a standoff, with both sides declaring victory. When the election was called for the Republican, Chamberlain, Gary led an army to march on the capitol in Columbia. They stormed the building and occupied it until finally Hampton was declared the legitimate governor. Martin Gary had executed a coup.

I. M. Woods named a son after Gary fifteen years later. The newspaper noted I. M.'s service to the cause, noting that "whenever the Democratic party is endangered, there is no man in the country that will do more to dispel the threatening clouds than Doctor Woods."

When the red hats stormed the Capitol in 2021 the same way the Red Shirts had in 1876, I felt a sort of culminating, existential break. Time was doubling up on itself. The arc of history was not bending toward justice, but it was bending. It was history and hate that rhymed.

The next day, on the phone, following our contentious Zoom, I called Dad a coward.

"Why do you always just try to push everything away?" I demanded. "If you support the attack on the Capitol, you can just say it. That's what your ancestors did, and they turned their insurrectionists into 'Redeemers.' And you played along with them, but you're just a coward."

I was furious because I knew the January 6 storming of the Capitol would not have been possible if white people like Dad hadn't whitewashed the crimes of the Ku Klux Klan, of I. M. Woods, of Martin Gary and Wade Hampton and Robert E. Lee and all the rest of them. And I knew that his silence would help whitewash the Proud Boys and militias and QAnon acolytes who had tried to overthrow the government.

I thought about the parallels between Dad and his grandfather I. M. Woods. Both were raised to exist in a state of vast inequality—Dad in Jim Crow and I. M. in the slavocracy—and suddenly, at around the time they became adults, they found themselves facing a world whose beliefs were contrary to those upon which they had been reared.

Instead of realizing the horror in which he had been raised and repenting, I. M. did everything possible to restore the slavocracy. He helped create a phantasmagoric version of whiteness that insists on its own outraged innocence even as it revels in violence. That was the whiteness Dad inherited, the whiteness of lynching and of Jim Crow and of the "massive resistance" to school integration, which resulted in the Lamar Riot, where angry white crowds rocked and overturned school buses carrying Black kids. That was in 1970, two years before I was born.

Lamar was in Darlington County, the home of Dad's favorite racetrack. Two years before the riot, in 1968, George Wallace, the segregationist governor of Alabama, campaigned at Darlington as part of his presidential run. "George Washington founded this country, and George Wallace will save it," NASCAR founder Bill France announced before the race.

Then Wallace spoke. The crowd of more than fifty thousand people went crazy. "Damn, the crowd cheered him more than Richard Petty," one observer noted in a news story I found online.

When Dad tried to teach me to love NASCAR, he didn't mention any of this history. Because by the time I was born, the whiteness Dad had inherited from I. M. had entered a new, post–Civil Rights stage where it no longer spoke of itself openly. Instead, it used terms like *crime*, *welfare*, *busing*, and *affirmative action* to air its grievances and consolidate the power and property gathered over the centuries.

Dad told me to be a proud rebel, to be proud of being southern, to wave a Confederate flag, but he never told me about the horrors of our family holding people in concentration camps of tortured bondage. He told me that the family had owned slaves, but in telling me, as his mother had told him, that the slaves were happy, he covered up the true nature of the institution, which, far from being benign, or even peculiar, is a unique and epochal evil, demanding a moral response from the descendants of its perpetrators.

And so I tried to tell these things to him. But now he would no longer listen.

I write my name, his name, and I cross it out.

I must let the crimes in my name remain legible while acknowledging the rank horror of their criminality. Nothing is adequate, but something is required. The only possible solution, as flawed and makeshift as it may be, is to cross my name out, allowing both the word and the slash through it to stand.

~~Baynard Woods~~.

The slash through my name serves as full disclosure, bright-yellow tape, cordoning off the crime scene without hiding it.

Chapter 28

I WOKE UP EARLY. I put on a pot of coffee in my parents' suburban South Carolina kitchen. Dad was still asleep. Since he had been diagnosed with ALS, the devastating and invariably fatal neurodegenerative disease, a few months earlier, he had been sleeping much later—getting up and going to bed were both so difficult now, he put them off as long as possible.

Mom was sitting in her little sunroom built off the back of the house, drinking decaf and studying her Bible as birds bounced around the various feeders she had placed outside her window.

She refused to recognize the reality of the disease and the death that would ineluctably follow in its wake, praying every day for a miracle. Because she would not listen to doctors when they talked about the grim progression of ALS, she didn't know how much worse this ordeal would get. The historian Tony Judt, who died of ALS in 2010, described it as "being in a prison cell that gets steadily smaller. You don't know when it's going to get so small it's going to crush you to death. But you know it is going to happen, the only question is when."

But Mom would not hear this.

This was only my second time seeing my parents in over a year, and Dad's decline seemed catastrophic. During the quarantine, he'd had two spinal surgeries before they realized that it was ALS rendering his legs increasingly useless, and none of us knew yet how to address this certain calamity.

I had arrived the night before, in a rental car, and helped Dad into the bed, going through the elaborate ritual required to help him get up from his chair, lift his legs enough to change into pajamas, and get into the bed. This morning I was going to return to his hometown of Manning in a small and tentative first step toward addressing at least one of the horrors I'd found in our family's history with some kind of concrete, collaborative action.

Of all the countless atrocities committed by our white family, I devoted the most attention to the murder Dad had told me about twenty-five years earlier, the murder that had forced his grandfather Dr. Irvin McSwain Woods to flee from South Carolina.

I thought that somehow this crime might hold the key to help me understand my own whiteness, to comprehend what it was that inspired Dylann Roof to murder, the Nazis to rally, and the rest of us to refuse to see reality. Somehow, all of those questions around the role of whiteness in the world and in my life funneled into the figure of I. M. Woods.

Though I could not find definitive proof—which is the purpose of a cover-up—I had come to believe that my great-grandfather was involved in the assassination of a Black county commissioner named Peter J. Lemon in April 1871, exactly 150 years before.

"What time will you be back?" Mom asked.

"I'm not sure. It takes two and a half hours to drive to Manning," I said. "I'm meeting the guy at eleven, but he has a funeral to go to later."

Mom and I walked to the door of Dad's room to look in on him sleeping before I left. The light streaming in through his bedroom window made everything a golden color. Mom, impossibly thin now, squeezed my hand.

Dad had told me that he wouldn't be able to stay in this room much longer without some major renovations because, the doctor said, soon he would be entirely confined to a wheelchair and we would need to use a lift to get him out of bed and into the chair and then again to get back into bed, and the lift couldn't make it through the awkward angle of the two doors leading into what had been intended as a guest room.

As it was now, he had a series of straps and cords and pulleys he'd set up on the bed to help him adjust his increasingly paralyzed body, using the little strength left in the limbs he could still control. But that would not last long. He could barely use his right hand at all now. And both of his legs refused to answer his calls to muster.

"I need to finish the interview by two so I can go by McCabe's and get barbecue for Dad," I said.

"He wishes so much he could go," she said.

"I know he does," I said.

I did not want Dad to come with me this time.

I'd been sharing my research with the Clarendon County Archives—where Dad and I had been the previous year, just before the pandemic broke out—and one day the archivist M. L. Witherspoon had written to tell me that a man named George Frierson wanted to talk with me. He had come into the archive asking about the assassination of Peter J. Lemon, and Witherspoon asked if I'd be willing to talk to him.

When I Googled Frierson, I saw that he was known for helping post-humously overturn the conviction and death sentence of George Stinney, a fourteen-year-old Black boy whom white South Carolinians sentenced to death after a two-hour trial in 1947, making him the youngest person ever legally executed in the United States.

Frierson, like Stinney, had grown up in Clarendon County, and he had made it his mission to do whatever he could to rectify the horror of this history, which haunted his hometown like a ghost. I admired him for this, but it also made me think less of my own father.

It should not have been necessary for Frierson to lead that fight, to point out the injustice perpetrated by the whites. The white people who had grown up under the Jim Crow regime that executed the young boy should have risen up in contrition, disgust, or anger. They should have pulled down the white supremacist monument in front of the courthouse and all the other white supremacist propaganda. Instead, so many southern whites of my parents' generation, the last generation to grow up under the de jure segregation of the Jim Crow apartheid regime, just remained silent, as if they had simply moved beyond it all.

"We don't see color," became the most effective way for them to maintain the power open white supremacy had gained them. Because now, in order to recognize those advantages, one would have to invoke race. If you refuse to acknowledge race, then you don't have to acknowledge those advantages.

Though Dad wouldn't talk about politics or race anymore, I had tried to explain this to Mom.

"It's like playing basketball where your team stole the other team's shoes and so they're having to play barefoot. When they say both sides should have shoes, the shod team says, 'Shoes aren't important. We don't even see shoes,'" I said.

She nodded, but she was too overwhelmed with worry about Dad to really listen. I believe that Mom, like a lot of other white people, and perhaps especially women, who have themselves been the victims of discrimination in the patriarchal South, had truly believed that raising her children to be "color blind" was the best way to respond to the hate that had reared her. But in passing on an innocent and naive view of the world she grew up in, she had helped transmit the miasma to me that had been passed on to her. Whiteness is the name we give this curse.

I did not want to pass the miasma on. I was happy to be able to help in uncovering the injustice perpetrated by my great-grandfather's generation of whites in the hope that, by dismantling the illusion of innocence that permeates our sense of the past and of ourselves, we white people might be able to save ourselves and thereby stop causing so much harm to people of color—and to the planet itself.

I felt certain that there was a connection between the climate-change denial that was threatening life on our planet and the erasure of the reality of colonization, genocide, and slavery. White supremacy is ignoring reality to the point of its annihilation. It would rather destroy the world than admit it is wrong.

The ideologies of race and capitalism were born together, cocreated, and together they have emitted the vast majority of the carbon changing the atmosphere and the climate and putting the earth in jeopardy. If greed and power prevented white people from seeing the humanity of other people, if they were willing to pass the moral curse of their concentration camp luxury on to their children, how could we expect them, us, to care about the mostly invisible species going extinct each day?

Race, I realized, was a lot like capitalism in another way. I could call myself an anarchist, a communist, or a socialist, and I would still have to participate in the capitalist system in order to eat. Similarly, I can attempt to extract myself from whiteness, try to dismantle it from within, to transform it, but I am still a part of the racial economy. There is no individual salvation, no state of racial grace that I can attain as a white person.

And yet, I can try to be better, to be more graceful, which is to say more liberatory, every day. I can decide, as I. M. Woods could have decided 150 years ago, to be an abolitionist. Or I can choose to support white power.

This was the kind of thinking that made me feel I owed something to Lemon, the Black county commissioner who had been ambushed and murdered by a gang of white men who subsequently enlisted the entire white community in covering up the crime. The only time I could find Lemon's name in the historical record in the years after his assassination was when the *Manning Times* printed a threat, in 1887, that warned an official who had hired a Black police officer, "You will be done like Peter Lemon the radical, you can guess what became of him."

I thought my great-grandfather was one of the men responsible, but I could not be sure—because no one was ever charged or tried for the assassination, despite a $500 reward. So the cover-up was my inheritance. I could not allow Lemon's name to exist only as a racist threat. I wanted to help Frierson with anything he wanted to do for Lemon.

On the phone, he talked to me of absolution. He said, "There is conspiracy and there is complicity" and told me the Biblical story of how Saul, who later became Saint Paul, held the coats of the men who murdered Saint Stephen.

I understood him to be saying that if I knew of this evil and I did not try to rectify it, I would be holding the lynchers' coats. Despite my resistance to the New Testament example, I felt he was right.

We decided to find the place where the white men had ambushed and assassinated Peter J. Lemon, as soon as vaccines made travel safe. We were looking for a place, but more than that we were looking for the meaning in that place, for a way to memorialize what had been suffered there and to start undoing the conspiracy it had helped solidify. And I did not want Dad along for that, with all of his what-abouts to diminish it.

I needed to go there to feel contrition, and I did not think, even before he fell ill, that Dad was capable of contrition.

Following our big fight after January 6—and his diagnosis, which came at about the same time—he refused to discuss race or politics any further. Just after the white army of red hats stormed the Capitol and lost, Dad outlawed all conversation about it.

"I don't watch the news, and I just can't talk about politics anymore," he told me and his Democratic brothers. "I have too much on my mind as it is."

ALS could insulate him, but it could not absolve him, at least not to me. Having supported a racist president and racist policies, he should not be cleared of wrongdoing on account of his illness, acting as if none of it had mattered—as if the world he had helped make, the world I had inherited from him, was no longer of any import in the face of his own death.

Once again, he exercised the power he had wielded as the "head of the household" when I was a child—telling me when the conversation had to stop. But now, in the face of his illness, I could not rebel, I could not push him. I was furious, but I had to acquiesce. I wanted him to think about his mistakes, make an assessment of his life, but I could not make him do that. I loved him and he was suffering and I had to help however I could.

As I stood there that morning with Mom looking in on him sleeping, so weak and so frail, his skin grayish in the morning light, his hair wild, his beard long, I still felt that fury gnawing at me. I needed him to be better, even at this extreme moment, and he refused. I looked at him with anger, with pity, and still also with love.

Driving to Manning, I passed through the counties that had been at the heart of the Ku Klux conspiracy in which I believed my great-grandfather had been involved. On April 19, 1871, Congress signed what was called the Ku Klux Klan Act, a bill giving President Grant the power to suspend habeas corpus and declare martial law in the "formerly insurrectionist" states in an attempt to put down the guerrilla war being waged against Reconstruction's multiracial democracy by the white planters. The conspiracy was most violent in the northern counties I was now passing through, resulting in the murder and torture of thousands of newly emancipated Black people wishing to exercise their constitutional rights and also of the white scalawags and carpetbaggers who supported this new democracy.

The KKK Act was signed into law the same morning that two men found the body of Peter Lemon, riddled with buckshot, in the back of his buggy, still attached to a bay horse at the edge of a lonely road just outside Manning.

In October 1871, a few months after the lynching of Lemon, Grant declared martial law, and Klansmen from all over the state fled, either to Texas or to Canada. I. M. Woods sold a piece of land that September in what I believe was a bid to fund his escape.

As in the legend Dad had told me about his grandfather, I found that most of the Klansmen who fled eventually received amnesty and returned to their hometowns, where they were greeted as heroes. And now, passing numerous Confederate flags in the course of my two-hour drive, I could see the remnants of that amnesty.

The fields glowed like blood with a crimson cover crop as I pulled into Clarendon County, following my phone's directions back to the center of the small town. I was returning to the town of I. M. Woods in an attempt to pull the mask off his head, if only so I might finally see my own face.

As I pulled up in front of the squat brick archives building with its twin white columns, I saw a man get out of a car that was parked in the shade of a tree at the back of the lot. He was brown skinned, wearing a black hat with a small brim and a tall crown perched lightly atop his head. Thick glasses covered his eyes and a mask fit snugly over his nose and mouth. I knew it was Frierson.

While I was interested in excavating the crime of my ancestor in order to try to find a way to undo whiteness, Frierson, a veteran and former county school board commissioner, wanted to memorialize a forgotten Black hero of Clarendon County. Two sides of the same situation, and our interests aligned—both things needed to be done, and we could only do them together.

When we first started talking, I told Frierson everything I had learned about the lynching of Peter Lemon, sharing all my documents with him.

Peter J. Lemon had been born in bondage in Clarendon County. He left and joined the Fifth Massachusetts Regiment after the Civil War started, serving under Daniel Chamberlain, who would later be elected the state's governor. Lemon won the county commissioner seat in the election of 1868, despite white violence and voter suppression. He also seems to have commanded a Black militia, organized to defend against the Klan. He leased land from a carpetbagger, refusing to submit to the sharecropping system the former slavers were attempting to create.

All of this made him a prime target of the unreconstructed white terrorists attempting to restore some simulacrum of the old slave regime.

The first time the Ku Klux terrorists came for Lemon, they pulled him from his house and subjected him to physical abuse so bad he would not describe it to friends and allies. He left the county briefly but refused to be scared away and returned to fulfill his duties to the county that had elected him and the Reconstruction regime the racist whites were desperate to overthrow.

This time, the Klan sent him a letter, warning him to leave or die. Where the letter was addressed to him, Lemon wrote the name of a white man above his own and sent the Klan threat to that man.

Congressional testimony described the man as an "eccentric druggist" and treated this gesture as a joke—but I thought of it more as a fuck-you. Lemon was going to show them he was not scared. Upon receiving the letter, the "druggist," who may have been the letter's original author and my great-grandfather, attacked Lemon with a pistol, but was deterred by other white men, who calmed him down.

Soon after that, Lemon received another letter, purportedly from a friend, summoning him to Manning for county business. The man he was supposed to meet never showed up. When Lemon was on his way home, a group of white men ambushed him. Six or eight of them shot, making it impossible to say exactly who took his life.

Whiteness is an anonymity granting immunity to those who defend it.

After Lemon's death, Black militias and their supporters marched to Manning in what was essentially a massive Black Lives Matter protest, demanding justice, while the white press did its best to demonize Lemon, calling him "vicious," "low," and "drunk" and essentially blaming him for his own murder. I was not surprised to find that the protesters never got anything resembling justice and no one was ever charged with the murder.

It was frustrating not to be able to pin the crime on specific individuals, to prove that my great-grandfather had pulled a trigger, but then I realized that was the point of whiteness. It is a conspiracy of violence and silence, a compact whereby white people, often unwittingly, work together to bestow upon ourselves as much power as possible while freeing ourselves from all culpability. The violence requires silence, but the silence also requires violence. The cover-up, which insists that I be protected and not bound by the law, is my inheritance.

Whiteness is plausible deniability. To combat it, I offer a plausible culpability.

Frierson and I approached each other and bumped knuckles, pandemic style. Under his black Members Only jacket he wore a purple shirt and a purple paisley-patterned tie. It felt as if we had known each other for a long time.

"I'll ride with you," Frierson said, indicating it was time to go. "My car is big, which means it uses a lot of gas."

Using the GPS on my phone, we determined that the Lemon Branch, a body of water that had taken the name of the man assassinated there, was off Raccoon Road just past where it meets 301. He gave me directions as we made our way through Manning, turning right to avoid a stretch of stoplights at the small town's busiest strip.

"One hundred and fifty years to the day, almost," he said.

Eventually, after some exploratory wandering, we walked a sandy old farming road until we came to a cut in the trees. The path through the woods was damp and lush. The fronds of ferns quivered in the shadows, the way they do near the banks of a cold mountain stream.

We emerged into a clearing, the sky above us a blinding blue. And there, ringed by a mix of pine, oak, holly, and various scrub trees and weeds, a deep-green pond reflected all of that, the chlorophyll of the leaves and luminous shapelessness of the sky, back up to itself. Pond scum hugged the banks in pastel patches of pale green.

"There it is," Frierson said. "The Peter J. Lemon Branch."

We stood there solemnly.

"I have lived here all my life, and you've brought me somewhere I've never been," he said. "This is a blessing."

"I wouldn't be here without you," I said. "I am grateful."

On a pathway to one side of the branch was a wagon—a flatbed with three horizontal slats making the sides and a hitch on the front—resting crooked in the old dirt road. In the background was a small, old house, its tin roof a glinting streak of silver in the day's zenith.

"When they shot him, he was coming along the road in a buggy," I said. "His friend could hear the shots from his house. It's almost eerie to see this trailer here with that house in the distance."

"It is indeed," he said.

I imagined my great-grandfather hiding in the woods, taking cover in a patch of ferns or behind a rock, waiting for the ambush, and I shivered in the spring air. Even standing here, I could not fathom the form that whiteness had taken when it pulled that trigger. We white people have not even started to plumb the depths of our ancestors' depravity—which makes us ever more susceptible to its return.

I saw a deer stand and realized that waiting out here in the woods to kill a man would be a lot like hunting. I recalled the way Dad had called Black people "bears" when I was a kid, and I wondered if that name had come down from I. M., as if the name justified the hunt.

I knelt and put my fingers in the dirt. Though we would never know the precise place Lemon was murdered, just as we would never know exactly who pulled the triggers or who carried out the cover-up, I was certain that this moment here on this piece of earth mattered, even if I couldn't say how.

"Are you still thinking about a monument for Lemon?" I asked, standing up.

"Well now," Frierson said, and laughed. "You're the one who got this started."

"I am all for it," I said. "I'll help in any way I can."

"Yes, there's a way we have to go about doing things," he said.

"Right," I said. "I'm just a carpetbagger. You're here all the time. And you have done this before. I only want to follow your lead."

"But you've brought me somewhere today I've never been before. I'll have to tell my son that," he said.

He stared off into space for a minute, as if something was on his mind.

"Yes, I'll have to tell my son. I give all these people counsel. But who is going to counsel me?" he said. "My son is a preacher, but it must be strange for him to counsel his father."

Frierson and I shared a sense of obligation to the past, to time itself, and he seemed to appreciate, like me, the mystery of human generations, and so we walked on a little, both thinking about the difficult relations of fathers and sons, of race and place, crime and time, our feet marking off more minutes, increasing the interest we owed to the past.

I bent down and put my fingers in the dirt again in something akin to prayer and let Frierson get a bit ahead of me, his gait at once determined, elegant, and plodding, each step kicking up small clouds of dust from between the flattened strands of grass and onto the ankles of his dark pants as his heavy shoes slapped the earth.

I thought of my dad transmitting the story of his grandfather's crime to me. He couldn't recall the circumstances or the tone in which he'd first heard it from his father. And he'd never asked his father how he had learned of the story. But other relatives had heard the tale as well, and they had each let it sit on the outskirts of family history.

Maybe that was why the murder committed by I. M. Woods had become so important to me. In a lifetime of deferral, denial, pride, and political bluster, telling that story, on the river years ago, was the only time Dad had acknowledged the horror of our history, speaking words that pointed to the truth of the past, rather than the fantasy that southern whites had concocted for themselves and their children. It was the one time he'd confessed that he was descended from white supremacists.

This instance of evil was given to me as an awareness. All the others— the thousands of people tortured and bound and murdered and raped, those who suffered under the unjust laws passed by the legislature of which I. M. was a part—haunted me in a different form, unknown ghosts lurking always at the edge of my perception.

My education had begun with whiteness as an illusion of innocence and the freedom not to notice race. But in that story Dad told me that day on the river, I had seen a glimpse of the possibility of whiteness as the recognition of an obligation.

But I had no idea how to fulfil that obligation. That was why I was so grateful to be here with Frierson. Unlike most people, he had asked those questions for himself, he had tallied what he owed a dead boy wrongfully executed, and he had followed through until he had paid that debt as well as he could, acknowledging it would never be enough. He could not change history, he could not bring the boy back to life, he could not enact justice; he could only embrace his own humanity by attempting to do right by the living and the dead.

I don't know what we can do to make the past right. But I feel as if the blood is crying out for something.

"Did you find what you were looking for today?" Frierson asked, his voice quiet but full of intensity.

We were back in the parking lot of the archives, and location lent the question a practical air. I had spent the last year looking for information. But we both knew that was not what he meant right now. Neither of us had gone out to the Lemon Branch in search of information. We were both looking for something deeper than that. Perhaps a word he had used earlier was right. I'd been seeking absolution.

But I'd found something else. I'd found with Frierson not absolution but engagement. To absolve is to set free. But I had discovered a way of acting to form a community of concern—of being bound more tightly to the world.

We agreed to work together to find a way to memorialize Peter Lemon. For me that would be one step in undermining the conspiracy of whiteness. In the law, for a person implicated by a conspiracy to be removed from it, that person must act directly to proclaim separation from the criminal enterprise. Whiteness can become an obligation to denounce it, revealing the conspiracy.

Frierson and I said goodbye, promising to talk again soon.

"Call and let me know you made it home safe," he said.

I made it to McCabe's just in time to get barbecue to bring home for Dad. They only took cash and I was twenty dollars short, and they spotted me because of my dad. Eating there before we went to the archives had been the last time he had been in a restaurant. First the pandemic hit, and then, by the time he'd had a vaccine, he was too weak to want to go out.

I had been wary of a white savior complex during my research. The problem with white saviors, as I learned when I worked at the school, is that we always try to save the wrong person. As I drove back, I realized that, with my research, I had, at least in part, been trying to save my dad. On some subconscious level, I had thought that if I could find the key to the clue he had given me, maybe I could convince him, maybe I could save him from his own whiteness.

It was too late for that now. This was not religion, and a deathbed conversion did no one any good. It was just one more instance of my desire to win the argument, whatever the cost.

On a larger level, I had also found hope in my search for the crime of I. M. Woods because in that moment of Reconstruction, following the Wo-ah, there was a time when whiteness could have been dismantled. I. M. and his fellow Klansmen and red shirts derailed that possibility. But it was there for me to see. I had seen the promise of Reconstruction in the Baltimore Uprising and in the antifascists risking their lives to fight against the Nazis in Charlottesville. I was pissed off at Dad because he did nothing to dismantle his whiteness, but I knew that I too still had a lot of work to do.

As I walked into my parents' house, carrying a cooler full of Manning barbecue, and saw Dad sitting there in his wheelchair with his wild white beard, I knew I could not save my father, but neither could I blame him for my own racist mistakes and oversights.

I had to recognize the crimes of my forebears and transform them so that I might transform myself. Whiteness is not only an inheritance but also a bequest. It is an obligation to repair our history. But it has to happen in the present, for each of us in the course of our lives. The horizons of whiteness lie not in the past but in the future, when it may be reborn as repair.

"I brought you some cue," I said to Dad, knowing he might not be able to eat much longer, as he wheeled toward me in his chair.

Looking at him, I could see myself in his features, beneath his wizened white hair, and I knew I had to go back and examine my own life with the same eye I had given to I. M. Woods.

I am Woods. I am whiteness, imbued with the wretched history of my people. Whiteness is a reckoning, a responsibility, and an ever-present threat. I can save no one but myself. But as I told Dad about my trip to the Lemon Branch and our plans to memorialize Peter Lemon, I thought that perhaps I could somehow be of service.

Whiteness can be a hope for its own nonexistence, a hope for the future, a hope that we may one day know what it means to live outside our own lies. Whiteness must fight against itself with all the weapons at its disposal—even love.

Acknowledgments

In a book that is partly about unacknowledged debts, the acknowledgments seem to take on a greater weight because I am aware that debts can never be fully paid. But they can be acknowledged, as can the gratitude I feel at the completion of this project. But as this book has taught me, we are always forgetting our obligations and our debts. To those I've neglected here, even though you have nourished me, I am sorry. My mistakes are mine alone.

I owe a great debt to all the archivists who helped me discover the factual basis of my inheritance in what once seemed like the intractable past. I owe a special debt of gratitude to M. L. Witherspoon, who was essential to this project and always met my inquiries with patience and kindness. Jessica Douglas, an archivist and a friend, helped me work through digital archives when the world shut down and ultimately found the coroner's inquest that followed the death of Peter J. Lemon. That handwritten document in the state archive helped open up the world of 1871 Clarendon County and what I believe is the cover-up of the murder of Peter J. Lemon. I could never have found it without Jess.

In writing about one's own life, family, friends, and acquaintances become supporting characters, which is always a little unjust. This is a book about warped perspectives, so I am painfully aware that this presents the world solely through my eyes and my memory and that no one else in the book has a chance to respond. I've worked as a reporter for a long time, but this is mostly not a work of journalism. I changed the names of many of the people in this book because consenting to hang out with me in 1988 doesn't constitute consent to have your name and business in a book. But you know who you are. I did my best to capture the world we shared. I am sure you saw it differently because that's how life works and why we are different people.

There was some reporting involved in the book, and I did not change the names of historical figures or those who are public in some way. Which brings me to George Frierson. I owe a tremendous debt to him for the example he provided me with his work on the George Stinney case and the grace he showed me in our attempt to uncover a crime committed 150 years ago. When I first talked to him, I knew I was on the right path. Mr. Frierson, thank you for showing me how an obligation to the past can manifest in present action.

Various family members helped me greatly in piecing together our history. Though I tried to be open with my intentions, this may not be the book you were expecting. I'm sure you might have expected a lot more genealogy and a lot less autobiography.

Lottie McCowan sent me innumerable documents that were of great value to my research. Richard and Susan Woods have assisted me in my work in countless ways over the years. As I began research in state archives, they allowed me and Nicole to stay in their home for the month of February 2020. We had no way to know that the archives would be closed for in-person visits just a few weeks later. Because of the pandemic, that time was even more essential. Thank you.

Uncle Bully also contributed considerable insight and inspiration, sharing contacts and perspectives. Irvin and Nancy Woods, Gus Woods and Alice Stevens, Jay Woods, Trisha Woods, Michael Woods, Raynell Woods, Robin Woods, Bailey Woods, Trevor Woods, Jennings Woods, Ryan Devoe, Harry Devoe, Eric Mooney, and Dan Beaman have all helped me understand my inheritance in various ways.

So many people, including my dad's brothers and their wives, helped as he suffered through ALS. None of us could have made it through the illness without the home health aides who assisted him, especially Stephanie, Mary Lou, and Shawna. Y'all were real heroes who helped us walk to the end.

My dad helped with the book more than he knew, and whenever a story came up, he'd ask, "Did that make the book?" He died just as I was finishing it. I wish you were here to read it. He, my mom, my brother, and I lived so much of this together. Mom and Chris, y'all are the only ones who knew some of these stories—and now I've blabbed it all to the world. At least I can say I always said I was going to be a writer. I love y'all so much and I am so thankful for all the ways y'all have loved me. I owe you so much, Mom.

The King family, my aunt Gaile, John Scoff, Sarah Blazer, Marilyn Alls, and so many others have been there for me. Grandmother Woods, Nanny, Summey, Mike King, and the others of earlier generations gave me glimpses.

I've learned so much from my students over the years. I'm sorry for when I failed you. Special thanks to Anthony Anderson, Jayro Cruz, Ayanna Brooks, Rajon Jones, Marsha Collins, and Brian Jerry, who have continued to teach me.

D. Watkins read nearly every iteration of this book, and whenever we traded manuscripts, I knew I needed to up my game. Your work prompted the best kind of competition, making me want to be better as a writer and as a person.

I ended up recording myself reading each chapter aloud and then listening back to it as I walked around the city, which proved an essential part of the book's composition. I developed the technique in an attempt to re-create the energy of walking around and talking with Brandon Soderberg about the book we were writing together as I began to think about this one. And, since probably no one knows me better as a writer, his insight into this book was crucial. I'm looking forward to getting the band back together.

Laura Wexler, with her unerring eye for what is essential to a story, and Wil Hylton, with his critical enthusiasm, gave me much needed pushes at various points. The Barnyard Sharks gave me rhythm for my stories. Aaron Henkin, Ruby Fulton, Dan Pavlik, Michael Shank, Albert Garcia-Romeu, and Beth Harper, y'all rule. Wendel Patrick, Dharna Noor, Rebekah Kirkman, Lawrence Weschler, Lisa Snowden, Brian Charles, Lafayette Gilchrist, Kris Riddle, Chris Farmer, Kondwani Fidel, Devin Allen, Kim Rice, Wayne Polston, Issac J. Bailey, Frank Wilhoit, Eddie Conway, Gerald Dent, Marc Steiner, DeRay Mckesson, Kelly Davis, Erica Green, Ivan Bates, PFK Boom, Shorty, Mary Finn, Kevin Abrams, Levar Mullen,

ACKNOWLEDGMENTS

Clay Risen, Joanna Osbourne, Jeff Lewandowski, Natalie Kahla, Alex Orr, Damien Ober, Andreja Sisic, Davi Peterson, Patti Provance, Terrance Sims, Patchen Mortimer, Jaisal Noor, Eze Jackson, J. M. Giordano, Joe Formichella, Suzanne Hudson, Teri Henderson, Ailish Hopper, Paul Rucker, Sari Weissbard, Frank Wilhoit, and many others have supported me as I grappled with the ideas in this book. Thank you all.

This book would never have come to be without my truly top-notch agent and friend Brandi Bowles. When you called me after reading the revised proposal, it was one of the best moments of my life. I'm so grateful for your support.

Coming up as a writer, I read about people working with these great editors who really shaped their work. Krishan Trotman, you are that editor. When I wrote the first draft "from the outside," you pushed me to make it personal and to write it from the inside—which was a lot scarier. You always told me when my work sucked, and that meant so much to me because I knew I could believe your praise when it came. You made the book what it is. I am forever indebted.

Amina Iro, Kathryn Gordon, Abimael Ayala-Oquendo, Mari C. Okuda, S. B. Kleinman, and the rest of the team at Legacy were a pleasure to work with, and the book wouldn't be what it is without y'all. I'm so happy to be part of the team.

It's strange that a dog could help with a book, but old Jang was my Night Editor. You were the best. Thanks for everything. Most of all, I need to thank Nicole, because no one has ever given me so much joy, insight, companionship, criticism, and love. Pretty much every day for more than twenty years now, you've challenged and fascinated me. Growing and changing with you is the greatest journey of my life. I couldn't ask for more.

In many ways, this book is an attempt to reckon with myself. There are many wrongs not acknowledged here, of course, and I'm still unaware of much of the harm I've done in the world and of even more I have inherited. To everyone who I have hurt—I am sorry.